THE SECOND ADMINISTRATION

OF

THOMAS JEFFERSON

1805—1809

HISTORY OF THE UNITED STATES.

BY

HENRY ADAMS.

HISTORY

OF THE

UNITED STATES OF AMERICA

DURING THE SECOND ADMINISTRATION OF

THOMAS JEFFERSON

By HENRY ADAMS

VOL. I.

ANTIQUARIAN PRESS LTD.
New York
1962

First Published
1891-1896
by
Charles Scribner's Sons

———

Reprinted 1962
by
Antiquarian Press, Ltd.
New York, N.Y.

Edition Limited to 750 Sets

Library of Congress Catalog Card Number: 61-8054

Printed in the U.S.A.

———

NOBLE OFFSET PRINTERS, INC.
NEW YORK 3, N.Y.

CONTENTS OF VOL. I.

HISTORY OF THE UNITED STATES.

———◆———

CHAPTER I.

A SECOND time President Jefferson appeared at the Capitol, escorted with due formalities by a procession of militia-men and other citizens ; and once more he delivered an inaugural address, " in so low a voice that not half of it was heard by any part of the crowded auditory." [1] The second Inaugural roused neither the bitterness nor the applause which greeted the first, although in part it was intended as a cry of triumph over the principles and vanishing power of New England.

Among Jefferson's manuscripts he preserved a curious memorandum explaining the ideas of this address. As the first Inaugural declared the principles which were to guide the government in Republican hands, the second should report the success of these principles, and recall the results already reached. The task deserved all the eloquence and loftiness of thought that philosophy could command ;

[1] Diary of J. Q. Adams (March 4, 1805), i. 373.

for Jefferson had made a democratic polity victorious
at home and respectable in the world's eyes, and the
privilege of hearing him reaffirm his doctrines and
pronounce their success was one that could never be
renewed.   The Moses of democracy, he had the glory
of leading his followers into their promised and conquered Canaan.

Jefferson began by renewing the professions of his
foreign policy : —

" With nations, as with individuals, our interests,
soundly calculated, will ever be found inseparable from
our moral duties ; and history bears witness to the fact
that a just nation is taken on its word, when recourse is
had to armaments and wars to bridle others."

The sentiments were excellent ; but many of Jefferson's followers must have asked themselves in
what history they could find the fact, which the
President asserted, that a just nation was taken on
its word ; and they must have been still more perplexed to name the nation, just or unjust, which was
taken on its word by any other in the actual condition of the world.   Without dwelling on this topic,
which had already become one of interest in the
councils of his Cabinet, Jefferson, passing to practical
questions involved in redemption of debt, advanced
a new idea.

" Redemption once effected," he said, " the revenue
thereby liberated may, by a just repartition among the
States and a corresponding amendment of the Constitution, be applied, *in time of peace*, to rivers, canals, roads,

arts, manufactures, education, and other great objects within each State. *In time of war*, — if injustice, by ourselves or others, must sometimes produce war, — increased as the same revenue will be increased by population and consumption, and aided by other resources reserved for that crisis, it may meet within the year all the expenses of the year without encroaching on the rights of future generations by burdening them with the debts of the past. War will then be but a suspension of useful works, and a return to a state of peace a return to the progress of improvement."

Ten years earlier, in the mouth of President Washington, this sentiment would have been generally denounced as proof of monarchical designs. That Jefferson was willing not only to assume powers for the central government, but also to part from his State-rights associates and to gratify the Northern democrats by many concessions of principle, his first Administration had already proved; but John Randolph might wonder to see him stride so fast and far toward what had been ever denounced as Roman imperialism and corruption; to hear him advise a change of the Constitution in order to create an annual fund for public works, for the arts, for education, and even for such manufactures as the people might want, — a fund which was to be distributed to the States, thus putting in the hands of the central government an instrument of corruption, and making the States stipendiaries of Congress. Every principle of the Republican party, past or to come, was put to nought by a policy which contradicted the famous sentiment of Jefferson's first annual message : " Sound principles will not justify our taxing the industry of our fellow-citizens to accumulate treasure for wars to happen we know not when, and which might not perhaps happen but from the temptations offered by that treasure." Yet pregnant as this new principle might be in connection with the Constitution and the Union, its bearing on foreign affairs was more startling. Jefferson, the apostle of peace, asked for a war fund which should enable his government to wage indefinite hostilities without borrowing money ! His mind dwelt on the possibility of conquests !

Quitting this dangerous ground, the President spoke of the Louisiana purchase. Then followed a paragraph upon religion. Next he came to the subject of the Indians, and chose this unusual medium for enforcing favorite philosophical doctrines. The memorandum written to explain his address declared the reasons that led him to use the mask of Indian philanthropy to disguise an attack upon conservatism.

" Every respecter of science," said this memorandum, " every friend to political reformation, must have observed with indignation the hue-and-cry raised against philosophy and the rights of man ; and it really seems as if they would be overborne, and barbarism, bigotry, and despotism would recover the ground they have lost by the advance of the public understanding. I have thought the occasion justified some discountenance of these anti-social

doctrines, some testimony against them ; but not to commit myself in direct warfare on them, I have thought it
best to say what is directly applied to the Indians only,
but admits by inference a more general extension."

In truth, under the lead of Napoleon and Pitt,
Europe seemed bent on turning back the march of
time and renewing the bigotry and despotism of the
Middle Ages ; but this occasion hardly dignified
Jefferson's method of bearing testimony against the
danger, by not committing himself to direct warfare
upon it, but by applying to Indians the homily which
by inference included the churches of New England.

" The aboriginal inhabitants of these countries," said
the President to his great audience, " I have regarded with
the commiseration their history inspires.   Endowed with
the faculties and the rights of men, breathing an ardent
love of liberty and independence, and occupying a country which left them no desire but to be undisturbed, the
stream of overflowing population from other regions
directed itself on these shores."

If the Boston newspapers were not weary of ridi-
culing Jefferson's rhetoric, this sentence was fitted to
rouse their jaded amusement ; but in a few moments
they had reason to feel other emotions.   He said that
he had done what humanity required, and had tried
to teach the Indians agriculture and other industries
in order to prepare them for new conditions of life, —
a claim not only true, but also honorable to him.
Unfortunately these attempts met with obstacles from
the Indians themselves : —

"They are combated by the habits of their bodies, prejudice of their minds, ignorance, pride, and the influence of interested and crafty individuals among them, who feel themselves something in the present order of things, and fear to become nothing in any other. These persons inculcate a sanctimonious reverence for the customs of their ancestors; that whatsoever they did must be done through all time; that reason is a false guide, and to advance under its counsel, in their physical, moral, or political condition, is perilous innovation; that their duty is to remain as their Creator made them, ignorance being safety, and knowledge full of danger. In short, my friends, among them is seen the action and counteraction of good sense and bigotry; they too have their anti-philosophers, who find an interest in keeping things in their present state, who dread reformation, and exert all their faculties to maintain the ascendency of habit over the duty of improving our reason and obeying its mandates."

Gallatin remonstrated in vain against this allusion to New England habits;[1] the President could not resist the temptation to strike once more his old enemies. Gallatin, whose sense of humor was keener than that of Jefferson, must have been amused by the travesty of New England under the war-paint and blankets of the Choctaws and Kickapoos; but Jefferson was never more serious than in believing that the people of Massachusetts and Connecticut were held in darkness by a few interested "medicine-men," and that he could, without committing him-

[1] Gallatin's Writings, i. 227.

self in direct warfare, insult the clergy, lawyers, and keen-witted squirarchy of New England, thus held up "by inference" to the world as the equivalent to so many savages.

The rest of the Inaugural was chiefly devoted to the press and its licentiousness. Jefferson expressed himself strongly in regard to the slanders he had received, and even hinted that he would be glad to see the State laws of libel applied to punish the offenders; but he pointed out that slander had no political success, and that it might safely be disregarded as a political weapon. He urged "doubting brethren" to give up their fears and prejudices, and to join with the mass of their fellow-citizens. "In the mean time let us cherish them with patient affection; let us do them justice, and more than justice, in all competitions of interest." Finally, as though to silence the New-England pulpit, he closed with a few words which the clergy might perhaps think misplaced in the mouth of so earnest a deist, — an invocation of "that Being in whose hands we are, who led our forefathers, as Israel of old," to the "country flowing with all the necessaries and comforts of life, . . . and to whose goodness I ask you to join with me in supplications."

The Second Inaugural strode far beyond the first in the path of democracy, away from the landmarks of Virginia republicanism, betraying what Jefferson's friends and enemies alike thought a craving for popularity. If this instinct sometimes led him to

forget principles he had once asserted, and which
he would some day again declare vital, the quality
was so amiable as to cover many shortcomings ; but
its influence on national growth could not be disputed. Jefferson cherished but one last desire, —
to reach the end of his next term without disaster.
He frankly expressed this feeling in a letter written to General Heath soon after the autumn election of 1804, which gave him the electoral vote of
Massachusetts : —

" I sincerely join you," said he, " in congratulations
on the return of Massachusetts into the fold of the Union.
This is truly the case wherein we may say, ' This our
brother was dead, and is alive again ; and was lost, and
is found.' It is but too true that our Union could not be
pronounced entirely sound while so respectable a member
as Massachusetts was under morbid affection. All will
now come to rights. . . . The new century opened itself
by committing us on a boisterous ocean ; but all is now
subsiding ; peace is smoothing our path at home and
abroad ; and if we are not wanting in the practice of justice and moderation, our tranquillity and prosperity may
be preserved until increasing numbers shall leave us nothing to fear from abroad. With England we are in cordial
friendship ; with France in the most perfect understanding ; with Spain we shall always be bickering, but never
at war till we seek it. Other nations view our course
with respect and friendly anxiety. Should we be able to
preserve this state of public happiness, and to see our
citizens, whom we found so divided, rally to their genuine
principles, I shall hope yet to enjoy the comfort of that

general good-will which has been so unfeelingly wrested from me, and to sing at the close of my term the *Nunc dimittis, Domine*, with a satisfaction leaving nothing to desire but the last great audit." [1]

He could not forgive the New England clergy their want of feeling in wresting from him ever so small a share of the general good-will, and he looked for-ward with impatience to the moment when he should enjoy universal applause and respect. In Decem-ber, 1804, when this letter was written, he felt confi-dent that his splendid triumph would last unchecked to the end of his public career ; but the prize of general good-will, which seemed then almost won, continually eluded his grasp. The election of Novem-ber, 1804, was followed by the session of 1804–1805, which stirred bad blood even in Virginia, and betrayed a spirit of faction among his oldest friends. His In-augural Address of March, 1805, with its mixture of bitter-sweet, was answered within a few weeks by Massachusetts. At the April election the Federalists reversed the result of November, and re-elected Caleb Strong as governor by a vote of about 35,200 against 33,800, with a Federalist majority in the Legislature. Even in Pennsylvania divisions among Jefferson's fol-lowers increased, until in the autumn of 1805 Duane and Leib set up a candidate of their own choice for governor, and forced McKean, Dallas, and Gallatin's friends to unite with the Federalists in order to re-elect McKean. Jefferson balanced anxiously between

[1] Jefferson to General Heath, Dec. 13, 1804; Jefferson MSS.

these warring factions, trying to offend neither Duane nor John Randolph, nor even Burr, while he still drew the mass of moderate Federalists to sympathize in his views.

Thus the new Presidential term began, bringing with it little sign of change. The old arrangements were continued, with but one exception. Madison, Gallatin, Robert Smith, and Dearborn remained in the Cabinet; but Attorney-General Lincoln resigned, and Robert Smith asked to be transferred from the Navy Department to the Attorney-General's office.[1] After some hesitation Jefferson yielded to Smith's request and consented to the transfer. As Smith's successor in the Navy Department Jefferson selected Jacob Crowninshield, a member of Congress from Massachusetts, who was then at Washington. Crown-inshield, in consequence of his wife's objection to leaving her family, declined the offer, Jan. 29, 1805,[2] but the President nevertheless sent the nomination to the Senate, March 2, 1805, together with that of Robert Smith, " now Secretary of the Navy to be Attorney-General of the United States." The same day the Senate confirmed both appointments, and the commissions were regularly issued, March 3, — Robert Smith apparently ceasing thenceforward to possess any legal authority over the Navy Department.

Nevertheless Crowninshield persisted in declining

[1] Jefferson to Robert Smith, Jan. 3, 1805; Jefferson MSS.

[2] Crowninshield to Jefferson, Jan. 29, 1805; Jefferson MSS. State Department Archives.

the office, and Robert Smith continued to act as Secretary of the Navy, probably by the verbal request of the President.   At length he consented to retain his old position permanently, and Jefferson sought for a new attorney-general.   He offered the post, June 15, to John Julius Pringle of South Carolina, who declined.   He then offered it, July 14, to John Thompson Mason, who also declined.   August 7, Jefferson wrote to Senator Breckinridge of Kentucky, asking him to accept the office of attorney-general, and a temporary commission was the same day issued to him.

When Congress met, Dec. 2, 1805, Breckenridge was attorney-general under a temporary commission, and Robert Smith, who had ceased to be Secretary of the Navy on the confirmation of his successor, March 3, was acting as secretary under no apparent authority.   Dec. 20, 1805, the President sent a message to the Senate making nominations for vacancies which had occurred during the recess, for which commissions had been granted " to the persons herein respectively named."   One of these persons was John Breckinridge of Kentucky to be Attorney-General of the United States, and the nomination was duly confirmed.   Breckenridge's permanent commission bore date Jan. 17, 1806.

These dates and facts were curious for the reason that Robert Smith, who had ceased to be Secretary of the Navy, March 3, 1805, ceased necessarily to be attorney-general on the confirmation of Breckin-

ridge, and continued to act as Secretary of the Navy
without authority of law.   The President did not
send his name to the Senate, or issue to him a new
commission either permanent or temporary.   On the
official records of the Department of State, not Robert
Smith but Jacob Crowninshield was Secretary of the
Navy from March 3, 1805, till March 7, 1809, when
his successor was appointed, although Jacob Crowninshield died April 15, 1808, and Robert Smith never
ceased to act as Secretary of the Navy from his appointment in 1801 to his appointment as Secretary
of State in 1809.   During the whole period of Jefferson's second administration, his Secretary of the
Navy acted by no known authority except the verbal
request or permission of the President.

In perfect quiet, disturbed only by rumors of wars
abroad, spring crept forward to summer, summer
ripened to autumn.   Peace was restored with Tripoli;
commerce grew apace; the revenue rose to $14,000,-
000; the Treasury was near a surfeit; no sign appeared of check to the immense prosperity which
diffused itself through every rivulet in the wilderness, and the President could see no limit to its
future increase.   In 1804 he had sent out an expedition under Captain Meriwether Lewis to explore the
Louisiana purchase along the course of the Missouri
River.   May 14, 1804, Lewis and his party began
their journey from St. Louis, and without serious
difficulty reached the Mandan towns, sixteen hundred and nine miles from the starting point, where,

Nov. 1, 1804, they went into winter quarters. April 8, 1805, Lewis resumed his journey to the westward, sending the report of his wanderings to Washington. This report told only of a vast region inhabited by Indian tribes and disturbed by the restless and murderous Sioux ; but it served to prove the immensity of the new world which Jefferson's government had given to the American people. Other explorations had been begun along the line of the Red and Washita rivers. In such contributions to human knowledge Jefferson took keen interest, for he had no greater delight than in science and in whatever tended to widen the field of knowledge.

These explorations of the territory beyond the Mississippi had little immediate bearing on the interests of commerce or agriculture ; but the government was actively engaged in measures of direct value. July 4, 1805, William Henry Harrison, Governor of the Indiana Territory, closed a bargain with the Wyandots, Ottawas, and other Indian tribes, by which the Indian title over another part of Ohio was extinguished. The Indians thenceforward held within the State of Ohio only the country west of Sandusky and north of the old line fixed by the treaty of Greenville. Within the year the Piankeshaw tribe sold for a small annuity a tract of land in southern Indiana, along the Ohio River, which made the United States government master of the whole north bank of the Ohio to its mouth. These concessions, of the utmost value, were obtained at a trifling cost. " The average price

paid for the Indian lands within the last four years,"
wrote the Secretary of War,[1] " does not amount to
one cent per acre." The Chickasaws and Cherokees
sold a very large district between the Cumberland
and Tennessee rivers in Tennessee, so that thenceforward the road from Knoxville to Nashville passed
through no Indian land. In Georgia the Creeks were
induced to sell an important territory between the
Oconee and Ocmulgee rivers. In these treaties provision was also made for horse-roads through the
Creek and Cherokee country, both from Knoxville
and from central Georgia to the Mobile River.

Besides the many millions of acres thus gained for
immediate improvement, these treaties had no little
strategic value in case of war. No foreign country
could fail to see that the outlying American settlements were defenceless in their isolation. Even
the fort and village at Detroit were separated from
the nearest white village by a wide Indian country
impassable to wagons or artillery; and the helpless-
ness of such posts was so evident as to impress every
observer.

" The principles of our government," said **Jefferson**
when danger at last arose,[2] " leading us to the employment of such moderate garrisons in time of peace as may
merely take care of the post, and to a reliance on the

[1] Dearborn to Robertson, March 20, 1805 ; State Papers, vol.
v. ; Indian Affairs, i. 700.

[2] Message of Jan. 30, 1808 ; State Papers, vol. v. ; Indian
Affairs, i. 752.

neighboring militia for its support in the first moments of war, I have thought it would be important to obtain from the Indians such a cession in the neighborhood of these posts as might maintain a militia proportioned to this object."

This "principle of our government" that the settlers should protect the army, not the army the settlers, was so rigorously carried out that every new purchase of Indian lands was equivalent to providing a new army. The possession of Sandusky brought Detroit nearer its supports; possession of the banks of the Ohio strengthened Indiana. A bridle-path to New Orleans was the first step toward bringing that foreign dependence within reach; and although this path must necessarily pass through Spanish territory, it would enable the government in an emergency to hear from Louisiana within six weeks from the despatch of an order.

In spite of these immense gains, the military situation was still extremely weak. The Indians held in strong force the country west of Sandusky. The boundary between them and the whites was a mere line running from Lake Erie south and west across Ohio, Indiana, and Illinois to the neighborhood of St. Louis. Directly on this boundary line, near Greenville, lived the Shawanese, among whom a warrior named Tecumthe, and his brother called the Prophet were acquiring an influence hostile to the white men. These Indians, jealous of the rapid American encroachments, maintained relations with the British

officials in Canada, and in case of a war between
the United States and England they were likely to
enter into a British alliance. In this case unless the
United States government could control Lake Erie,
nothing was more certain than that Detroit and
every other post on the Lakes beyond must fall into
British hands, and with them the military possession of the whole Northwest. Whether Great Britain
could afterward be forced to surrender her conquests
remained to be seen.

Even in Kentucky the country between the Tennessee River and the Mississippi still belonged to the
Chickasaws ; and south of the Tennessee River as far
as the Gulf of Mexico, and east to the Ocmulgee, all
belonged to Cherokees, Creeks, and Choctaws, who
could not boast, like the Chickasaws, that " they had
never spilt the blood of a white man." These tribes
maintained friendly relations with the Spanish authorities at Mobile and Pensacola, and, like the Shawanese and Northwestern Indians, dreaded the grasping
Americans, who were driving them westward. In
case of war with Spain, should New Orleans give
trouble and invite a Spanish garrison, the Indians
might be counted as Spaniards, and the United States
government might be required to protect a frontier
suddenly thrust back from the Floridas to the Duck
River, within thirty miles of Nashville.

The President might well see with relief every
new step that brought him within nearer reach of
his remote military posts and his proconsular prov-

ince at New Orleans. That he should dread war was natural, for he was responsible for the safety of the settlements on the Indian frontier, and he knew that in case of sudden war the capture of these posts was certain, and the massacre of their occupants more than probable. New Orleans was an immediate and incessant danger, and hardly a spot between New Orleans and Mackinaw was safe.

Anxiety caused by these perils had probably much to do with the bent of the President's mind toward internal improvements and democratic rather than Virginia principles. In 1803 the United States government became owner of a territory which dwarfed the States themselves, and which at its most important point contained a foreign population governed by military methods. Old political theories had been thrown aside both in the purchase and in the organization of this New World ; their observance in its administration was impossible. The Louisiana purchase not only required a military system of government for itself, but also reacted on the other national territory, and through it on the States in their relations to Washington. New England was thrown to the verge of the political system ; but New York and Pennsylvania, Georgia and Tennessee, Ohio and Kentucky found many new interests which they wanted the central government to assist, and Virginia, holding the power and patronage of the central government, had every inducement to satisfy these demands.

So it happened that Jefferson gave up his Virginia dogmas, and adopted Gallatin's ideas. They were both jealous of the army and navy; but they were willing to spend money with comparative liberality on internal improvements; and the wisdom of this course was evident. Even in a military point of view, roads and canals were more necessary than forts or ships.

The first evidence of change was the proposed fund for internal improvements and war purposes described in the second Inaugural Address. The suggestion was intended to prepare the public for a relaxation of Gallatin's economy. Although the entire debt could not be paid before 1817, only ten and a half millions of bonds remained to be immediately dealt with. By the year 1809 these ten and a half millions would be discharged; and thereafter Gallatin might reduce his annual payments of principal and interest from $8,000,000 to $4,500,000, freeing an annual sum of $3,500,000 for use in other directions. During the next three years Gallatin was anxious to maintain his old system, and especially to preserve peace with foreign nations; but after the year 1808 he promised to relax his severity, and to provide three or four millions for purposes of internal improvement and defence. The rapid increase of revenue helped to create confidence in this calculation, and to hasten decision as to the use of the promised surplus. The President had already decided to convert it into a permanent reserve fund. He looked forward to the moment when, as he expressed it, he could " begin upon canals, roads, colleges, etc." [1] He no longer talked of " a wise and frugal government which shall restrain men from injuring one another, which shall leave them otherwise free to regulate their own pursuits of industry and improvement, and shall not take from the mouth of labor the bread it has earned; " he rather proposed to devote a third of the national revenues to improvements and to regulation of industries.

This theory of statesmanship was broader than that which he had proclaimed four years earlier. Jefferson proved the liberality and elevation of his mind; and if he did this at some cost to his consistency, he did only what all men had done whose minds kept pace with the movement of their time. So far as he could see, at the threshold of his second term, he had every reason to hope that it would be more successful than his first. He promised to annihilate opposition; and no serious obstacle seemed in his path. No doubt his concessions to the spirit of nationality, in winning support from moderate Federalists and self-interested democrats, alienated a few State-rights Republicans, and might arouse uneasiness among old friends; but to this Jefferson resigned himself. He parted company with the " mere metaphysical subtleties" of John Randolph. Except in his aversion to military measures and to formal etiquette, he stood

[1] Jefferson to Gallatin, May 29, 1805; Gallatin's Writings, 232.

nearly where President Washington had stood ten
years before.

The New England hierarchy might grumble, but
at heart Massachusetts was already converted. Only
with the utmost difficulty, and at the cost of avoiding every aggressive movement, could the Federalists keep control of their State governments. John
Randolph flattered himself that if Jefferson's personal authority were removed from the scale, Virginia
would again incline to her old principles; but he was
mistaken. So long as Virginia held power, she was
certain to use it. At no time since the Declaration
of Independence had the prospects of nationality
seemed so promising as in the spring of 1805. With
the stride of the last four years as a standard for the
future, no man could measure the possible effects of
the coming four years in extending the powers of the
government and developing the prosperity of the nation. Gallatin already meditated schemes of internal
improvements, which included four great thorough-
fares across the Alleghanies, while Fulton was nearly
ready with the steamboat. The Floridas could not
escape the government's grasp. Even New England
must at last yield her prejudices to the spirit of
democratic nationality.

No one could wonder if Jefferson's head was somewhat turned by the splendors of such a promise. Sanguine by nature, he felt that every day made more
secure the grandeur of his destiny. He could scarcely
be blamed for putting a high estimate on the value

of his services, for in all modesty he might reasonably ask what name recorded in history would stand higher than his own for qualities of the noblest order in statesmanship. Had he not been first to conceive and to put in practice the theories of future democracy? Had he not succeeded in the experiment? Had he not doubled the national domain? Was not his government a model of republican virtues? With what offence against the highest canons of personal merit could he be charged? What ruler of ancient or modern times, what Trajan or Antonine, what Edward or Louis, was more unselfish or was truer to the interests intrusted to his care? Who had proposed to himself a loftier ideal? Among all the kings and statesmen who swayed the power of empire, where could one be found who had looked so far into the future, and had so boldly grappled with its hopes?

CHAPTER II.

DURING the administrations of Jefferson and Madison, the national government was in the main controlled by ideas and interests peculiar to the region south of the Potomac, and only to be understood from a Southern stand-point. Especially its foreign relations were guided by motives in which the Northern people felt little sympathy. The people of the Northern States seemed almost unwilling to know what the people of the Southern States were thinking or doing in certain directions, and their indifference was particularly marked in regard to Florida. Among the varied forms of Southern ambition, none was so constant in influence as the wish to acquire the Floridas, which at moments decided the action of the government in matters of the utmost interest; yet the Northern public, though complaining of Southern favoritism, neither understood nor cared to study the subject, but turned impatiently away whenever the Floridas were discussed, as though this were a local detail which in no way concerned the North. If Florida failed to interest the North, it exercised the more control over the South, and over a government Southern in character and purpose. Neither

the politics of the Union nor the development of
events could be understood without treating Florida
as a subject of the first importance.   During the
summer and autumn of 1805, — a period which John
Randolph justly regarded as the turning point of Republican administration, — Florida actually engrossed
the attention of government.

On arriving at Madrid, Jan. 2, 1805, Monroe found
Charles Pinckney waiting in no happy temper for a
decision in regard to himself.   Pinckney's recall was
then determined upon, and his successor chosen.   He
was anxious only to escape the last humiliation of
being excluded from the new negotiation by Monroe.
From this fear he was soon relieved.   Monroe shared
his views ; allowed him to take part in the conferences,
and to put his name to the notes.   The two ministers
acted in harmony.

Nearly a month was consumed in the necessary
preliminaries.   Not until Jan. 28, 1805, were matters
so far advanced that Monroe could present his first
note.[1]   Following his instructions, he put forward all
the claims which had been so often discussed, — the
Spanish and French spoliations ; the losses resulting
from suppression of the *entrepôt* at New Orleans in
1802; the claim of West Florida, and that to the Rio
Bravo.   With the note the two envoys enclosed the
projet of a treaty, — to which could be made only the
usual objection to one-sided schemes, that it required

[1] Monroe and Pinckney to Cevallos, Jan. 28, 1805 ; State
Papers, ii. 636.

Spain to concede every point, and offered no equivalent worth mention. Spain was to cede both the
Floridas, and also Texas as far as the Rio Colorado,
leaving the district between the Colorado and the
Rio Bravo as a border-land not to be further settled. She was to create a commission for arranging
the spoliation and *entrepôt* claims ; and this commission should also take cognizance of all claims
that might be made by Spanish subjects against the
United States government.

To this note and *projet* Don Pedro Cevallos quickly
replied.[1] Availing himself of an inadvertent sentence
in Monroe's opening paragraph, to the effect that it
was necessary to examine impartially the several
points at issue in each case, Cevallos informed the
Americans that in accordance with their wish he
would first examine each point separately, and then
proceed to negotiation. He proposed to begin with
the claims convention of August, 1802.

Commonly nothing gratified American diplomatists
more than to discuss questions which they were
ordered to take in charge. Yet the readiness shown
by Cevallos to gratify this instinct struck Monroe as
a bad sign ; he saw danger of lowering the national
tone, and even of becoming ridiculous, if he allowed
the Spaniards to discuss indefinitely claims which
the United States had again and again asserted to
be too plain for discussion. He felt too the influ-

[1] Cevallos to Monroe and Pinckney, Jan. 31, 1805 ; State
Papers, ii. 636.

ence of Pinckney, who had never ceased to urge that nothing could be done with the Spanish government except through fear or force. He could not refuse discussion, but he entered into it with the intention of promptly cutting it short.[1]

To cut the discussion short was precisely what Cevallos meant should not be done; and a contest began, in which the Spaniard had every advantage. Monroe replied to the Spanish note of January 31 by imposing an ultimatum at once.[2] " We consider it our duty to inform your Excellency that we cannot consent to any arrangement which does not provide for the whole subject " of the claims, including the French spoliations. " It is in his Majesty's power, by the answer which you give, to fix at once the relations which are to subsist in future between the two nations." Cevallos, leaving the ultimatum and the French spoliations unnoticed, rejoined by discussing the conditions which the King had placed on his consent to ratify the claims convention of 1802.[3] Taking up first the Mobile Act, he expressed in strong terms his opinion of it, and of the explanation given to it by the President. Nevertheless, he withdrew his demand that the Act should be annulled. The King's " well-founded motives of complaint in respect to that

[1] Monroe and Pinckney to Madison, May 23, 1805 ; State Papers, ii. 667.

[2] Pinckney and Monroe to Cevallos, Feb. 5, 1805 ; State Papers, ii. 640.

[3] Cevallos to Monroe and Pinckney, Feb. 10, 1805 ; State Papers, ii. 541.

Act still exist," he said, " and his Majesty intends to keep them in mind, that satisfaction may be given by the United States ; but as it relates to ratifying the convention of August, 1802, his Majesty agrees from this time to be satisfied in this respect." The question of French spoliations he reserved for separate discussion.

Monroe replied briefly by referring to his ultimatum, and by inviting discussion of the boundary question ; but Cevallos, instead of taking up the matter of boundaries in his next note, discussed the French spoliation claims and the right of deposit at New Orleans.[1]   To rebut the first, he produced a letter from Talleyrand dated July 27, 1804, in which Napoleon announced that neither Spain nor the United States must touch these claims, under penalty of incurring the Emperor's severe displeasure.   In regard to the right of deposit, Cevallos took still stronger ground : —

" The edict of the Intendant of New Orleans, suspending the deposit of American produce in that city, did not interrupt, nor was it the intention to interrupt, the navigation of the Mississippi ; consequently these pretended injuries are reduced to this small point, — that for a short time the vessels loaded in the stream instead of taking in their cargoes at the wharves. . . . If the erroneous opinions which were formed in the United States, if the complaints published in the papers of your country, —

[1] Cevallos to Monroe and Pinckney, Feb. 16, 1805 ; State Papers, ii. 643.

as false as they were repeated, — that the navigation of
the Mississippi was interrupted, if the virulent writings
by which the public mind was heated, and which led to
compromit the American government and tarnish the
good name of that of Spain, were causes that the inhabitants of the western territory of the United States
could not form a correct idea of what passed at New
Orleans ; and if, in this uncertainty, they were disappointed in the extraction of their produce, or suffered
other inconveniences, — they ought to attribute the same
to internal causes, such as the writings before mentioned,
filled with inflammatory falsehoods, the violence of enthusiastic partisans, and other occurrences which on
those occasions served to conceal the truth.   The Government of Spain, so far from being responsible for the
prejudices occasioned by these errors and erroneous ideas,
ought in justice to complain of the irregular conduct pursued by various writers and other individuals in the
United States, which was adapted to exasperate and mis-
lead the public opinion, and went to divulge sentiments
the most ignominious, and absurdities the most false,
against the government of his Majesty and his accredited
good faith."

Not satisfied with this rebuttal, Cevallos added that
the persons who complained of this trifling inconvenience " had been enjoying the rights of deposit for
four years more than was stipulated in the treaty,
and this notwithstanding the great prejudice it occasioned to his Majesty's revenue, by making New
Orleans the centre of a most scandalous contraband
trade, the profits of which it is not improbable but
that some of those individuals have in part received."

Finally, he affirmed the Intendant's right to prohibit the deposit.

On receiving this paper, Monroe hesitated whether to break off the negotiation; but quickly came to the decision not to do so. His instructions expressly authorized him to abandon the *entrepôt* claims; while a rupture founded on the French spoliations, in the face of Talleyrand's threats, was rupture with France as well as with Spain, and exceeded his authority. He concluded to go on, although he saw that every new step involved new dangers.

Before Monroe had prepared a reply to the sharp letter on the claims convention, Cevallos wrote again.[1] In this letter, dated February 24, he discussed the West Florida boundary, and contented himself with stating the Spanish case as it stood on the treaties and public evidence. His argument contained no new points, but was evidently intended to lure the Americans into endless discussion. Monroe was obliged to follow where Cevallos led. February 26 he replied to the Spanish note on the claims. Beginning with complaints that Cevallos had not met with directness the American proposals; branching into other complaints that he had renewed propositions which Monroe had already declared incompatible with the rights of the United States; that he had charged the American government with trying to obtain double payment for the same loss, and had branded

[1] Cevallos to Monroe and Pinckney, Feb. 24, 1805; State Papers, ii. 644.

the whole American people as being in league with smugglers; that he had attacked the freedom of the press, and had called the right of deposit a charity of King Charles, — after adding that "it was impossible for us to have received a note which could have been more unexpected," the two American envoys began to discuss the French spoliation claims, "on the presumption that no premeditated outrage was intended." [1]

After a long argument on the French spoliations, Monroe's note next reached the most delicate point in discussion, — the positive order of Napoleon forbidding recognition of the claims. Treating the order as though it were only an expression of opinions, Monroe said, "We have received them with the consideration which is due to the very respectable authority from which they emanate. On all treaties between independent Powers each party has a right to form its own opinion. Every nation is the guardian of its own honor and rights; and the Emperor is too sensible of what is due to his own glory, and entertains too high a respect for the United States, to wish them to abandon a just sense of what is due to their own." Appealing finally to the positive orders of his own government, Monroe repeated that on these claims he must insist. Cevallos replied with a disavowal of "premeditated outrage;" and there, March 1, 1805, after Monroe had passed two months

[1] Monroe and Pinckney to Cevallos, Feb. 26, 1805; State Papers, ii. 646.

in Spain, he found himself at his starting-point, at a loss how to go forward or to recede.

Monroe received early in February Talleyrand's letter of Dec. 21, 1804, on the boundary of West Florida;[1] he next suffered the mortification of listening to Talleyrand's order of July 27, 1804, forbidding Spain to "condescend" to pay or even to discuss the French spoliation claims; and from these documents he saw that for nearly a year past the French and Spanish governments had combined to entrap and humiliate him. The fault was his own, for he had received plain, not to say rude, warning; but he was perhaps only the more angry on that account, and in his irritation he undertook to terrify Napoleon. March 1, 1805, under the full consciousness of his situation, he wrote to Armstrong at Paris;[2] —

"It cannot be doubted that if our Government could be prevailed on to give ground, that of France would be very glad of it, as it would be to take us and all our concerns, especially our funds, under its care. We are inclined to believe, with almost equal confidence, if we are firm, and show that we are not only able but resolved to take care of ourselves, that she will let us do so, and in regard to this question with Spain throw her weight into our scale to promote an adjustment between us on the fair principles insisted on by our Government. To bring her to this, she must clearly understand that the negotiation

[1] Monroe's diary at Aranjuez, March 16, 1805; Monroe MSS.

[2] Monroe to Armstrong, March 1, 1805; MSS. State Department Archives.

is about to break up without doing anything, and that the failure is entirely owing to the part she has taken against us. When she sees that this is the literal fact, I do not think that her government will expose itself to the consequences resulting from it. It is not prepared to quarrel with us for many reasons : first, as we are a republic, and that system of government too recently overset there, and the one established in its stead too feebly founded, to make it a desirable object with the Emperor ; second, as she relies altogether for supplies on our flag, and on our merchants and people for many other friendly offices in the way of trade, which none others can render ; third, as our government pursues, by prohibiting our trade with St. Domingo, and in many other respects, a system of the most friendly accommodation to the interests of France, she ought not to hazard those advantages if there were no other objections to a rupture with us ; fourth, — but there are other and much stronger objections to it, — we should come to a good understanding with England. . . . These considerations incline us to think that a rupture with us is an event which of all others she least seeks at the present time ; and that it is only necessary to let her see distinctly that one with Spain is on the point of taking place, and will be owing altogether to her support of her pretensions, to induce France to change her policy and tone in the points depending here."

Pursuing this train of reasoning, Monroe tested its correctness by challenging a direct issue of courage. His letter, thus inspired, reached Paris in due time, and its ideas were pressed by Armstrong on members of the French government. Their answer was prompt and final ; it was instantly reported by Armstrong to

Monroe in a letter [1] so pregnant with meaning that two of its sentences may be said to have decided the fate of Jefferson's second administration : —

" On the subject of indemnity for the suspended right of deposit (professing to know nothing of the ground on which the interruption had been given) they would offer no opinion. On that of reparation for spoliations committed on our commerce by Frenchmen within the territory of his Catholic Majesty, they were equally prompt and decisive, declaring that our claim, having nothing of solidity in it, must be abandoned.

" With regard to boundary, we have, they said, already given an opinion, and see no cause to change it. To the question, What would be the course of this government in the event of a rupture between us and Spain? they answered, We can neither doubt nor hesitate, — we must take part with Spain ; and our note of the 30th Frimaire [Dec. 21, 1804] was intended to communicate and impress this idea."

This stern message left Monroe helpless. To escape from Madrid without suffering some personal mortification was his best hope ; and fortunately Godoy took no pleasure in personalities. The Spaniard was willing to let Monroe escape as soon as his defeat should be fairly recorded. The month of March had nearly passed before Monroe received Armstrong's letter ; meanwhile Cevallos consumed the time in discussing the West Florida boundary. At the end of the month Monroe, fully aware at last

[1] Armstrong to Monroe, March 12 and 18, 1805; State Papers, ii. 636.

of his situation, attempted to force an issue. March 30 he wrote to Cevallos that he was weary of delay : [1]

" It neither comports with the object of the present mission nor its duties to continue the negotiation longer than it furnishes a well-founded expectation that the just and friendly policy which produced it, on the part of the United States, is cherished with the same views by his Catholic Majesty."

Unfortunately he had no excuse for breaking abruptly a negotiation which he had himself invited ; and Cevallos meant to give him at that stage no such excuse, for the important question of the Texan boundary remained to be discussed, and Talleyrand's instructions on that point must be placed on record by Spain.

Monroe wrote to Cevallos, April 9, that he considered " the negotiation as essentially terminated by what has already occurred.[2] . . . Should his Majesty's government think proper to invite another issue, on it will the responsibility rest for the consequences. The United States are not unprepared for, or unequal to, any crisis which may occur." Three days later he repeated the wish to " withdraw from a situation which, while it compromits the character of our government, cannot be agreeable to ourselves." [3] Cevallos

[1] Pinckney and Monroe to Cevallos, March 30, 1805; State Papers, ii. 657.

[2] Monroe and Pinckney to Cevallos, April 9, 1805; State Papers, ii. 658.

[3] Monroe and Pinckney to Cevallos, April 12, 1805; State Papers, ii. 660.

took no notice of the threats, and contented himself
with repelling the idea that the blame of breaking off
the negotiation should rest upon him.   Nevertheless
he hastened to record the opinion of his Government
in regard to the last claim of the United States, —
the Texan boundary.

Here again Cevallos followed the guidance of Talleyrand.   The dividing-line between Louisiana and
Texas, he said, ought to be decided by the line between the French and Spanish settlements.   The
French post of Natchitoches, on the Red River, was
distant seven leagues from the Spanish post of Nues-
tra Señora de los Adaes ; and therefore the boundary
of Louisiana should run between these two points
southward, along the watershed, until it reached the
Gulf of Mexico between the Marmentou and the Cal-
casieu, — a boundary which deprived the United
States not only of Texas, but of an important territory afterward included in the State of Louisiana.[1]

Eager as Monroe was to close the negotiation, he
could not leave this note without reply ; and accordingly he consumed another week in preparing more
complaints of Cevallos' dilatory conduct, and in proving that Texas was included in the grant made by
Louis XIV. to Anthony Crozat in 1712.   After dis-
posing of that subject, he again begged for a conclusion.   " As every point has been thus fully discussed,
we flatter ourselves that we shall now be honored

[1] Cevallos to Pinckney and Monroe, April 13, 1805; State
Papers, ii. 660.

with your Excellency's propositions for the arrangement of the whole business." [1] He flattered himself
in vain ; ten days passed without an answer.   May 1,
at a private interview, he tried to obtain some promise
of action, without better result than the usual oblig-
ing Spanish expressions ; a week afterward he made
another attempt, with the same reply, followed on
Monroe's part by an offer to concede even the point
of dignity.   " Would Señor Cevallos listen to a new
and more advantageous offer on the part of the
United States ? "   Cevallos replied that such a step
would be premature, as the discussion was not yet
ended.[2]   Monroe had no choice but to break through
the diplomatic net in which he had wound himself ;
and at length, May 12, 1805, he sent a general ultimatum to the Spanish government : If Spain would
cede the Floridas, ratify the claims convention of
August, 1802, and accept the Colorado as the Texan
boundary, the United States would establish a neutral
territory a hundred miles wide on the eastern bank of
the Colorado, from the Gulf to the northern boundary
of Louisiana ; would assume the French spoliation
claims, abandon the *entrepôt* claims, and accept the
cession of West Florida from the King, thereby abandoning the claim that it was a part of Louisiana.[3]

[1] Monroe and Pinckney to Cevallos, April 20, 1805; State
Papers, ii. 662.

[2] Monroe and Pinckney to Madison, 23 May, 1805; State
Papers, ii. 668.

[3] Pinckney and Monroe to Cevallos, May 12, 1805; State
Papers, ii. 665.

To this note Cevallos replied three days afterward by a courteous but decided letter, objecting in various respects to Monroe's offers, and summing up his objections in the comment that this scheme required Spain to concede everything and receive nothing; she must give up both the Floridas, half of Texas, and the claims convention, while she obtained as an equivalent for these concessions only an abandonment of claims which she did not acknowledge : [1] —

" The justice of the American government will not permit it to insist on propositions so totally to the disadvantage of Spain ; and however anxious his Majesty may be to please the United States, he cannot on his part assent to them, nor can he do less than consider them as little conformable to the rights of his Crown."

Three days later Monroe demanded his passports. For once, Cevallos showed as much promptness as Monroe could have desired. Without expressing a regret, or showing so much as a complimentary wish to continue the negotiation, Cevallos sent the passports, appointed the very next day for Monroe's audience of leave, and bowed the American envoy out of Spain with an alacrity which contrasted strongly with the delays which had hitherto wasted five months of time most precious to the American minister at the Court of St. James. In truth, the Prince of Peace had no longer an object to gain

[1] Cevallos to Monroe and Pinckney, May 15, 1805; State Papers, ii. 666.

by detaining Monroe; he had won every advantage
which could be wrung from the situation, except
that of proving the defeat of the United States by
publishing it to the world. For this, he could trust
Monroe.

After writing an angry letter to the French ambassador at Madrid, Monroe went his way, May 26, leaving Pinckney to maintain the forms of diplomatic
relations with the Spanish government. Pinckney
had still more to suffer before escaping from the
scene of his diplomatic trials. The Spaniards began
to plunder American commerce ; the spoliations of
1798 were renewed; the garrisons in West Florida
and Texas were reinforced; Cevallos paid no attention to complaints or threats. In October Pinckney
took leave and returned to America, and George W.
Erving was sent from London to take charge of the
legation at Madrid. Erving made an excellent representative within the narrow field of action open to
him as a mere *chargé d'affaires;* but he could do
little to stem the current of Spanish desperation.
The Prince of Peace, driven by France, England, and
America nearer and nearer to the precipice that
yawned for the destruction of Spain, was willing to
see the world embroiled, in the hope of finding some
last chance in his favor. When Erving in December,
five months after Monroe's departure, went to remonstrate against seizures of American ships in flagrant
violation of the treaty of 1795, Godoy received him
with the good-natured courtesy which marked his

manners. " How go our affairs ? " he asked ; " are we to have peace or war ? " Erving called his attention to the late seizures. The Prince replied that it was impossible for Spain to allow American vessels to carry English property. " But we have a treaty which secures us that right," replied Erving. " Certainly, I know you have a treaty, for I made it with Mr. Pinckney," rejoined Godoy ; and he went on with entire frankness to announce that the " free-goods " provision of that treaty would no longer be respected. Then he continued, with laughable coolness, —

" You may choose either peace or war. 'T is the same thing to me. I will tell you candidly, that if you will go to war this certainly is the moment, and you may take our possessions from us. I advise you to go to war now, if you think that is best for you ; and then the peace which will be made in Europe will leave us two at war." [1]

Defiance could go no further. Elsewhere the Prince openly said that the United States had brought things to such a point as to leave Spain indifferent to the consequences. In war the President could only seize Florida ; and Florida was the price he asked for remaining at peace. Mexico and Cuba were beyond his reach. Meanwhile Spain not only saved the money due for the old claims, but plundered American commerce, and still preserved her title to the Floridas and Texas, — a title which, at least as con-

[1] Erving to Madison, Dec. 7. 1805; MSS. State Department Archives.

cerned the Floridas, the Americans must sooner or later extinguish.

Such was the result of the President's diplomacy in respect to Spain. War was its only natural outcome, — war with Spain ; war with Napoleon, who must make common cause with King Charles ; coalition with England ; general recurrence to the ideas and precedents of the last Administration. Jefferson had exasperated Spain and irritated France. He must next decide whether this policy should be pursued to its natural result.

Meanwhile Monroe returned to Paris, where he passed six weeks with Armstrong and with his French acquaintances in conference on the proper course to be pursued. Talleyrand was absent in Italy with the Emperor, who May 26 received at Milan the iron crown of the Lombard kings. That Napoleon was the real element of danger was clear to both envoys. A policy which should force France to interfere on behalf of the United States was their object ; and on this, as on many points, Armstrong's ideas were more definite than those of Monroe, Madison, or Jefferson. Even before Monroe left Madrid, he received a letter from Armstrong in which the outline of a decisive plan was sketched : —

" It is simply to take a strong and prompt possession of the northern bank of the Rio Bravo, leaving the eastern limit *in statu quo*. A stroke of this kind would at once bring Spain to reason, and France to her rescue, and without giving either room to quarrel. You might then negotiate, and shape the bargain pretty much as you pleased." [1]

Evidently the seizure of Texas, leaving West Florida untouched, was the only step which the President could properly take ; for Texas had been bought and paid for, whereas West Florida beyond doubt had never been bought at all. Armstrong saw the weak point of Napoleon's position, and wished to attack it. He had no trouble in bringing Monroe to the same conclusion, although in yielding to his arguments Monroe tacitly abandoned the ground he had been persuaded by Livingston to take two years before, that West Florida belonged to Louisiana.

" There is no shade of difference in our opinions," wrote Armstrong to Madison after Monroe's arrival at Paris,[2] " and so little in the course to be pursued with regard to Spain that it is scarcely worth noticing. The whole may be reduced to this : that instead of assailing the Spanish posts in West Florida, or even indicating an intention to do so, I would (from motives growing more particularly out of the character of the Emperor) restrict the operations to such as may have been established in Louisiana. This, with some degree of demonstration that we meditate an embargo on our commercial intercourse with Spain and her colonies, would compel this government to interpose promptly and efficiently, and with dispositions to prevent the quarrel from going further."

[1] Armstrong to Monroe, May 4, 1805; MSS. State Department Archives.

[2] Armstrong to Madison, July 3, 1805; MSS. State Department Archives.

Throughout these Spanish negotiations ran a mysterious note of corruption which probably came not from Cevallos, Godoy, or King Charles; for Spain was always the party to suffer, and France was always the party to profit by Spanish sacrifices. That the jobbery had its origin in Napoleon was improbable, for he too suffered from it. Neither Napoleon nor Godoy was open to bribery in such a sense; they were so high in power that small pecuniary motives had no influence on their acts. Yet the Treasuries both of France and Spain were in trouble, and were seeking resources. That Talleyrand had private motives for conniving in their expedients cannot be proved; but in 1805, as in 1798, every attempt to turn negotiation into a job came from Talleyrand's intimate circle, the subordinates of the French Foreign Office.[1] In June, Monroe found at Paris the same hints at the influence of money which had irritated him in the preceding autumn ; and he wrote to Madison in a tone which showed that he gave them weight.

" I have conferred much," he said,[2] " with the gentleman alluded to in my letter from Bordeaux of December 16, and from what I can gather am led to believe that France has withheld her opinion on the western limits [Texas], to favor our pretensions when she thinks proper to take a part in it ; that she does not think it proper so to do in the present stage, or until our Government acts

[1] Cf. Correspondance de Napoleon, xxxii. 321.

[2] Monroe to Madison, June 30, 1805 ; MSS. State Department Archives.

so as to make Spain apply to her. He thinks she will then act; and settling the Spanish spoliation business as by the treaty of 1802, and getting all that can be got for Florida (he says eight millions of dollars are expected), promote an adjustment."

If Jefferson's administration cared to commit an error of colossal proportions, it had but to follow the hints of these irresponsible agents of Marbois and Talleyrand, who presumed to say in advance what motives would decide the mind of Napoleon. No man in France — neither Talleyrand nor Berthier, nor even Duroc — knew the scope of the Emperor's ambition, or could foretell the expedients he would use or reject. Monroe's friend was ill-informed, or deceived him. France had not withheld her opinion on the western limits; on the contrary, her opinion had been exactly followed by Spain. Not Talleyrand, much less Napoleon, but Cevallos himself had withheld that opinion from Monroe's knowledge, doubtless because he wished to keep a weapon in reserve for use at close quarters if his antagonist should come so near. Had Monroe not been discomfited before Cevallos exhausted his arsenal, this weapon would certainly have been used for a final blow. Cevallos still held it in reserve.

Leaving the Spanish affair embroiled beyond disentanglement, Monroe recrossed the Channel, and July 23 found himself again in London. During a century of American diplomatic history a minister of the United States has seldom if ever within six months

suffered, at two great Courts, such contemptuous
treatment as had then fallen to Monroe's lot. That
he should have been mortified and anxious for escape
was natural. He returned to England, meaning to
sail as quickly as possible for America. "It was very
much my wish," he wrote.[1] Hoping to sail at latest
by November 1, he selected his ship, and gave notice
to the British Foreign Office. In his own interests
no step could have been wiser, but it was taken too
late; the time lost in Spain and at Paris had been
fatal to his plan, and he could no longer avoid another defeat more serious, and even more public, than
the two which had already disturbed his temper.

That the American minister in London at any time
should for six months leave his post, even in obedience to instructions, was surprising ; but that he
should have done this in 1804, after Pitt's return
to power, was matter of amazement. Monroe expected an unfriendly change of policy in the British
government. As early as June, 1804, he wrote to
Madison : " My most earnest advice is to look to
the possibility of such a change." [2] Four months
later, although the attitude of the British ministry
had become more threatening, Monroe started for
Madrid, leaving Pitt in peace, unwatched, to take his
measures and to fix beyond recall his change of
policy. July 23, 1805, when the American minister
at last returned from his Spanish journey and arrived

[1] Monroe to Madison, Oct. 18, 1805 ; State Papers, iii. 106.
[2] Monroe to Madison, June 3, 1805 ; State Papers, iii. 93.

in London, after some weeks lost at Paris, he found a state of affairs such as might have alarmed the most phlegmatic of men.

Pitt had made good use of Monroe's absence. During the winter of 1804–1805 Parliament passed several Acts tending to draw all the West Indian commerce into British hands. Throughout the West Indies free ports were thrown open to the enemy's vessels, which were encouraged to bring there the produce of their colonies, receiving British merchandise in return, while the Act further provided for the importation of this enemy's produce into Great Britain in British ships. Other Acts and Orders extended the system of licenses, by which British subjects were allowed to trade with their enemies in neutral vessels, and concluded by requiring that all their trade with the French islands should be carried on through the free ports alone.[1]

These measures were intended to force the trade of the French and Spanish colonies into a British channel; but all were secondary to a direct attack on American commerce. While Parliament and Council devised the legislation and rules necessary for taking charge of the commerce of Cuba, Martinique, and the other hostile colonies, the Lords of Appeals were engaged in providing the law necessary for depriving America of the same trade. July 23, 1805, Sir William Scott pronounced judgment in the case

[1] Act of April 10, 1805; Instructions of June 29, 1805 ; Orders of Aug. 3, 1805.

of the " Essex." Setting aside his ruling in the case
of the " Polly," [1] he held that the neutral cargo which
came from Martinique to Charleston, and thence to
London, was good prize unless the neutral owner
could prove, by something more than the evidence
of a custom-house entry, that his original intention
had been to terminate the voyage in an American
port. In consequence of this decision, within a few
weeks American ships by scores were seized without
warning; neutral insurance was doubled; and the
British merchantmen vied with the royal navy in
applauding the energy of William Pitt.

Of the decision as a matter of morality something
might be said. That Pitt should have planned such
a scheme was not surprising, for his moral sense had
been blunted by the desperation of his political struggle; but the same excuse did not apply to Sir William
Scott. The quarrel between law and history is old,
and its source lies deep. Perhaps no good historian
was ever a good lawyer: whether any good lawyer
could be a good historian might be equally doubted.
The lawyer is required to give facts the mould of a
theory; the historian need only state facts in their
sequence. In law Sir William Scott was considered
as one of the greatest judges that ever sat on the
English bench, a man of the highest personal honor,
sensitive to any imputation on his judicial independence, — a lawyer in whom the whole profession took
pride. In history he made himself and his court a

[1] See First Administration, ii. 400.

secret instrument for carrying out an act of piracy. The law defends him by throwing responsibility upon the political chiefs who were bound to make compensation to the plundered merchants if compensation was due. The judge's duty began and ended by declaring what was law. Experience had proved that the evidence previously required to convince the court of a certain fact was insufficient. The judge said this, and no more. History replies that whatever may be the strictly professional aspect of this famous judgment, in its nature it was a political act, and was known by the judge to be such. As a political measure its character was equivalent to a declaration of war, and did not materially differ from the more violent seizure of the Spanish treasure-ships by Pitt's order in the previous October. The lawyers justified that seizure also; the King's Advocate defended it in the House of Commons by the simple explanation that England was not in the habit of declaring war, but usually began hostilities by some act of force.[1] Lord Grenville, whom Pitt had entreated, only a few months before, to join the new ministry, and who was certainly considered as, next to Pitt himself, the highest political authority in England, was not deterred by this reasoning from denouncing the seizure of the Spanish galleons as an atrocious act of barbarity, contrary to all the law of nations, which stamped indelible infamy on the English name.

[1] Speech of Sir John Nicholl (Advocate-General), Feb. 11, 1805 ; Cobbett's Debates, iii. 407.

Lord Grey, another high authority, stigmatized it as combining violence, injustice, and bad faith. The seizure of the American ships was an act different in its nature only in so far as Sir William Scott condescended to throw over it in advance the ermine that he wore.

Monroe reached London on the very day when Sir William Scott pronounced his fatal decision in the case of the " Essex." Lord Harrowby no longer presided over the Foreign Office ; he had taken another position, making way for Lord Mulgrave. The new Foreign Secretary was, like most of Pitt's ministers in 1805, a Tory gentleman of moderate abilities. Except as a friend of Pitt he was unknown. His character and opinions seemed wholly without importance. To Lord Mulgrave, Monroe addressed himself ; and he found the Foreign Secretary as ready to discuss, and as slow to concede, as Don Pedro Cevallos had ever been.[1] " He assured me in the most explicit terms that nothing was more remote from the views of his Government than to take an unfriendly attitude toward the United States ; he assured me also that no new orders had been issued, and that his Government was disposed to do every. thing in its power to arrange this and the other points to our satisfaction." Yet when Monroe called his attention to the seizure of a score of American vessels in the Channel, by British naval officers who declared themselves to be acting by order, Lord Mulgrave

[1] Monroe to Madison, Aug. 16, 1805 ; State Papers, iii. 103.

quietly replied that the Rule of 1756 was good law, and that his Government did not mean to relax in the slightest degree from the rigor of Sir William Scott's decision.[1]

Monroe had felt the indifference or contempt of Lord Harrowby, Talleyrand, and Cevallos : that of Lord Mulgrave was but one more variety of a wide experience. The rough treatment of Monroe by the Englishman was a repetition of that which he had accepted or challenged at the hands of the Frenchman and Spaniard. Lord Mulgrave showed no wish to trouble himself in any way about the United States. He would not discuss the questions of impressment and commerce ; and his only sign of caring to explain or excuse the measures of his Government was in regard to Captain Bradley of the "Cambrian," who had been recalled from the American station for violations of neutrality. Monroe complained that Bradley had since been given a ship of the line. Mulgrave explained that the command of a line-of-battle ship was not necessarily a promotion, especially to an active officer accustomed to the independence and prize-money of the "Cambrian's" cruising ground.

With this result Monroe's diplomatic activity for the year 1804–1805 came to an end. The only conclusion he drew from it was one which Jefferson seemed little likely to adopt. He urged his Government to persevere in its course, and to threaten war

[1] Monroe to Madison, Aug. 20, 1805; State Papers, iii. 105.

upon France, Spain, and England at once.[1] "We probably shall never be able to settle our concerns with either Power without pushing our just claims on each with the greatest decision. . . . I am strong in the opinion that a pressure on each at the same time would produce a good effect with the other."

Nevertheless, Monroe had not yet reached the bottom of his English disaster. Neither the Acts of Parliament, the Orders in Council, nor the Judgment of the Lords of Appeal satisfied the suffering interests of England, however harsh they might seem to the interests of America. The new rules, the extension of licenses, the opening of free ports, tended to please the navy and shipping interests, but left the British colonists in a worse position than before; for as matters stood the whole produce of the West Indian Islands, French, Spanish, and British, was to be collected in a single mass and thrown on the London market. The warehouses on the Thames were to be overfilled with sugar, on the chance that neutral ships might convey it to France. For five years the colonists had insisted that their distress was due to excess in production ; but how could they check production when the French and Spanish islands were encouraged to produce ? Forgetting in their despair the attachment they felt to America, the colonists attributed all their troubles to American competition. The East

[1] Monroe to Madison, Oct. 18, 1805 ; State Papers, iii. 106. Monroe to Colonel Taylor, Sept. 10, 1810 ; Monroe MSS., State Department Archives.

India Company, whose warehouses were also loaded
with unsalable goods, could discover no better reason than the same neutral rivalry for the cessation
of Continental demand.   The shipowners, not yet
satisfied by Sir William Scott's law, echoed the same
cry.   All the interested classes of England, except
the manufacturers and merchants who were concerned in commerce with the United States, agreed
in calling upon government to crush out the neutral trade.   Sir William Scott had merely required
an additional proof of its honesty ; England with
one voice demanded that, honest or not, it should
be stopped.

This almost universal prayer found expression in
a famous pamphlet that has rarely had an equal for
ability and effect.   In October, 1805, three months
after the " Essex " decision, while Monroe was advising Madison to press harder than ever on all the
great belligerent Powers, appeared in London a book
of more than two hundred pages, with the title :
" War in Disguise ; or, the Frauds of the Neutral
Flags."   The author was James Stephen, a man not
less remarkable for his own qualities than for those
which two generations of descendants have inherited
from him ; but these abilities, though elevating him
immensely above the herd of writers who in England bespattered America with abuse, and in America
befouled England, were yet of a character so peculiar as to bar his path to the highest distinction.
James Stephen was a high-minded fanatic, passion-

ately convinced of the truths he proclaimed. Two
years after writing " War in Disguise," he published
another pamphlet, maintaining that the Napoleonic
wars were a divine chastisement of England for her
tolerance of the slave-trade; and this curious thesis
he argued through twenty pages of close reasoning.[1]
Through life a vehement enemy of slavery, at a time
when England rang with abuse of America, which he
had done much to stimulate, he had the honesty and
courage to hold America up as an example before
Europe, and to assert that in abolishing the slave-
trade she had done an act for which it was impossible
to refuse her the esteem of England, and in consequence of which he prayed that harmony between
the two countries might be settled on the firmest
foundation.

This insular and honest dogmatism, characteristic
of many robust minds, Stephen carried into the question of neutral trade. He had himself begun his
career in the West Indies, and in the prize-court at
St. Kitt's had learned the secrets of neutral commerce. Deeply impressed with the injury which this
trade caused to England, he believed himself bound
to point out the evil and the remedy to the British
public. Assuming at the outset that the Rule of 1756
was a settled principle of law, he next assumed that
the greater part of the neutral trade was not neutral at all, but was a fraudulent business, in which
French or Spanish property, carried in French or

[1] New Reasons for abolishing the Slave-Trade, 1807.

Spanish ships, was by means of systematic perjury protected by the prostituted American flag.

How much of this charge was true will never be certainly known. Stephen could not prove his assertions. The American merchants stoutly denied them. Alexander Baring, better informed than Stephen and far less prejudiced, affirmed that the charge was untrue, and that if the facts could be learned, more British than enemy's property would be found afloat under the American flag. Perhaps this assertion was the more annoying of the two; but to prove either the one or the other was needless, since from such premises Stephen was able to draw a number of startling conclusions which an English public stood ready to accept. The most serious of these was the certain ruin of England from the seduction of her seamen into this fraudulent service; another was the inevitable decay of her merchant marine; still another pointed to the loss of the Continental market; and he heightened the effect of all these evils by adding a picture of the British admiral in the decline of life raised to the peerage for his illustrious actions, and enjoying a pension from the national bounty, but still unable. to spend so much money as became an English peer, because his Government had denied to him the " safe booty " of the neutral trade![1] Humor was not Stephen's strongest quality, or he never would have caricatured the British mind so coarsely; but coarse as the drawing might be, England was

[1] War in Disguise, pp. 131–133.

not conscious of the caricature. Cobbett alone could have done justice to the pecuniary sanctity of the British peerage; but on this point humor was lost to the world, for Cobbett and Stephen were in accord.

Thus a conviction was established in England that the American trade was a fraud which must soon bring Great Britain to ruin, and that the Americans who carried on this commerce were carrying on a " war in disguise " for the purpose of rescuing France and Spain from the pressure of the British navy. The conclusion was inevitable. " Enforce the Rule of 1756!" cried Stephen; "cut off the neutral trade altogether!" This policy, which went far beyond the measures of Pitt and the decision of Sir William Scott, was urged by Stephen with great force; while he begged the Americans, in temperate and reasonable language, not to make war for the protection of so gross a fraud. Other writers used no such self-restraint. The austere and almost religious conviction of Stephen could maintain itself at a height where no personal animosity toward America mingled its bitterness with his denunciations; but his followers, less accustomed than he to looking for motives in their Bibles, said simply that the moment for going to war with the United States had come, and that the opportunity should be seized.[1]

[1] Bosanquet, Causes of the Depreciation, etc. p. 42.

CHAPTER III.

THE Eighth Congress had hardly expired, March 3, 1805, amid the confusion and ill-temper which followed the failure of impeachment, when President Jefferson and Secretary Madison began to hear the first mutterings of European disaster. Talleyrand's letter to Armstrong, Dec. 21, 1804, arrived with its blunt announcement that Napoleon meant to oppose every step of Monroe's negotiation at Madrid, and with its declaration that West Florida had not been included in the retrocession of Louisiana to France, but had been refused to France by King Charles. Jefferson was then at Monticello, and thither the documents from Paris followed him. He wrote to Madison that Monroe's case was desperate.

"I consider," said the President,[1] "that we may anticipate the effect of his mission. On its failure as to the main object, I wish he may settle the right of navigating the Mobile, as everything else may await further peaceable proceedings ; but even then we shall have a difficult question to decide, — to wit, whether we will let the present crisis in Europe pass away without a settlement."

[1] Jefferson to Madison, March 23, 1805 ; Madison MSS.

This letter showed that as early as the month of March, 1805, the President foresaw Monroe's disasters, and began to speculate upon the next step to be taken. The attempt to obtain Florida through Spanish fears had failed; but his first impression was that everything might go on as before, if the Spaniards would consent to a free navigation of the Mobile. Madison was still more vague; his first impulse was to retrace his steps. He wrote to the President a singular letter of contradictions.

"I cannot entirely despair," said he, March 27,[1] "that Spain, notwithstanding the support given by France to her claim to West Florida, may yield to our proposed arrangement, partly from its intrinsic value to her, partly from an apprehension of the interference of Great Britain; and that this latter consideration may, as soon as France despairs of her pecuniary object, transfer her weight into our scale. If she [France] should persist in disavowing her right to sell West Florida to the United States, and above all can prove it to have been the mutual understanding with Spain that West Florida was no part of Louisiana, it will place our claim on very different ground, — such probably as would not be approved by the world, and such certainly as would not with that approbation be maintained by force. If our right be good against Spain at all, it must be supported by those rigid maxims of technical law which have little weight in national questions generally, and none at all when opposed to the principles of universal equity. The world would decide that France having sold us the territory of

' Madison to Jefferson, March 27; 1805; Jefferson MSS.

a third party, which she had no right to sell, that party having even remonstrated against the whole transaction, the right of the United States was limited to a demand on France to procure and convey the territory, or to remit *pro tanto* the price, or to dissolve the bargain altogether."

For eighteen months every French and Spanish agent in Washington, Paris, and Madrid had assured Madison, in language varying between remonstrance and insult, that Spain had not ceded West Florida to France; the records of the State Department proved that France had asked for West Florida and had been refused; Jefferson had not ventured to record a claim to West Florida when he received possession of Louisiana, and had been obliged to explain, in language which Gallatin and Randolph thought unsatisfactory, the words of the Mobile Act. In spite of this, Madison committed himself and government to the claim that West Florida was a part of Louisiana; he pressed that claim, not against France, but against Spain; he brought Monroe to a rupture with the Spanish government on that issue, — yet with these recollections fresh in his mind, he suddenly told Jefferson that if France could prove a matter of common notoriety, the world would decide that the United States had acted without regard to law or equity, while in any case the claim to West Florida as against Spain was a mistake.

That Madison should have followed a train of reasoning so singular, was less surprising than that he should have advanced so far without showing a sign that he was prepared for the next step. Knowing as early as March, 1805, that his plans were defeated, and that he might expect a repulse from Spain and France, he selected a new minister to succeed Pinckney at Madrid. This diplomatist, whose career was to be as futile if not as noisy as that of his predecessor from South Carolina, was James Bowdoin of Massachusetts, son of a celebrated governor of that State. Jefferson wrote privately to him, April 27, announcing the appointment; and the tone of the letter implied that in the month's interval since the arrival of Talleyrand's manifesto the President's pacific views had suffered a change.

" Our relations with that nation are vitally interesting," he wrote.[1]   " That they should be of a peaceable and friendly character has been our most earnest desire. Had Spain met us with the same disposition, our idea was that her existence on this hemisphere and ours should have rested on the same bottom, should have swum or sunk together. We want nothing of hers, and we want no other nation to possess what is hers ; but she has met our advances with jealousy, secret malice, and ill-faith. Our patience under this unworthy return of disposition is now on its last trial, and the issue of what is now depending between us will decide whether our relations with her are to be sincerely friendly or permanently hostile. I still wish, and would cherish, the former, but have ceased to expect it."

[1] Jefferson to Bowdoin, April 27, 1805; Jefferson MSS.

Jefferson had the faculty, peculiar to certain temperaments, of seeing what he wished to see, and of believing what he willed to believe. Few other Americans could have seriously talked of the Spanish empire in America as swimming or sinking with that of the United States; but Jefferson, for the moment, thought that the earthen pot of Spanish dominion could trust itself to float safely under charge of the iron energy of American democracy. He could gravely say in regard to Spain, " we want nothing of hers," when for eighteen months he had exhausted every resource, short of force, to gain Baton Rouge, Mobile, and Pensacola, not to speak of East Florida and Texas. He charged that Spain met his advances with jealousy, secret malice, and ill-faith, after his ministers had intrigued with Napoleon for nearly two years, in the constant hope of depriving her of her property. Dec. 13, 1804, he wrote to General Heath: " With Spain we shall always be bickering, but never at war till we seek it; "[1] and six months later he wrote to Bowdoin that her secret malice and ill faith were leading to permanently hostile relations. He had not much further to go; for if he meant to maintain his authority among rulers, the war that would never come till he sought it must be sought.

As Monroe's overthrow became more and more evident, the President grew uneasy, and turned restlessly from one device to another. In the first days of August Monroe's despatches arrived, announcing

[1] See p. 8.

that he had left Madrid, and that all his offers had
been rejected by Spain. Madison was in Philadelphia, where his wife was detained by a long and
troublesome lameness. The President was at Monticello. A brisk interchange of letters took place,
marking from day to day the fluctuations of feeling
peculiar to the characters of the two men. One question alone was to be decided, — should they seize this
moment to break with Napoleon ?

Madison's first reflections reached no result. He
shrank from admitting that the government stood between war and humiliation more dangerous than war.

" The business at Madrid," he said, August 2,[1] " has
had an awkward termination, and if nothing, as may be
expected, particularly in the absence of the Emperor,
should alleviate it at Paris, involves some serious questions. After the parade of a mission extraordinary, a
refusal of all our overtures in a haughty tone without
any offer of other terms, and a perseverance in with-
drawing a stipulated provision for claims admitted to be
just, without *ex post facto* conditions manifestly unreasonable and inadmissible, form a strong appeal to the
honor and sensibility of this country."

The conclusion drawn from this somewhat mild
review was not such as Monroe, Armstrong, or Livingston had recommended.

" I find that, as was apprehended from the tenor of
former communications," continued the secretary, " the
military *status quo* in the controverted districts, the navi-

[1] Madison to Jefferson, Aug. 2, 1805; Jefferson MSS.

gation of the rivers running through West Florida, and the spoliations subsequent to the convention of 1802 have never had a place in the discussions. Bowdoin may perhaps be instructed, consistently with what has passed, to propose a suspension of the territorial questions, the deposit, and the French spoliations, on condition that those points be yielded, with an incorporation of the convention of 1802 with a provision for subsequent claims. This is the utmost within the Executive purview. If this experiment should fail, the question with the Legislature must be whether or not resort is to be had to force, to what extent, and in what mode. Perhaps the instructions to Bowdoin would be improved by including the idea of transferring the sequel of business hither. This would have the appearance of an advance on the part of Spain, the more so as it would be attended with a new mission to this country, and would be most convenient for us also, if not made by Spain a pretext for delay."

Madison, after enduring one " refusal of all our overtures in a haughty tone," suggested that another be invited. The slightly patronizing air which characterized Jefferson's attitude toward Madison, but which he never betrayed toward Gallatin, was explained by this want of directness in Madison's nature, and by the habitual slowness of his decisions. The action suggested by Madison threw the control of events into the hands of France. This at least was the opinion of Jefferson, whose mind was wrought by the news from Pinckney to a state of steadily growing alarm.

" I think the *status quo*, if not already proposed, should be immediately offered through Bowdoin," wrote Jefferson, August 4, before receiving Madison's letter of August 2.[1] " Should it even be refused, the refusal to settle a limit is not of itself a sufficient cause of war, nor is the withholding a ratification worthy of such a redress. Yet these acts show a purpose, both in Spain and France, against which we ought to provide before the conclusion of a peace. I think, therefore, we should take into consideration whether we ought not immediately to propose to England an eventual treaty of alliance, to come into force whenever (within —— years) a war shall take place with Spain or France."

Three days later he wrote again, and his alarm had increased : [2] —

" The papers now enclosed to you confirm me in the opinion of the expediency of a treaty with England, but make the offer of the *status quo* [to Spain] more doubtful ; the correspondence will probably throw light on that question. From the papers already received I infer a confident reliance on the part of Spain on the omnipotence of Bonaparte, but a desire of procrastination till peace in Europe shall leave us without an ally."

Ten days more passed ; the whole mortification became evident ; the President's anger and alarm rose to feverishness.[3] He wrote to Madison, August 17, —

" I am anxious to receive opinions respecting our procedure with Spain, as should negotiations with England

[1] Jefferson to Madison, Aug. 4, 1805 ; Madison MSS.
[2] Jefferson to Madison, Aug. 7, 1805 ; Works, iv. 583.
[3] Jefferson to Madison, Aug. 17, 1805; Jefferson MSS.

be advisable they should not be postponed a day unnecessarily, that we may lay their result before Congress
before they rise next spring. Were the question only
about the bounds of Louisiana, I should be for delay.
Were it only for spoliations, just as this is as a cause
of war, we might consider if no other expedient were
more eligible for us. But I do not view peace as within
our choice. I consider the cavalier conduct of Spain as
evidence that France is to settle with us for her, — and
the language of France confirms it, — and that if she
can keep us insulated till peace, she means to enforce by
arms her will, to which she foresees we will not truckle,
and therefore does not venture on the mandate now. We
should not permit ourselves to be found off our guard
and friendless."

The President's plan presented difficulties which
Madison could not fail to see. That Jefferson should
wish Pitt to fight the battles of the United States
was natural; but Pitt was little in the habit of doing
gratuitous favors, and might reasonably ask what
price he was to receive for conquering the Floridas
and Texas for the United States. Madison's comments on the President's proposed British treaty
pointed out this objection. Madison agreed that the
Executive should take provisional measures, on which
Congress might act.[1] "An eventual alliance with
Great Britain, if attainable from her without inadmissible conditions, would be for us the best of
all possible measures; but I do not see the least
chance of laying her under obligations to be called

[1] Madison to Jefferson, Aug. 20, 1805; Jefferson MSS.

into force at our will without correspondent obligations on our part." Objection to the President's plan was easy; but when the secretary came to a plan of his own, he could suggest nothing more vigorous than to renew a moderate degree of coquetry with Merry, which would have the side advantage of alarming France and Spain, "from whom the growing communication with Great Britain would not be concealed."

Such a weapon was no doubt as effective against Napoleon as heelless slippers against Pitt; but the President thought the situation to have passed beyond such tactics. Madison's proposed coquetry with Merry met with less favor in Jefferson's eyes than his own proposed one-sided alliance with England had met in the eyes of Madison. Upon a treaty of alliance with England the President was for the moment bent, and he met Madison's objections by arguments that showed lively traits of the writer's sanguine temper. He complained that Madison had misconceived the nature of the proposed British treaty. England should stipulate not to make peace without securing West Florida and the spoliation claims to America, while American co-operation in the war would be sufficient inducement to her for making this contract.[1]

"Another motive much more powerful would indubitably induce England to go much further. Whatever ill humor may at times have been expressed against us

[1] Jefferson to Madison, Aug. 27, 1805; Works iv. 585.

by individuals of that country, the first wish of every
Englishman's heart is to see us once more fighting by
their sides against France; nor could the King or his
ministers do an act so popular as to enter into an alliance with us.   The nation would not weigh the consideration by grains and scruples; they would consider it
as the price and pledge of an indissoluble friendship.   I
think it possible that for such a provisional treaty they
would give us their general guaranty of Louisiana and
the Floridas.   At any rate we might try them; a failure would not make our situation worse.   If such a one
could be obtained, we might await our own convenience
for calling up the *casus fœderis*.   I think it important
that England should receive an overture as early as
possible, as it might prevent her listening to terms of
peace."

If Jefferson was right in thinking that every
Englishman's heart yearned toward America, he was
unfortunate in delaying his offer of indissoluble
friendship until the moment when Sir William Scott
delivered his opinion in the case of the " Essex."
Madison's scheme was equally unpromising, because
he had made a personal enemy of Merry, on whom
the success of Madison's tactics depended.   Each of
the two high authorities felt the weakness of the
other, and the secretary even went so far as to hint,
in courteous language, that the President's idea was
unpractical : —

" The more I reflect on the papers from Madrid, the
more I feel the value of some eventual security for the
active friendship of Great Britain, but the more I see at

the same time the difficulty of obtaining it without a like
security to her of ours. If she is to be *bound*, we must
be *so too*, either to the same thing, — that is to join her
in the war, — or to do what she will accept as equivalent
to such an obligation. What can we offer to her? A
mutual guaranty, unless so shaped as to involve us pretty
certainly in her war, would not be satisfactory. To offer
commercial regulations or concessions on points in the
law of nations as a certain payment for aids which might
never be received or required, would be a bargain liable
to obvious objections of the most serious kind. Unless,
therefore, some arrangement which has not occurred to
me can be devised, I see no other course than such an
one as is suggested in my last letter." [1]

In this state of things, the remaining members of
the Cabinet were asked for their opinions ; and in
the course of a few days the President received
written papers from Gallatin and Robert Smith.
Gallatin was annoyed at the results of Jefferson's
diplomacy. Emphatically a Northern man, he cared
little for Florida ; and a war with Spain would have
been in his eyes a Southern war. He made no concealment of his opinion that the whole negotiation
rested on a blunder ; and he told Madison as much,
with a bluntness which the secretary could scarcely
have relished.

"The demands from Spain were too hard," said he,[2]
"to have expected, even independent of French inter-

[1] Madison to Jefferson, Sept. 1, 1805; Jefferson MSS.

[2] Gallatin to Madison, Aug. 6, 1805 ; Gallatin's Writings,
i. 237.

ference, any success from the negotiation. It could only be hoped that the tone assumed by our negotiators might not be such as to render a relinquishment or suspension of some of our claims productive of some loss of reputation. If we are safe on that ground, it may be eligible to wait for a better opportunity before we again run the risk of lowering the national importance by pretensions which our strength may not at this moment permit us to support. If from the manner in which the negotiation has been conducted that effect has already been produced, how to save character without endangering peace will be a serious and difficult question."

These words were written before he had seen Monroe's despatches. When the whole correspondence was put into his hands he read it, and in returning it to Madison made the dry comment that the business had not ended quite so badly as he had previously supposed.[1] The phrase bore a double meaning, for even Madison must have admitted that the business could not have ended much worse.

Gallatin sent to the President a remarkable paper,[2] in substance an argument for peace, and in tenor a criticism of the grounds which Jefferson, Madison, Monroe, Livingston, and Pinckney had thought proper to take in their dispute with Spain. Gallatin held that, owing to the " unpardonable oversight or indifference " of Livingston and Monroe in failing to in-

[1] Madison to Jefferson, Sept. 1, 1805; Jefferson MSS.

[2] Gallatin to Jefferson, Sept. 12, 1805; Gallatin's Writings, i. 241.

sist on a boundary to Louisiana, the United States government was debarred from holding Spain responsible for the inevitable consequences of its own fault. Neither Spain's qualified refusal to ratify the claims convention of 1802 nor her rejection of the French spoliation claims would justify war. As a matter of abstract justice, war was not to be defended; as a matter of policy, it could not be recommended. The expense and loss would exceed the value of Florida; the political result would entangle America in alliance with England; and, " in fine, a subversion of all our hopes must be the natural consequence." Renewal of negotiation was the proper step, with the Sabine and Perdido as boundaries and a temporary arrangement under the *status quo*, acceptance of the Spanish condition precedent to ratifying the claims convention, and insistence against the new spoliations which French and Spanish privateers were daily making on American commerce in the West Indies. Pending the result of this negotiation Congress might spend some money on the militia, and might appropriate a million dollars annually to build ships of the line.

In effect, Gallatin threw his influence on the side of Madison against the President's semi-warlike views. The opinion of Robert Smith did not weaken the force of Gallatin's reasoning. Already a perceptible division existed in the Cabinet between the Treasury and the Navy. Hardly three months before the Spanish embarrassment, Gallatin had spoken to the President in strong terms of Robert Smith's administration, and had added,[1] —

" On this subject, — the expense of the Navy greater than the object seemed to require, and a merely nominal accountability, — I have, for the sake of preserving perfect harmony in your councils, however grating to my feelings, been almost uniformly silent."

Smith's present views tended to confirm Gallatin in his irritation, and to reconcile Jefferson to abandoning his energetic schemes. The Secretary of the Navy said that throughout these negotiations Spain had presumed much on American predilection for peace, and on the want of means to annoy her either by land or by water. He urged the necessity of working on her fears, and advised that Congress be recommended to provide additional gunboats, to put all the frigates in commission, and to build twelve seventy-fours. With these means he was disposed to take a commanding attitude; and if Spain were supported by France, to make an alliance with England.[2]

Gallatin and Robert Smith agreed only on one point, — that the affair had been mismanaged. Both secretaries held that America had made pretensions which she had not strength at the moment to support. Rather than " again run the risk of lowering national importance," Gallatin preferred to submit to

[1] Gallatin to Jefferson, May 30, 1805; Gallatin's Writings, i. 233.

[2] Robert Smith to Jefferson, Sept. 10, 1805 ; Jefferson MSS.

the consequent loss of reputation, and return to a true peace-policy. Robert Smith wished to maintain a high tone, and to arm. All Jefferson's instincts were with Gallatin; but the path that Gallatin proposed was hard and mortifying, and although he made it as little abrupt as possible, he could not prevent it from seeming what it was, — a severe humiliation to the President. Not without some inward struggle could a President of the United States bow his neck to such a yoke as Spain and France imposed.

At that moment, the middle of September, arrived Armstrong's letter advising the military occupation of Texas and a cessation of intercourse with Spain. His plan was the first well-considered suggestion yet made for carrying out the policy hitherto pursued; and although contrary to Gallatin's advice, it agreed so well with the President's views that he caught at it with the relief of a man unable to solve his own problem, who hears another explain what to himself is inexplicable. Jefferson seized Armstrong's idea, and uniting it with his own, announced the result to Madison as the true solution of the difficulty: [1] —

" Supposing a previous alliance with England to guard us in the worst event, I should propose that Congress should pass acts (1) authorizing the Executive to suspend intercourse with Spain at discretion; (2) to dislodge the new establishments of Spain between the Mississippi

[1] Jefferson to Madison, Sept. 16, 1805; Works, iv. 587.

and Bravo ; (3) to appoint commissioners to examine and ascertain all claims for spoliation."

Here at length was a plan, — uncertain, indeed, because dependent on British help, but still a scheme of action which could be discussed. The President appointed October 4 as the day on which the Cabinet should reunite at Washington to consider his project, but Madison replied that he could not return so soon; and in order that the Cabinet should know his views, he explained at some length the course he advised, which differed widely from that of the President.

"With respect to Great Britain," he said,[1] "I think we ought to go as far into an understanding on the subject of an eventual coalition in the war as will not preclude us from an intermediate adjustment, if attainable, with Spain. I see not, however, much chance that she will positively bind herself not to make peace, while we refuse to bind ourselves positively to make war, — unless, indeed, some positive advantage were yielded on our part in lieu of an engagement to enter into the war. No such advantage as yet occurs as would be admissible to us and satisfactory to her."

In regard to England, therefore, Madison had nothing to propose except negotiation without end. Having settled this point, he went on : —

"At Paris I think Armstrong ought to receive instructions to extinguish in the French government every hope of turning our controversy with Spain into a French job, public or private; to leave them under apprehensions

[1] Madison to Jefferson, Sept. 30, 1805; Jefferson MSS.

of an eventual connection between the United States and Great Britain ; and to take advantage of any change in the French Cabinet favorable to our objects with Spain."

To leave Bonaparte " under apprehensions " was to be the object of Madison's diplomacy at Paris, — a task which several European governments were then employing half a million armed men to accomplish, hitherto without success, but which Madison hoped to effect by civilities to Merry.

After this decision, nothing remained but to mark out a line of conduct in regard to Spain. In the course of the summer Bowdoin, the new minister, had sailed ; but on arriving in Spain, and learning the failure of Monroe's negotiation, he went to Paris and London without visiting Madrid.

" As to Spain herself," continued Madison, " one question is, whether Bowdoin ought to proceed or not to Madrid. My opinion is that his trip to Great Britain was fortunate, and that the effect of it will be aided by his keeping aloof until occurrences shall invite him to Spain. . . . The nicest question, however, is whether any, or what, steps should be taken for a communication with the Spanish government on the points not embraced by the late negotiation. On this question my reflections disapprove of any step whatever other than such as may fall within the path to be marked out for Armstrong, or as may be within the sphere of Claiborne's intercourse with the Marquis of Casa Calvo. Perhaps the last may be the best opportunity of all for conveying to Spain the impressions we wish, without committing the government in any respect more than may be advisable. In general it seems to me proper that Claiborne should hold a pretty strong language in all cases, and particularly that he should go every length the law will warrant against Morales and his project of selling lands. If Congress should be not indisposed, proceedings may be authorized that will be perfectly effectual on that as well as other points; but before their meeting there will be time to consider more fully what ought to be suggested for their consideration."

Having brought the government face to face with the government of Spain, in the belief that Spain and France must yield to a peremptory demand, — finding that Spain not only refused every concession, but renewed depredations on American commerce and took an attitude of indifference to threats or entreaties, — Madison proposed no more vigorous measure than to " go every length the law will warrant" against certain Spanish land-grants.

Such a course pleased no one, and threatened to create new dangers. Monroe and Armstrong urged that a supposed devotion to peace on the part of the President weighed heavily against him with Spain and France. Jefferson approved their proposed aggressive policy, as he wrote to Madison, chiefly because it would " correct the dangerous error that we are a people whom no injuries can provoke to war." [1] He shrank from war, except under the shield of England, and yet he feared England for an ally even more than Spain for an enemy. His perplexity ended in help-

[1] Jefferson to Madison, Sept. 18, 1805; Jefferson MSS.

lessness.   The Cabinet meeting was held October 4 ; but he reported to Madison that nothing came of it : [2]

" The only questions which press on the Executive for decision are whether we shall enter into a provisional alliance with England, to come into force only in the event that *during the present war* we become engaged in war *with France*, leaving the declaration of the *casus fœderis* ultimately with us ; whether we shall send away Yrujo, Casa Calvo, Morales ; whether we shall instruct Bowdoin not to go to Madrid till further orders.   But we are all of the opinion that the first of these questions is too important and too difficult to be decided but on the fullest consideration, in which your aid and counsel should be waited for."

Again Madison wrote back his opinion.   More than six months had elapsed since the President, March 23, despaired of Monroe's mission ; every alternative had been repeatedly discussed ; every advice had been taken.   Congress would soon meet ; something must be decided, — in reality delay was itself a decision ; yet the President and Secretary of State seemed no nearer a result than they had been six months before.   Meanwhile the European packets brought news that put a different face on the problem.   Sir William Scott's decision in the case of the " Essex " arrived ; seizures of American ships by England began ; Pitt's great coalition with Russia and Austria against Napoleon took the field, and August 27 Napoleon broke up the camp at Boulogne

[1] Jefferson to Madison, Oct. 11, 1805; Jefferson MSS.

and began his long-intended movement across the Rhine. Upon Madison's mind this European convulsion acted as an additional reason for doing nothing: [1] —

" Considering the probability of an extension of the war against France, and the influence that may have on her temper toward the United States, the uncertainty of effecting with England such a shape for an arrangement as alone would be admissible, and the possible effects elsewhere of abortive overtures to her, I think it very questionable whether a little delay may not be expedient, especially as in the mean time the English pulse will be somewhat felt by the discussions now on foot by Mr. Monroe."

Accordingly the Secretary advised that Morales, Casa Calvo, and Yrujo should be ordered out of the country, while Bowdoin should remain in England, — and so left it.

Madison's measures and conduct toward Europe showed the habit of avoiding the heart of every issue, in order to fret its extremities. This mark of Madison's character as a diplomatist led him into his chief difficulties at home and abroad; but the Spanish imbroglio of 1805 first brought the weakness into public notoriety, and he recovered from the subsequent revelation only after years of misfortune. The same habit of mind made him favor commercial restrictions as a means of coercion. So he disregarded Armstrong's idea of seizing Texas,

[1] Madison to Jefferson, Oct. 16, 1805; Jefferson MSS.

but warmly approved of his passing suggestion as to an embargo : [1] —

" The efficacy of an embargo cannot be doubted. Indeed, if a commercial weapon can be properly shaped for the Executive hand, it is more and more apparent to me that it can force all the nations having colonies in this quarter of the globe to respect our rights."

This mental trait was closely connected with Madison's good qualities, — it sprang from the same source as his caution, his respect for law, his instinctive sense of the dangers that threatened the Union, his curious mixture of radical and conservative tastes ; but whatever its merits or defects, it led to a strange delusion when it caused him to believe that a man like Napoleon could be forced by a mere pin-prick to do Jefferson's will.

Jefferson himself was weary of indecision. He had rested his wish for an English alliance on the belief that Napoleon meant to make peace in Europe in order to attack America ; and this idea, never very reasonable, could have no weight after Napoleon had plunged into a general European war. No sooner did he receive Madison's letter of October 16, than he again changed his plan.

" The probability of an extensive war on the continent of Europe, strengthening every day for some time past, is now almost certain," he wrote October 23 to Madison.[2] " This gives us our great desideratum, time. In truth it

[1] Madison to Jefferson, Sept. 14, 1805; Jefferson MSS.
[2] Jefferson to Madison, Oct. 23, 1805; Jefferson MSS.

places us quite at our ease.   We are certain of one year
of campaigning at least, and one other year of negotiation for their peace arrangements.   Should we be now
forced into war, it is become much more questionable
than it was whether we should not pursue it unembar-
rassed by any alliance, and free to retire from it whenever we can obtain our separate terms.   It gives us time,
too, to make another effort for peaceable settlement.
Where should this be done?   Not at Madrid, certainly.
At Paris! through Armstrong, or Armstrong and Monroe as negotiators, France as the mediator, the price of
the Floridas as the means.   We need not care who gets
that, and an enlargement of the sum we had thought of
may be the bait to France, while the Guadeloupe as the
western boundary may be the soother of Spain ; providing for our spoliated citizens in some effectual way.   We
may announce to France that determined not to ask justice of Spain again, yet desirous of making one other effort
to preserve peace, we are willing to see whether her interposition can obtain it on terms which we think just ;
that no delay, however, can be admitted ; and that in the
mean time should Spain attempt to change the *status quo*,
we shall repel force by force, without undertaking other
active hostilities till we see what may be the issue of her
interference."

A similar letter was sent on the same day to Gallatin ; and the next day Jefferson wrote to Robert
Smith, suggesting the same idea, with some characteristic additions.[1]

Jefferson's idea that Napoleon would require two
years of war seemed reasonable; for how could Jeffer-

[1] Jefferson to Robert Smith, Oct. 24, 1805; Jefferson MSS.

son know that Ulm had already surrendered, that
Austerlitz would be fought within six weeks, and
that peace would be restored before the new year,
with the Emperor Napoleon more terrible than ever?
In truth Jefferson only reverted to his policy of peace
which he had seemed to abandon, but to which he
really clung even when most earnest for a British
alliance. His conduct in that sense was at least
consistent. So much could hardly be said for Madison, even though the President apparently yielded to
the secretary's advice. Of all the points on which
Madison, and Monroe in obedience to his orders, had
most strongly insisted, even to the extent of offend-
ing Talleyrand, the strongest was that under no circumstances should the Florida negotiation be turned
into a bribe to France. As late as September 30,
in writing the opinion intended to guide the Cabinet, Madison asked authority " to extinguish in the
French government every hope of turning our controversy with Spain into a French job, public or private." [1] The President's suggestion of October 23
avowedly turned the controversy with Spain into a
French job, which must inevitably become private as
well as public.

Madison made no protest. He soon returned to
Washington, and there, Nov. 12, 1805, a Cabinet
meeting was held, whose proceedings were recorded
by the President in a memorandum, probably written
at the moment. This memorandum closed a record,

[1] Madison to Jefferson, Sept. 30, 1805; Jefferson MSS.

unusually complete, of an episode illustrating better than any other the peculiarities of Jefferson and Madison, and the traits of character most commonly alleged as their faults.[1]

" 1805, *Nov.* 12.   Present, the four secretaries ; subject, Spanish affairs. — The extension of the war in Europe leaving us without danger of a sudden peace, depriving us of the chance of an ally, I proposed we should address ourselves to France, informing her it was a last effort at amicable settlement with Spain, and offer to her, or through her, (1) A sum of money for the rights of Spain east of Iberville, say the Floridas ; (2) To cede the part of Louisiana from the Rio Bravo to the Guadeloupe ; (3) Spain to pay within a certain time spoliations under her own flag, agreed to by the convention (which we guess to be a hundred vessels, worth two millions), and those subsequent (worth as much more), and to hypothecate to us for those payments the country from Guadeloupe to Rio Bravo.   Armstrong to be employed.   The first was to be the exciting motive with France, to whom Spain is in arrears for subsidies, and who will be glad also to secure us from going into the scale of England ; the second, the soothing motive with Spain, which France would press *bonâ fide*, because she claimed to the Rio Bravo ; the third, to quiet our merchants.   It was agreed to unanimously, and the sum to be offered fixed not to exceed five million dollars.   Mr. Gallatin did not like purchasing Florida under an apprehension of war, lest we should be thought in fact to purchase peace.   We thought this overweighed by taking advantage of an opportunity which might not occur

[1] Cabinet Memoranda; Jefferson MSS.

again of getting a country essential to our peace and to the security of the commerce of the Mississippi. It was agreed that Yrujo should be sounded through Dallas whether he is not going away, and if not, he should be made to understand that his presence at Washington will not be agreeable, and that his departure is expected. Casa Calvo, Morales, and all the Spanish officers at New Orleans are to be desired to depart, with a discretion to Claiborne to let any friendly ones remain who will resign and become citizens, as also women receiving pensions to remain if they choose."

CHAPTER IV.

PRESIDENT JEFFERSON'S decision, in October, 1805, to retrace his steps and reverse a policy which had been publicly and repeatedly proclaimed, was the turning-point of his second Administration. No one can say what might have happened if in August, 1805, Jefferson had ordered his troops to cross the Sabine and occupy Texas to the Rio Bravo, as Armstrong and Monroe advised. Such an act would probably have been supported, as the purchase of Louisiana had been approved, by the whole country, without regard to Constitutional theories; and indeed if Jefferson succeeded to the rights of Napoleon in Louisiana, such a step required no defence. Spain might then have declared war; but had Godoy taken this extreme measure, he could have had no other motive than to embarrass Napoleon by dragging France into a war with the United States, and had this policy succeeded, President Jefferson's difficulties would have vanished in an instant. He might then have seized Florida; his controversies with England about neutral trade, blockade, and impressment would have fallen to the ground; and had war with France continued two years, until Spain

threw off the yoke of Napoleon and once more raised
in Europe the standard of popular liberty, Jefferson
might perhaps have effected some agreement with
the Spanish patriots, and would then have stood at
the head of the coming popular movement throughout the world, — the movement which he and his
party were destined to resist. Godoy, Napoleon, Pitt,
Monroe, Armstrong, John Randolph, and even the
New England Federalists seemed combined to drag
or drive him into this path. Its advantages were so
plain, even at that early moment, as to overmaster
for a whole summer his instinctive repugnance to
acts of force.

After long hesitation, Jefferson shrank from the
step, and fell back upon his old policy of conquering
by peace; but such vacillations were costly. To Gallatin the decision was easy, for he had ever held that
on the whole the nation could better afford a loss of
dignity than a war; but even he allowed that loss
of dignity would cost something, and he could not
foretell what equivalent he must pay for escape from
a Franco-Spanish war. Neither Jefferson nor Gallatin could expect to be wholly spared; but Madison's
position was worse than theirs, for he had still to
reckon with his personal enemies,—John Randolph,
Yrujo, and Merry, — and to overawe a *quasi* friend
more dangerous than an enemy, — the military diplo-
mate, Turreau.

Turreau during this summer kept his eye fixed on
the Secretary of State, and repeatedly hinted, in a

manner extremely frank, that he meant to tolerate no
evasions. He wrote to Talleyrand in a tone of cool
confidence. July 9 he said that the Emperor's measures for the protection of Florida were sufficient:

" The intervention of France in the negotiations with
Spain has stopped everything. They have been affected
by it here, but have not shown to me any discontent at
it. ' Well,' said Mr. Jefferson to me lately, ' since the
Emperor wishes it, the arrangement shall be adjourned
to a more favorable time.' "

That Jefferson made this remark could be believed
only by his enemies, for it contradicted the tenor of
his letters to Madison; but although Turreau doubtless overstated the force of the words, he certainly
gave to Talleyrand the impression that the President was reduced to obedience. The impression was
enough; correct or not, it strengthened Napoleon's
natural taste for command.

A few weeks afterward, Turreau wrote to Madison
a note in regard to General Moreau's reception in
the United States. In a tone excessively military he
said : [1] —

" General Moreau ought not (*ne doit point*) to be, in
a foreign country, the object of honors which the consideration of his services would formerly have drawn upon
him ; and it is proper (*il convient*) that his arrival and his
residence in the United States should be marked by no demonstration which passes the bounds of hospitality."

[1] Turreau to Madison, 26 Thermidor, An xiii. (Aug. 14,
1805) ; MSS. State Department Archives.

Madison was indignant at this interference, and proposed to resent it. The President encouraged him to do so, on the express ground that they had not ventured to resent the conduct of France in regard to Monroe's negotiation:[1] —

" The style of that government in the Spanish business was calculated to excite indignation ; but it was a case in which that might have done injury. But the present is a case which would justify some notice in order to let them understand we are not of those Powers who will receive and execute mandates."

Meanwhile General Smith, who had not resented the repudiation of his niece by the Emperor, and to whom Madison showed the offensive letter, undertook to soothe the irritation. " He says," wrote Madison in his next letter to the President,[2] " that Turreau speaks with the greatest respect, and even affection, toward the Administration ; and such are the dispositions which it is certain he has uniformly manifested to me." Upon these assurances Madison toned down the severity he had intended.

Turreau had resided hardly six months in the United States before he announced to Talleyrand the conviction of all American politicians that any war would end in driving from office the party which made it:[3] —

[1] Jefferson to Madison, Aug. 25, 1805; Works, iv. 584.

[2] Madison to Jefferson, Sept. 1, 1805; Jefferson MSS.

[3] Turreau to Talleyrand, 20 Messidor, An xiii. (July 9, 1805); Archives des Aff. Étr., MSS.

" To such an extent is the actual Administration convinced of this fact, that it allows itself to be outraged
every day by the English, and accepts all the humiliations
they care to impose ; and notwithstanding the contempt
generally felt here for Spain, against whom a war was
last year quite openly provoked, the members of the
United States government have not dared to undertake
it, although sure of beginning it with public opinion in
their favor.   And no one need think that this indisposition
to war depends only on the personal character and the
philanthropic principles of Mr. Jefferson, for it is shared
by all the party leaders, even by those who have most
pretensions and well-founded hopes to succeed the actual
President, — such as Mr. Madison."

Turreau's sketch of American character and ambition was long and interesting, and suggested the
vulnerable point where France should throw her
strength against this new people.   Neither as a military nor as a naval power did he think the United
States formidable.   Their government made no concealment of its weakness : —

" They especially lack trained officers.   The Americans
are to-day the boldest and the most ignorant navigators in
the universe.   In brief, it seems to me that, considering
the weakness of the military constitution, the Federal
government, which makes no concealment of this weakness, will avoid every serious difference which might lead
to aggression, and will constantly show itself an enemy to
war.   But does the system of encroachment which prevails here agree with a temper so pacific?   Certainly not,
at first sight ; and yet unless circumstances change, the

United States will succeed in reconciling the contradiction. To conquer without war is the first fact in their politics (*Conquérir sans guerre, voilà les premiers faits politiques.*) "

These reflections were written early in July, 1805, before the President and his Cabinet had begun to discuss Monroe's failure and the policy of a Spanish war, and more than three months before the President wholly abandoned the thought of warlike measures. Turreau's vision was keen, but he had no excuse for short-sightedness. Madison made little effort to disguise his objects or methods.

" I took occasion to express to Mr. Madison," wrote Turreau in the same despatch, " my astonishment that the schemes of aggrandizement which the United States government appeared to have, should be always directed toward the south, while there were still in the north important and convenient territories, such as Canada, Nova Scotia, etc. ' Doubtless ! ' replied the secretary, ' but the moment has not yet come ! When the pear is ripe it will fall of itself.' "

Had Turreau asked why, then, Madison gave so violent a shaking to the Florida pear-tree, Madison must have answered, with the same candor, that he did so because he supposed the Florida pear to be ripe. The phrase was an admission and an invitation, — an admission that Florida would have been left alone if Spain had been as strong as England; and an invitation to Turreau to interpose with safety the sword of France. Turreau could not doubt the

effect of his own blunt interference. So confident
had the new French minister already become, in
July, 1805, that he not only told Madison to stop
these petty larcenies of Spanish property, but also
urged Napoleon to take the Floridas and Cuba into
his own hand solely to check American aggression.
" I believe that France alone can arrest these American enterprises and baffle (*déjouer*) their plan."

Had Turreau's discipline stopped there, much might
have been said in his favor; but in regard to still
another matter he used expressions and made demands such as Madison never yet had heard from a
diplomatic agent, although the secretary's experience
was already considerable. Neither Yrujo nor Merry
had succeeded in giving to their remonstrances or
requests the abruptness of Napoleon's style.

The Federalist newspapers during Jefferson's first
term had found so little reason for charging him with
subservience to France, that this old and stale reproach had nearly lost its weight. Neither the New
England merchants whom France had plundered,
and whose claims Jefferson consented to withdraw,
nor the British government or British newspapers
had thought it worth their while to press the charge
that Jefferson was led astray by love or fear of
Napoleon or the Empire. Not until the winter of
1805–1806 did the doctrine of French influence recover a certain share of strength; but as John Randolph and his friends, who detested Madison, were
outraged by the conduct of France in Spanish affairs,

so Timothy Pickering and the whole body of Federalists, who hated the South and the power which rested
on the dumb vote of slaves, were exasperated by the
conduct of France in regard to their trade with St.
Domingo. In both cases Madison was the victim.

St. Domingo was still in name and in international
law a colony of France. Although Rochambeau surrendered himself and his few remaining troops as
prisoners of war to the English in November, 1803;
although the negroes in January, 1804, proclaimed
their independence, and held undisputed control of
the whole French colony, while their ports were open,
and not an armed vessel bearing the flag of France
pretended to maintain a blockade, — yet Napoleon
claimed that the island belonged to him. General
Ferrand still held points in the Spanish colony for
France, and defeated an invasion attempted by Dessalines ; nor did any government betray a disposition
to recognize the black empire, or to establish relations with Dessalines or Christophe, or with a negro
republic. On the other hand, the trade of Hayti,
being profitable, was encouraged by every government in turn ; but because it was, even more than
other West Indian trade, unprotected by law, the vessels which carried it were usually armed, and sailed
in company. In the winter of 1804–1805, soon after
General Turreau's arrival at Washington, a flotilla
armed with eighty cannon and carrying crews to the
number of seven hundred men, set sail from New
York with cargoes which included contraband of war

of all kinds. Turreau remonstrated with Madison, who assured him that a law would soon be reported for correcting this abuse.

A Bill was accordingly reported; but it prohibited only the armed commerce and put the trade under heavy bonds for good behavior. To answer Turreau's object the trade must be prohibited altogether. Dr. Logan, one of the senators from Pennsylvania, who led the Northern democrats, with the "Aurora's" support, in hostility to the Haytian negroes, moved an amendment to the Bill when it came before the Senate. He proposed to prohibit every kind of commerce with St. Domingo; and the Senate was so closely divided as to require the casting vote of the Vice-President. Burr gave his voice against Dr. Logan's amendment, and the Bill accordingly passed, March 3, 1805, leaving the unarmed trade still open.

Turreau duly reported these matters to his Government.[1] The facts were public, and were given needless notoriety by the merchants themselves. On the return of the Haytian flotilla to New York, they celebrated the event in a public dinner, and the company drank a health to the government of Hayti. Another expedition was reported to be preparing. General Ferrand issued severe proclamations against the trade,[2] and Madison remonstrated strongly against Ferrand. One armed American ves-

[1] Turreau to Talleyrand, 30 Germinal, An xiii. (April 20, 1805); Archives des Aff. Étr., MSS.

[2] State Papers, ii. 728.

sel, which had carried three cargoes of powder to the
Haytians, was taken by a British cruiser, sent into
Halifax, and there condemned by the British court
as good prize for carrying on an unlawful trade.

Early in August, 1805, after Monroe's return to
London, and while Jefferson and Madison were discussing the problem of protecting themselves from
French designs, the Emperor Napoleon, who had returned from Italy and gone to the camp at Boulogne,
received Turreau's despatch, and immediately wrote
in his own emphatic style to Talleyrand : [1] —

" The despatch from Washington has fixed my attention. I request you to send a note to the American
minister accredited to me. You will join to it a copy
of the judgment [at Halifax] ; and you will declare
to him that it is time for this thing to stop (*que cela
finisse*) ; that it is shameful (*indigne*) in the Americans
to provide supplies for brigands and to take part in a
commerce so scandalous ; that I will declare good prize
everything which shall enter or leave the ports of St.
Domingo ; and that I can no longer see with indifference the armaments evidently directed against France
which the American government allows to be made in
its ports."

In this outburst of temper Napoleon's ideas of
law became confused. The American government
did not dispute his right to seize American vessels
trading with Hayti : the difficulty was that he did not
or could not do so, and for this reason he made the

[1] Napoleon to Talleyrand, 22 Thermidor, An xiii. (Aug. 10,
1805) ; Correspondance, xi. 73.

demand that the American government should help
him in doing what he was powerless to effect without
its aid. Talleyrand immediately wrote to Armstrong
a letter in which he tried to put the Emperor's commands into a shape more diplomatic, by treating the
Haytians as enemies of the human race, against whom
it was right that the United States should interpose
with measures of hostility : [1] —

" As the seriousness of the facts which occasion this
complaint obliges his Majesty to consider as good prize
everything which shall enter into the part of St. Domingo
occupied by the rebels, and everything coming out, he
persuades himself that the government of the United
States will take on its part, against this commerce at
once illicit and contrary to all the principles of the law
of nations, all the repressive and authoritative measures
proper to put an end to it. This system of impunity
and tolerance must last no longer (*ne pourrait durer
davantage*)."

For the third time within six months Talleyrand
used the word " must " to the President of the United States. Once the President had been told that
he must abandon his Spanish claims ; then that he
must show no public respect for Moreau ; finally
he was told still more authoritatively that he must
stop a trade which France was unable to stop, and
which would continue in British hands if Congress
should obey Napoleon's order. Talleyrand directed

[1] Talleyrand to Armstrong, 29 Thermidor, An xiii. (Aug. 16,
1805) ; State Papers, ii. 726.

Turreau to repeat at Washington the Emperor's remonstrance, and Turreau accordingly echoed in Madison's ear the identical words, "must last no longer." [1] His letter, to his indignation, received no answer or notice.

Thus at the moment when Congress was to meet, Dec. 2, 1805, serious problems awaited it. The conduct of Spain was hostile. At sea Spanish cruisers captured American property without regard to treaty-rights ; on land Spanish armed forces made incursions from Florida and Texas at will.[2] The conduct of France was equally menacing, for Napoleon not only sustained Spain, but also pressed abrupt demands of his own such as Jefferson could not hear without indignation. As though Congress had not enough difficulty in dealing with these two Powers, Great Britain also took an attitude which could be properly met by no resistance short of a declaration of war.

During the whole year the conduct of England changed steadily for the worse. The blockade of New York by the two frigates "Cambrian" and "Leander" became intolerable, exasperating even the mercantile class, who were naturally friendly to England, and who had most to dread from a quarrel. On board the "Leander" was a young midshipman named Basil Hall, who in later years described the mode of life he led in this service, and whose account of the blockade, coming from a British source, was

---

[1] Turreau to Madison, Jan. 3, 1806 ; State Papers, ii. **726.**

[2] State Papers, ii. 682–695.

less liable than any American authority to the charge
of exaggeration.

" Every morning at daybreak," according to his story,[1]
" we set about arresting the progress of all the vessels we
saw, firing off guns to the right and left to make every
ship that was running in heave to, or wait until we had
leisure to send a boat on board ' to see,' in our lingo,
' what she was made of.' I have frequently known a
dozen, and sometimes a couple of dozen, ships lying
a league or two off the port, losing their fair wind,
their tide, and worse than all their market, for many
hours, sometimes the whole day, before our search was
completed."

An informality in papers, a suspicion of French
ownership, a chance expression in some private letter found and opened in the search, insured seizure, a
voyage to Halifax, detention for months, heavy costs,
indefinite damage to vessel and cargo, and at best
release, with no small chance of re-seizure and condemnation under some new rule before the ship could
reach port.

Such vexations were incident to a state of war. If
the merchants of New York disliked them, the merchants might always ask Government to resent them;
but in truth commerce found its interest in submission. These vexations secured neutral profits; and
on the whole the British frigates and admiralty
courts created comparatively little scandal by in-

[1] Fragments of Voyages and Travels, by Captain Basil Hall,
R. N., F. R. S., London, 1856.

justice, while they served as a protection from the piratical privateers of Spain and France. Madison, Gallatin, and the newspapers grumbled and complained; but the profits of neutrality soothed the offended merchant, and the blockade of New York was already a fixed practice. Had the British commanders been satisfied with a moderate exercise of their power, the United States would probably have allowed the habit of neutral blockade to grow into a belligerent right by prescription. Neither the mercantile class nor the government would have risked profit or popularity on such a stake; but fortunately the British officers steadily became more severe, and meanwhile in their practice of impressment roused extreme bitterness among the seafaring classes, who had nothing to gain by submission. In Basil Hall's words, the British officers took out of American vessels every seaman " whom they had reason, or supposed or said they had reason, to consider " a British subject, " or whose country they guessed from dialect or appearance." By these impressments American vessels were often left short-handed, and were sometimes cast away or foundered. In such cases the owners were greatly irritated; but commonly the exasperation was most deeply felt by the laboring class and among the families of seafaring men. The severity with which impressment was enforced in 1805 excited hatred toward England among people who had at best no reason to love her. More than twenty years afterward, when Basil Hall revisited

New York, he was not surprised to find the name of his old ship, the " Leander," still held in detestation. Not only were the duties harsh, but, as he frankly admitted, they were harshly performed.

After Pitt's return to power impressments increased until they averaged about a thousand a year. Among them were cases of intolerable outrage; but neither President, Congress, nor people, nor even the victims themselves, cared as a body to fight in defence of their rights and liberties. Where an American-born citizen had been seized who could prove his birth, Madison on receiving the documents sent them to Monroe, who transmitted them to the British Admiralty, which ordered an inquiry; and if the man had not been killed in action or died of disease and hard usage, he was likely, after a year or two of service, to obtain a release. The American-born citizen was admitted to be no subject for impressment, and the number of such persons actually taken was never so large as the number of British-born sailors who were daily impressed; but both the mercantile and the national marine of the United States were largely manned by British seamen, and could not dispense with them. According to Gallatin's calculation,[1] American tonnage increased after 1803 at the rate of about seventy thousand tons a year; and of the four thousand two hundred men required to supply this annual increase, about two thousand five hundred were British. If the British marine lost two thousand five hundred men

[1] Gallatin to Jefferson, April 16, 1807; Works, i. 335.

annually by desertion or engagement in the American service, even after recovering one thousand seamen a year by impressment, the British navy made good only a fraction of the loss.   On the other hand, if the United States government went to war to protect British seamen, America would lose all her mercantile marine; and these same seamen for whom she was fighting must for the most part necessarily return to their old flag, because they would then have no other employer.   The immediate result of war must strengthen the British marine by sending back to it ten thousand seamen whom America could no longer employ.

Nations rarely submit to injury without a motive. If Jefferson and the Republican party, if Timothy Pickering and George Cabot, the merchants of Boston and New York, and even the seamen themselves, rejected the idea of war, it was because they found a greater interest in maintaining peace.   This interest consisted, as regarded England, in the large profits realized in neutral freights.   So long as the British navy protected this source of American wealth, Americans said but little about impressments; but in the summer of 1805 Pitt thought proper to obstruct this source, and suddenly the whole American seaboard, from Machias to Norfolk, burst into excitement, and demanded that the President should do something, — they knew not what, but at moments they seemed to ask for war.

The news of Sir William Scott's decision in the

case of the " Essex " reached America in the month
of September, while the President and Madison were
discussing an alliance with England to protect themselves against France and Spain.   The announcement
that Great Britain had suddenly begun to seize American ships by scores at the moment when Jefferson
counted most confidently on her willingness to oblige,
was a blow to the Administration so severe that a
long time elapsed before either Jefferson or Madison
realized its violence.   Their minds were intent on
the Spanish problem ; and with the question of war
pressing upon them from the south, they did not at
once perceive that another war was actually declared
against their commerce from the north.   Jefferson
disliked commercial disputes, and gladly shut his
eyes to their meaning; Madison felt their importance, but was never quick to meet an emergency.

Merry was near Philadelphia during the autumn,
when Mrs. Madison's illness obliged the secretary to
remain in that city.   Early in September Merry wrote
to his Government that the complete failure of
Monroe's Spanish mission was no secret, and that
Madison expected some collision with Spain in West
Florida, but would wait for the meeting of Congress
before taking action.   " Such a determination on the
part of the President," continued Merry,[1] " is so con-
sonant with his usual caution and temporizing system (to which the opposition here give the character
of timidity and irresolution), that I cannot but be

[1] Merry to Mulgrave, Sept. 2, 1805; MSS. British Archives.

disposed to give entire credit to the information." Shortly after the date of this despatch, news arrived that the British government had altered its rules in regard to the neutral carrying-trade, and that British cruisers were everywhere seizing American ships. Merry, who had not been forewarned by Lord Mulgrave, and who had no wish to see his own position made more uncomfortable than it already was, became uneasy. "The sensation and clamor," he wrote,[1] " excited by this news from England (which has already caused the insurance on such cargoes to be raised to four times the usual premium) is rendered the greater by such events having been totally unexpected, and by the merchants here having, on the contrary, considered themselves as perfectly secured against them." Merry saw that his Government had in the midst of peace taken a measure which Madison could hardly fail to denounce as an act of war. Dreading a violent explosion, the British minister waited anxiously ; but, to his surprise, nothing happened. " Although I have seen Mr. Madison twice since the attention of the public has been so much engaged with this object, he has not thought proper to mention it to me." [2] At first Merry could not account for this silence ; only by degrees was he taught to connect it with the Spanish quarrel, and to understand that Madison hoped to conciliate England in order to overawe France. In this play

[1] Merry to Mulgrave, Sept. 30, 1805 ; MSS. British Archives.
[2] Ibid.

of cross-purposes Merry's account of Madison's conversation was not calculated to alarm the British
government : [1] —

" Before I quitted the vicinity of Philadelphia to return
to this place [Washington], I had an interview with Mr.
Madison, who having then received accounts from Mr.
Monroe respecting the detention by his Majesty's ships
of several American vessels in consequence of their being
loaded with the produce of the enemy's colonies, brought
forward that subject to me, — speaking upon it, however,
with much more moderation than from his natural irritability, and the sensation which it had produced throughout this country, I could have expected on his part.   It
is unnecessary for me to trouble your Lordship by detail-
ing to you the several observations which he made to me
to endeavor to prove the impropriety of the principle upon which the detention of those vessels has taken place.
. . . As I had the honor to observe in the former part
of this letter, the American Secretary of State delivered
his sentiments on this subject with great temper, and
concluded by expressing only a wish that Mr. Monroe's
remonstrances upon it might prove so far efficacious as
at least to procure the liberation of the vessels and
cargoes which were already detained, as well as of those
which might be stopped before the new system adopted
by his Majesty's government in regard to the trade in
question should be generally known.   Our conversation
afterward turned upon some circumstances, the accounts
of which had just been received, of the recent conduct of
Spain toward this country, when Mr. Madison was much
less reserved in expressing his sentiments than on former

[1] Merry to Mulgrave, Nov. 3, 1805 ; MSS. British Archives.

occasions, and gave me the detail of the perfidious and insolent proceedings of some of the Spanish officers who still remain at New Orleans, and of others who command in the disputed territory, — which, combined with information he had received of the departure of four hundred troops with a quantity of military stores from the Havana, supposed to be destined to reinforce the garrisons in East and West Florida, and with a report which prevailed at New Orleans of a considerable force advancing from Mexico toward Louisiana, could not, he observed, fail to render the differences subsisting between the two governments still more difficult of accommodation."

This conversation took place about the middle of October, before the President had decided to acquiesce in the acts of Spain and France. As a result of the high tone taken toward England in the winter of 1803–1804, the secretary's mildness might well surprise a British minister, who was not quick of comprehension, and required to be told in plain language the meaning of Madison's manœuvres. No sooner had Merry returned to Washington than " a confidential person " was sent to him to explain the mystery : [1] —

" On this subject it has been remarked to me by a person in a confidential situation here that the detention of the American vessels by his Majesty's ships has happened very unseasonably to divert the attention of the people of the United States and of the Government from a proper consideration of the grievances and injuries

[1] Merry to Mulgrave, Nov. 3, 1805 : MSS. British Archives.

which they have experienced from Spain, and which the
Government were disposed and had actually taken the
measures to resent ; and he conceived that when the state
of the relations between the United States and other
Powers should be laid by the President before Congress
at their approaching meeting, the circumstance above-
mentioned, of what is considered to be so unfriendly a
proceeding on the part of Great Britain, will have the
same effect upon the resolutions of that body by blunting
the feelings which would otherwise have been excited by
the conduct of Spain, supported by France, against
this country."

The " confidential person " usually employed by
Jefferson and Madison on such errands was either
Robert or Samuel Smith ; partly because both these
gentlemen were a little inclined to officiousness, partly
because they were men of the world, or what Pichon
called " *hommes fort polis.*" In this instance the
agent was probably the Secretary of the Navy. In
telling the British minister that the President had
already taken measures to resent the conduct of
Spain, this agent was unwise, not so much because
the assertion was incorrect, as because Merry knew
better. In the same despatch, written Nov. 3, 1805,
Merry informed his Government of the President's
hopes of an agreement with Spain, founded on the war
in Europe, — hopes which had been entertained only
ten days, since October 23. He had the best reason
to be well informed on this subject, for he drew his
information directly from Jefferson himself.

That Merry should have been exceedingly perplexed

was no wonder. Two years had elapsed since his
first arrival in Washington, when he had been
harshly treated without sufficient reason, by President, Cabinet, and Congress ; and on returning to the
same place in this autumn of 1805, immediately after
his Government had made war on United States
commerce, he found himself received with surprising
cordiality. Immediately on his return, about October
20, he called at the White House. Instead of finding
the President in a passion, denouncing Pitt and the
British nation, as he might reasonably have expected,
Merry was delighted to find Jefferson in his most
genial humor. Not a word was said about British
outrages ; his conversation assumed the existence of
a close concert and alliance between England and the
United States : [1] —

" Upon my seeing the President on my return to this
place a fortnight ago, he spoke to me with great frankness respecting the state of affairs between this country
and Spain ; saying that it was possible that the accumu-
lation of the injuries which they had sustained might
produce a resolution on the part of the Congress to resent
them. With a view to the hostile situation of affairs, he
lamented that unfortunately [notwithstanding] the superiority of his Majesty's naval force and the vigilance
of his officers, it had not been possible to prevent the
enemy's fleet from crossing the Atlantic. He said that
this experience would render it necessary for the United
States to proceed with great caution and to gain time, in
order to put their principal seaports in a state of defence,

[1] Merry to Mulgrave, Nov. 3, 1805 ; MSS. British Archives.

for which he had already given directions. In the event of hostilities he considered that East and West Florida, and successively the Island of Cuba, the possession of which was necessary for the defence of Louisiana and Florida, as being the key to the Gulf of Mexico, would, in the manner in which that island might and would be attacked, be an easy conquest to them. He, however, expressed that his individual voice would constantly be for the preservation of peace with every Power, till it could no longer be kept without absolute dishonor."

Such speculations were not so practical as to affect Merry's antipathy to the American government, but he reported them to Lord Mulgrave without comment, as intended to express the President's plan in case of a Spanish war. Meanwhile the Secretary of State was engaged in composing a pamphlet, or book, to prove that the new rule adopted by Great Britain was an act of bad faith, in violation of international law. The task was not difficult.

Such was the diplomatic situation at Washington, Nov. 12, 1805, when the Cabinet adopted Jefferson's plan of reopening negotiations for the purchase of Florida on the line so persistently recommended by the irresponsible creatures of Talleyrand, and so steadily rejected to that moment by Madison and Monroe. Congress was to meet in three weeks, and within that time the diplomatic chaos must be reduced to order.

CHAPTER V.

August 27, 1805, President Jefferson, writing to Madison from Monticello, said : [1] " Considering the character of Bonaparte, I think it material at once to let him see that we are not of the Powers who will receive his orders." In Europe, on the same day, the Emperor broke up the camp at Boulogne and set his army in motion toward Ulm and Austerlitz. September 4 he was at Paris, busy with the thousand details of imminent war : his armies were in motion, his vast diplomatic and military plans were taking shape.

The United States minister at Paris had little to do except to watch the course of events, when during the Emperor's absence at Boulogne he received a visit from a gentleman who had no official position, but who brought with him a memorandum, written in Talleyrand's hand, sketching the outlines of an arrangement between the United States and Spain. The United States, said this paper, should send another note to the Government at Madrid, written in a tone and manner that would awaken Spain from

[1] Jefferson to Madison, Aug. 27, 1805 ; Writings, iv. 585.

her indifference. In this note the Prince of Peace should be warned of the consequences that would follow a persistence in his course, and should be encouraged to join with the United States in referring to Napoleon the matters in dispute. In case Spain would not unite in asking the good offices of France, a copy of the note must be sent by Armstrong to Talleyrand, with a request for the good offices of Napoleon. "The more you refer to the decision of the Emperor, the more sure and easy will be the settlement." If Spain, on the Emperor's representations, should consent to part with the Floridas, as she no doubt would do, France would propose the following terms : Commercial privileges in Florida as in Louisiana ; the Rio Colorado and a line northwestwardly, including the headwaters of all those rivers which fall into the Mississippi, as the western boundary of Louisiana, with thirty leagues on each side to remain unoccupied forever ; the claims against Spain, excluding the French spoliations, to be paid by bills on the Spanish colonies ; and, finally, ten million dollars to be paid by the United States to Spain.

Armstrong rejected the conditions on the spot. They sacrificed, he said, the whole country between the Colorado and the Rio Bravo ; abandoned the claim to West Florida, the claim to damages from the violation of *entrepôt* at New Orleans, and the claim, estimated at six millions, for French spoliations. They gave to Spain an accommodation for her payments beyond what she herself required; and they exacted the enormous sum of ten million dollars for a barren and expensive province.

September 4, the day of Napoleon's return to Paris, a long conversation followed. On both sides vigorous argument was pressed; but the Frenchman closed by saying: "I see where the shoe pinches. It is 'the enormous sum of ten million dollars;' but say seven! Your undisputed claims on Spain amount to two and a half or three millions. The arrangement as thus altered would leave four for Spain. Is not this sum within the limits of moderation?" Armstrong replied that he had nothing to say on the money transaction, but would immediately transmit Talleyrand's memorandum to the President. His despatch on the subject was accordingly sent, Sept. 10, 1805.[1]

Armstrong had little acquaintance with the person who brought the memorandum for his sole credential, and knew him only as a political agent of the government, who rested his claim to credit not on any authority from the Emperor, but on an unsigned document in Talleyrand's handwriting. " This form of communication he said had been preferred on account of greater security; it was a proof of ·the minister's habitual circumspection, and of nothing else." To most Frenchmen it might have seemed rather an example of Talleyrand's sup-

[1] Armstrong to Madison, Sept. 10, 1805 ; MSS. State Department Archives.

posed taste for jobbery, and the United States government had reason to know what was likely to be the outcome of such overtures ; but Armstrong was not unused to intrigue, and did not affect virtue above the comprehension of the society in which he lived.

A fortnight afterward the Emperor left Paris for his campaign in Germany. While Armstrong's despatch was still on its way to Washington, Napoleon captured Ulm, and November 13 entered Vienna. On the same day the despatch reached the United States.

Jefferson's Cabinet council of November 12 had barely come to its long-disputed conclusion, and decided to reopen the Florida negotiation as a French bargain, when Talleyrand's memorandum arrived, fixing definitely his terms. Naturally, the President supposed that Florida might thenceforward be looked upon as his own. At the next Cabinet he laid Armstrong's letter before the four secretaries ; and the result of their deliberation was recorded in his own hand : [1] —

"November 19. Present the same. — Since our last meeting we have received a letter from General Armstrong containing Talleyrand's propositions, which are equivalent to ours nearly, except as to the sum, he requiring seven million dollars. He advises that we alarm the fears of Spain by a vigorous language and conduct, in order to induce her to join us in appealing to the inter-

[1] Cabinet Memoranda, Nov. 19, 1805; Jefferson MSS

ference of the Emperor. We now agree to modify our propositions, so as to accommodate them to his as much as possible. We agree to pay five million dollars for the Floridas as soon as the treaty is ratified by Spain, a vote of credit obtained from Congress, and orders delivered us for the surrender of the country. We agree to his proposition that the Colorado shall be our western boundary, and a belt of thirty leagues on each side of it to be kept unsettled. We agree that joint commissioners shall settle all spoliations, and to take payment from Spain by bills on her colonies. We agree to say nothing about the French spoliations in Spanish ports which broke off the former convention. We propose to pay the five millions after a simple vote of credit, by stock redeemable in three years, within which time we can pay it. We agree to order to the commanding officer at Natchitoches to patrol the country on this side the Sabine and all the Red River as being in our possession, except the settlement of Bayou Pierre, which he is not to disturb unless they aggress ; he is to protect our citizens and repel all invasions of the preceding country by Spanish soldiers ; to take all offenders without shedding blood, unless his orders cannot otherwise be executed."

At last, after more than six months of hesitation, a Spanish policy was fixed ; and since it conceded every point which had been required by France, the President might reasonably hope that his difficulties were at an end. He did not venture to send instructions to Armstrong at once, because the authority of Congress was needed before pledging the government to pay so large a sum of money ; but Congress was to meet within a few weeks, and Jefferson could safely assume that the instructions would not be delayed beyond the New Year.

The President was greatly relieved to see the end of this annoying imbroglio; the more, because he could no longer shut his eyes to the conduct of Great Britain. The merchants of Boston, New York, Philadelphia, and Baltimore were frantic with rage and despair, hearing every day of new seizures, which swelled their losses to a sum then quite appalling, and carried ruin to their fairest fortunes. The carrying-trade was not a matter about which Jefferson cared to quarrel, for he held that Americans should not meddle with a commerce which did not belong to them; yet the public anger was far stronger against England than against Spain, and although the newspapers talked incessantly of a Spanish war, Jefferson soon felt that he should find great difficulty in preserving a British peace. That he should incline to a war with Spain in alliance with England was natural; but under no circumstances, and for no object, did Jefferson wish for war with Great Britain. From the first he had relied upon his power to coerce her by peaceable means; and the time had come when some coercion must be applied. No one could longer doubt that Pitt meant to keep what he had taken, and that the British policy was preconcerted with deliberate purpose.

When Merry next called at the State Department he heard nothing more about the misconduct of Spain or the advantages of a powerful British navy.

" The lively sensation " produced by the seizures, wrote Merry to Mulgrave,[1] December 2, " appears to have increased considerably since I had the honor of writing to your Lordship by the last mail. The commercial bodies at Philadelphia, Baltimore, and Norfolk have held public meetings on this subject, and come to resolutions to transmit to the Government of the United States particular statements of the injuries they allege to be sustaining daily in their trade. I am sorry to add that those public prints which are considered as the organs of the Government . . . have of late lost sight in a great measure of their complaints against Spain, with a view, as may be suspected, to excite and direct the whole national indignation against Great Britain. . . .

" In addition, my Lord, to these circumstances, I have been sorry to find in my recent conversations with Mr. Madison that he has treated this subject in a much more serious light than he had at first represented it to me. At my last interview with him, two days ago, he said that he had flattered himself that Mr. Monroe's remonstrances to your Lordship would not only have produced the liberation of all the vessels which should have been detained previously to the 1st November, but that, as that minister had been promised an answer in writing to his representations, the reconsideration of the matter which would probably have taken place before a written answer was given might have induced his Majesty's government, if not to give up entirely, at least to modify to a tolerable degree, the principle upon which they acted. It was true that the answer in question had not as yet reached him, nor had he heard lately from Mr. Monroe ; but he had recently received information from an authentic

[1] Merry to Mulgrave, Dec. 2, 1805; MSS. British Archives.

though not an official quarter, which gave him the strongest reason to apprehend that if any reply at all in writing should be made on the subject, it would contain nothing satisfactory."

Madison raised his tone awkwardly.   Mysterious " information from an authentic quarter " was scarcely sufficient ground for so abrupt a change, but Merry failed to press him on this point.   The secretary told the British minister that the government of England had committed " an act of commercial hostility on this country, and that the citizens of the United States would have a just claim of indemnity for whatever effective losses they might sustain in consequence of it; and he feared that these would be very considerable."   He hinted that measures would be taken to seek redress; and although he did not then foreshadow these measures, Merry read two days afterward in the " National Intelligencer " the Resolutions and speech in which Madison, in the year 1794, had urged commercial restrictions as the true policy of the United States against the same British outrages.   The motive of republication was plain.

At about the same time Madison finished his pamphlet called " Examination of the British Doctrine," which in the course of the coming session was laid on the desk of every senator and member.   The book was creditable to his literary and scholarly qualities. Clear, calm, convincing, it left the British government no excuse for its conduct; but, not without reason,

John Randolph objected that as an argument it was but a shilling pamphlet against eight hundred British ships of war. That Pitt could occasionally be convinced of his mistakes was certain; but no reasoners except Napoleon and Moreau had ever effectually convinced him.

Meanwhile the President prepared his Message. Of all Jefferson's writings none had a livelier interest than the Annual Message at the meeting of the Ninth Congress. The Second Inaugural, nine months before, prepared the public for new political opinions; but the Message surprised even those who looked for surprises. The Second Inaugural seemed to sweep old Republican principles to the common rubbish-heap of out-worn political toys. The Message went even further, and seemed to announce that the theory of foreign affairs on which the Republican Administration began its career must be abandoned. Jefferson intended it to carry such a meaning.

"The love of peace," he wrote to one of his old friends,[1] "which we sincerely feel and profess, has begun to produce an opinion in Europe that our government is entirely in Quaker principles, and will turn the left cheek when the right has been smitten. This opinion must be corrected when just occasion arises, or we shall become the plunder of all nations. The moral duties make no part of the political system of those governments of Europe which are habitually belligerent."

[1] Jefferson to Judge Cooper, Feb. 18, 1806; Jefferson MSS.

The Message began by an allusion to the yellow fever; from which it quickly turned to discuss the greater scourge of war : —

" Since our last meeting the aspect of our foreign relations has considerably changed. Our coasts have been infested and our harbors watched by private armed vessels ; some of them without commissions, some with illegal commissions, others with those of legal form, but committing piratical acts beyond the authority of their commissions. . . . The same system of hovering on our coasts and harbors, under color of seeking enemies, has been also carried on by public armed ships, to the great annoyance and oppression of our commerce. New principles, too, have been interpolated into the law of nations, founded neither in justice nor the usage or acknowledgment of nations. . . . With Spain our negotiations for a settlement of differences have not had a satisfactory issue. . . . Propositions for adjusting amicably the boundaries of Louisiana have not been acceded to. . . . Inroads have recently been made into the territories of Orleans and the Mississippi ; our citizens have been seized and their property plundered in the very parts of the former which had actually been delivered up by Spain, and this by the regular officers and soldiers of that government. I have therefore found it necessary at length to give orders to our troops on that frontier to be in readiness to protect our citizens and to repel by arms any similar aggressions in future. Other details necessary for your full information of the state of things between this country and that shall be the subject of another communication. In reviewing these injuries from some of the belligerent Powers, the moderation, the firmness, and the wisdom of the Legislature will all be called into action. We ought still to hope that time, and a more correct estimate of interest as well as of character, will produce the justice we are bound to expect; but should any nation deceive itself by false calculations, and disappoint that expectation, we must join in the unprofitable contest of trying which party can do the other the most harm. Some of these injuries may perhaps admit a peaceable remedy. Where that is competent it is always the most desirable. But some of them are of a nature to be met by force only, and all of them may lead to it."

From this preamble the public would naturally infer that measures of force were to be the object of the special message promised in regard to Spanish aggressions. As though to leave no doubt on the subject, the President urged the fortification of seaports, the building of gun-boats, the organization of militia, the prohibition of the export of arms and ammunition; and added that the materials for building ships of the line were on hand.

All this formality of belligerent language was little better than comedy. Jefferson could hardly be charged with a wish to deceive, since he could not wear the mask of deception. Both friends and enemies were amused to see how naturally he betrayed objects which his plan required should be concealed. In the first draft of the Message, sent for correction to Gallatin, the financial prospect was as pacific as the diplomatic was warlike; the Message not only announced a surplus for the coming year, but suggested the reduction of taxes. Gallatin pointed out that the English seizures alone would affect the revenue, and any measure of retaliation would still further diminish it; while the navy had increased its estimates from six hundred and fifty thousand dollars to one million and seventy thousand dollars. As for the hint at a reduction of taxes, Gallatin at once struck it out.[1] " As it relates to foreign nations, it will certainly destroy the effect intended by other parts of the Message. They never can think us serious in any intentions to resist, if we recommend at the same time a diminution of our resources." The President made these corrections, and returned the draft for revisal, with a note :[2] —

"On reviewing what had been prepared as to Great Britain and Spain, I found it too soft toward the former compared with the latter, and that so temperate a notice of the greater enormity of British invasions of right might lessen the effect which the strong language toward Spain was meant to produce at the Tuileries. I have therefore given more force to the strictures on Britain."

In studying "the effect which the strong language toward Spain was meant to produce at the Tuileries," Jefferson had in mind the effect which his strong language produced at the Tuileries in 1803.

[1] Gallatin to Jefferson, Nov. 21, 1805; Gallatin's Writings, i. 261.

[2] Jefferson to Gallatin, Nov. 24, 1805; Gallatin's Writings, i. 264.

He played a game of finesse hardly safe in the face of men like Godoy, Talleyrand, and Napoleon, whose finesse was chiefly used to cover force, and was not betrayed or derided by factious opposition in the press.   Besides being unsafe, it was unfair to himself. Jefferson was an honest man, and in putting on the outward appearance of a Talleyrand, he resembled an amateur imitating Talma and Garrick.   Gestures and tones alike were unnatural, awkward, and false; they exposed him to ridicule.   If President Jefferson had taken the public into his confidence, he would have told the people that under no circumstances would he consent to war; but that if the great Powers of Europe combined to injure America, she would close her ports, abandon her commerce, shut herself within her own continent, and let the world outside murder and rob elsewhere.   Such an avowal implied no disgrace; the policy it proclaimed was the alternative to war; and as the radical doctrine of the Republican party, the course was not only that which Jefferson meant to take, but it was that which he took.   The avowal might have invited aggression, and have been followed by failure; but he would have done better to fail on a direct issue of principle, than to fail after evading the issue until the issue itself was lost.

To carry out his scheme, the President put forward two policies, — a public and a secret; or, as he called it, an ostensible and a real one.   The warlike recommendations of the Annual Message were the public and ostensible policy; the real one was to be expressed in a secret message, announced in advance. To this coming message the President next turned his attention; but he found himself quickly involved in complications of his own creating. He had not only to recommend a double series of measures to Congress, but he had to frame a double series of replies which Congress was to return to him. He tried at first to combine the two answers in one. After writing a secret message asking for money to buy Florida, he drafted a series of Resolutions [1] which Congress was to adopt in reply to both messages at once, and in which " the citizens of the United States, by their Senate and Representatives in Congress assembled, do pledge their lives and fortunes " to maintain the line of the Sabine and the free navigation of the Mobile, pending negotiations, while the President should be authorized to take whatever unappropriated moneys might lie in the Treasury in order to carry these Resolutions into effect.

Clearly this would not do; and Gallatin undertook to set the matter right.

" The apparent difficulty in framing the Resolutions," he wrote to the President,[2] " arises from the attempt to blend the three objects together. The same reasons which have induced the President to send two distinct

[1] Jefferson to Gallatin: Spanish Resolutions, 1805 ; Gallatin's Writings, i. 277.

[2] Gallatin to Jefferson, Dec. 3, 1805; Gallatin's Writings, i. 278.

messages render it necessary that the public Resolutions of Congress should be distinct from the private ones; that those which relate to the war posture of the Spanish affairs, which are intended to express the national sense on that subject, and to enable the President to take the steps which appear immediately necessary on the frontier, should not be mixed with those proceedings calculated only to effect an accommodation."

The Secretary of the Treasury frequently corrected his chief, and still more frequently hinted a correction. Only a few days had passed since Jefferson had spoken to Gallatin of the " strong language toward Spain " as " meant to produce an effect at the Tuileries." Gallatin ignored this object, and spoke of the strong language toward Spain as intended to express the national sense, and as restricted in its bearing to the steps immediately necessary for protecting the frontier. The difference was worth noting. Evidently Gallatin felt no great confidence in producing an effect on the Tuileries.

" The course now recommended," he continued, " is precisely that which was followed in the Louisiana business when the deposit was withdrawn. A public Resolution . . . was moved by Randolph, and adopted by the House. A committee in the mean while brought in a confidential report sufficient to support and justify the President in the purchase he was going to attempt, and to this an appropriation law in very general terms was added. To follow a similar course appears not only best, but will also, as founded on precedent, be the smoothest mode of doing the business in Congress."

The President adopted Gallatin's suggestions.[1] The double messages breathing war and peace were prepared. The double answers were sketched out. Congress had only to act with the same quickness and secrecy which it had shown in the Louisiana business ; and of its readiness to do so, no one in the Cabinet seemed to doubt.

Yet nations could not so readily as individuals swing about on a course opposite to that which they had been led to expect. The American public had been wrought to anger against Spain. Of the negotiations little was publicly known. Monroe had come, and gone ; the Marquis Yrujo had remonstrated, and had written in newspapers ; but the rights and wrongs of the Spanish dispute remained a mystery to the public at large, which knew only that Spain had rejected all the offers made by the United States, had resumed her depredations on American commerce, and had taken a menacing attitude at Mobile and on the Sabine. Throughout the year the Republican press had followed hints from the Government at Washington, all looking toward a rupture with Spain. The same newspapers had shown at first a wish to make light of the late British seizures, — a course which misled the Federalist press into denunciations of England such as would never have been risked had the party in power not seemed disposed to apologize for England's conduct. The country at large

[1] Jefferson to Gallatin, Dec. 4, 1805; Gallatin's Writings, i. 281.

was prepared to hear the President advise a rupture with Spain, and upon that rupture to found his hope of success in negotiating with Pitt. The warlike tone of the Annual Message was certain to give additional strength to this expectation; and Jefferson might have foreseen that the sudden secret change of tone to be taken immediately afterward in the special message on Spanish affairs would produce bewilderment among his followers.

No one could doubt where the confusion would first appear. The last session had ended in a series of quarrels, in which party distinctions had been almost forgotten. The summer had done nothing to reunite the factions; on the contrary, it had done much to widen the breach. Already the " Aurora " announced that the Yazoo question was to determine " the relations, the principles, the characters, and the strength of parties in the next session of Congress;" and the public knew that the Yazoo question had passed beyond the stage of rational argument, and had become the test of personal devotion, the stepping-stone to favor or proscription with the next President. Three years before the election of 1808 Congress was already torn by a Virginia feud, — a struggle for power between John Randolph and James Madison.

As though to hurry and prolong this struggle, Jefferson announced, after his second inauguration, that he should retire at the close of his term, March 4, 1809. Without expressly recommending Madison as his successor, his strong personal attachment insured to the Secretary of State the whole weight of Executive influence. The whole weight was needed. The secretary, with all his amiable qualities, was very far from controlling the voice of Virginia. His strength lay rather among the Northern democrats, semi-Federalists, or "Yazoo men," as they were called, who leaned toward him because he, of all the prominent Virginians, was least Virginian. His diplomatic triumph in buying Louisiana had given him an easy advantage over his rivals; but even his reputation might sink with the failure of the Spanish treaty and the aggression of England.

No one who knew the men, or who had followed the course of President Jefferson's first Administration, could feel surprise that Madison's character should act on John Randolph as an irritant. Madison was cautious, if not timid; Randolph was always in extremes. Madison was apt to be on both sides of the same question, as when he wrote the "Federalist" and the Virginia Resolutions of 1798; Randolph pardoned dalliance with Federalism in no one but himself. Madison was in person small, retiring, modest, with quiet malice in his humor, and with marked taste for closet politics and delicate management; Randolph was tall in stature, abrupt in manner, self-asserting in temper, sarcastic, with a pronounced taste for publicity, and a vehement contempt for those silent influences which more practical politicians called legitimate and necessary, but which Randolph, when he could not control them, called corrupt.   Jefferson soon remarked, in regard to what Randolph denounced as back-stairs influence, " We never heard this while the declaimer was himself a back-stairs man." [1]   Just as the criticism was, no one could deny that Randolph seemed much out of place on the back-stairs of the White House, whereas Madison seemed to him in place nowhere else. The Spanish papers, which Randolph must read, were not likely to increase his respect for the Secretary of State; while Madison's candidacy made a counter-movement necessary for those Virginians who would not be dragged at the heels of the Northern democracy.

Long before the month of December Randolph foresaw the coming trouble.   The Yazoo men in the Ninth Congress were more numerous than ever; and they were credited with the wish to eject Speaker Macon from the chair, and to put some Northern democrat in Randolph's place at the head of the Committee of Ways and Means.   Oct. 25, 1805, Randolph wrote to Gallatin from Bizarre : —

" I look forward to the ensuing session of Congress with no very pleasant feelings.   To say nothing of the disadvantages of the place, natural as well as acquired, I anticipate a plentiful harvest of bickering and blunders ; of which, however, I hope to be a quiet, if not an unconcerned, spectator. . . .   I regret exceedingly Mr. Jefferson's resolution to retire, and almost as much the premature annunciation of that determination.   It

[1] Jefferson to Bidwell, July 5, 1806; Writings, v. 14.

almost precludes a revision of his purpose, to say nothing of the intrigues which it will set on foot. If I were sure that Monroe would succeed him, my regret would be very much diminished." [1]

Intrigue and dissension could not be confined to the House, but must spread to the Senate, and could hardly fail to affect even the Cabinet. While Gallatin's personal sympathies were with Madison, his political bias was on the opposite side. The old Republicans, with John Randolph at their head, had steadily protected the Treasury from jobs and extravagance; without their help Gallatin would lie at the mercy of the Northern democrats, who were not behind the Federalists in their willingness to spend money. He might expect an alliance between the Northern democrats and the Smith faction which controlled the Navy Department. To such a combination he must have foreseen that Madison would yield.

In the face of such latent feuds nothing could be more hazardous than to spring upon Congress, in Madison's interests, a new, tortuous, complicated Spanish policy, turning on the secret assurance that France could be bribed with five million dollars, at the moment when Congress would be required to begin a commercial war upon England. Whether Madison was responsible for these measures or not, his enemies would charge him with the responsibility; and even without such attacks from his own party, he

[1] Adams's Randolph, p. 161.

was struggling with enemies enough to have crushed Jefferson himself.

Early in December, all the actors in the drama assembled, to play another act in a tragi-comedy of increasing interest. With his old sanguine hopes, but not with all his old self-confidence, the President watched them slowly arrive, — Democrats, Federalists, Southern Republicans, all equally ignorant of what had been done, and what they were expected to do; but more curious, better-informed, and more sharp-sighted than these, the three diplomatists, Turreau, Merry, and Yrujo, waiting with undisguised contempt to see what species of coercion was to be employed against England, France, and Spain.

To impose on hostile forces and interests the compulsion of a single will was the task and triumph of the true politician, which had been accomplished, under difficult conditions, by men of opposite characters. A political leader might be combative and despotic, or pliant and conciliatory. The method mattered little, provided it obtained success, — but success depended more on character than on manœuvres. In the winter of 1805–1806 President Jefferson dealt with a problem such as few Americans have been required to solve. Other Presidents have met with violent opposition both within and without the ranks of their party; but no other President has been obliged to face a hostile minority, together with violent factiousness in the majority, and at the same time a spirit of aggression showing itself in acts of

war from three of the greatest Powers of Europe.
By what resources of skill or character President
Jefferson was to restrain this disorder from becoming
chaos, only a prophet could foretell. If ever the Federalist " crisis " seemed close at hand, it was in December, 1805.   Some energetic impulse could alone
save the country from drifting into faction at home
and violence abroad.

All might go well if England, France, and Spain
could be obliged to respect law. To restrain these
three governments was Jefferson's most urgent need.
The three envoys waited to see what act of energy he
would devise to break through the net which had been
drawn about him. Turreau enjoyed most of his confidence ; and soon after the meeting of Congress, at the
time when Jefferson was publicly using " strong language toward Spain," meant to produce an effect at
the Tuileries, Turreau wrote interesting accounts of
his private conversation for the guidance of Talleyrand and Napoleon : [1] —

" One may perhaps draw some inferences in regard to
the true sense of the Message from some words which
escaped the President in a private conversation with me.
' I see with pain,' he said, ' that our people have a tendency toward commerce which no other kind of interest
will be able to balance ; we should be essentially agri-
cultural, and yet agriculture will never be more than a
secondary interest here.' . . . In a preceding inter-

[1] Turreau to Talleyrand, Jan. 20, 1806; **Archives des Aff.**
Étr., MSS.

view the President invited me to a discussion of Spanish affairs. . . . After some complaints about Spanish privateers, and the protection which Spain granted to ours in particular, Mr. Jefferson expanded on the griefs of the Americans in regard to some excursions of Spanish patrols beyond the limits provisionally established, and, in consequence, within the territory of Louisiana. I replied that doubtless the Spanish government had not authorized these steps, and that the mistakes of a few subalterns could not produce serious differences between the two Powers. ‘ That is true; but,’ he added, ‘ these Spaniards are so stupid (*bêtes*), their government so detested,’ etc. It was not easy to contradict him on this point. As for the English, his complaints and reproaches have been much more serious. He has assured me that they have taken five hundred American ships; that they could not have done more harm had they been at war with America; yet that England would in vain try, as against the Americans, to destroy neutral rights. ‘ In that respect,’ added Mr. Jefferson, ‘ we have *principles* from which we shall never depart; our people have commerce everywhere, and everywhere our neutrality should be respected. On the other hand, we do not want war, — and all this is very embarrassing.’ ”

Turreau’s comment on these words may have affected the policy of Napoleon, as it must certainly have had weight with Talleyrand : —

“ If your Excellency was not already acquainted with the man and his government, this last phrase would be enough to enable you to judge the one and the other.”

CHAPTER VI.

THE Ninth Congress met Dec. 2, 1805. During no period of eight years did Congress contain a smaller number of remarkable members than during the two administrations of Jefferson, from 1801 to 1809; and if the few Federalists in opposition were left out of view, the American people had in the Ninth Congress hardly a single representative, except John Randolph, capable of controlling any vote but his own. In the Senate, when George Clinton took his seat as Vice-President, he saw before him, among the thirty-four senators, not less than twenty-seven who belonged to his own party; yet among these twenty-seven Republican members of the Senate was not one whose name lived. Senator Bradley of Vermont exercised a certain influence in his day, like Dr. Mitchill of New York, or Samuel Smith of Maryland, or William B. Giles of Virginia, or Abraham Baldwin and James Jackson of Georgia. These were the leaders of the Senate, but they were men whose influence was due more to their office than to their genius; the Government gave them more weight than they could give back to it. Breckenridge of Kentucky had become

attorney-general, and his seat was filled by John
Adair. In the whole Senate not a Republican member could be found competent to defend a difficult
financial or diplomatic measure as Gallatin or Madison could have done it, or would have wished it to
be done.

In the House the Administration could count upon
equally little aid. Setting aside John Randolph and
Joseph Nicholson, who were more dangerous than any
Federalist of New England to Government, the huge
Republican majority contained no man of note. Its
poverty was startling. Gallatin clung to Randolph as
the only member of the House competent to conduct
the public business ; and no small part of Randolph's
arrogance toward his own followers was due to his
sense of intellectual superiority, and to the constant
proof that they could do no business without his aid.
Randolph was rarely arrogant in the face of men
whose abilities were superior to his own, or whose will
was stronger ; he domineered over those whom he
thought his inferiors, but he liked no contest in which
he saw an uncertain hope of victory. In the Ninth
Congress he met no rival in his own party. Massachusetts sent a new member, from whose oratory
much was expected, — a certain Barnabas Bidwell ;
" but as a popular speaker he never can stand as the
rival of John Randolph," was the comment of a Massachusetts senator on listening to him in the House.[1]
New York, New Jersey, and Pennsylvania were repre-

[1] Diary of J. Q. Adams (March 8, 1806), i. 419.

sented by an almost solid mass of Democrats, without a single leader.   Virginia and the other Southern States sent many men of excellent character and of the best social position to Washington, but not one who made a national name or who tried to master the details of public business.   Perhaps the ablest new member was Josiah Quincy of Boston, whose positive temper, marked abilities, and vehement Federalism made him troublesome to the majority rather than useful in legislation.

When the House met, it proceeded at once to the election of a Speaker; and the old feuds of the last session broke out again.   Fifty-four votes were required to elect; and on the first ballot Macon had but fifty-one.   Twenty-seven Republicans voted for Joseph B. Varnum of Massachusetts, besides others who threw away their votes on candidates from Virginia and Pennsylvania.   Only at the third ballot did Macon get a majority, and even then he received but fifty-eight votes, while the full strength of his party was more than one hundred.   His first act was to reappoint Randolph and Nicholson on the Ways and Means Committee, where a place was also given to Josiah Quincy.

The President's Message was read December 3, and produced the effect to be expected.   The country received it with applause as a proof of vigor.   In Baltimore, and along the seaboard, it was regarded as equivalent to a declaration of war against Spain; it stopped trade, raised insurance, and encouraged piracy. The Federalist press throughout the country, except the "Evening Post," affected to admire and praise it. "Federalism revived!" said the bitter "Washington Federalist;" "dignified, firm, and spirited." "This day we have been astonished," wrote a correspondent to the "Boston Centinel;"[1] "the President's speech is, in principle, almost wholly on the Washington and Adams system. It has puzzled the Federalists and offended many of the Democrats. It is in perfect nonconformity to all the former professions of the party." The Federalists exaggerated their applause in order to irritate John Randolph and his friends, who could not fail to see that the Message strengthened Madison at the expense of the old Republicans. Jefferson's private language was not less energetic than his public message. Among the favorite ideas which the President urged was that of claiming for America the ocean as far as the Gulf Stream, and forbidding hostilities within the line of deep-sea soundings.[2] One of the Massachusetts senators to whom he argued this doctrine inquired whether it might not be well, before assuming a claim so broad, to wait for a time when the Government should have a force to maintain it. The President replied by insisting that the Government, "should squint at it;"[3] and he lost no chance of doing so. He assured his friends that no privateer

[1] Columbian Centinel, Dec. 21, 1805.
[2] Cabinet Memoranda, July 5, 1805; Jefferson MSS.
[3] Diary of J. Q. Adams (Nov. 30, 1805), i. 376.

would ever again be permitted to cruise within the Gulf Stream.[1]

Such an attitude, public and private, roused much interest. Congress waited anxiously for the promised special message on Spanish affairs, and did not wait long. December 6, only three days after the Annual Message was sent in, the special and secret message followed ; the House closed its doors, and the members listened eagerly to a communication which they expected to be, what it actually was, a turning-point in their politics.

The Message[2] very briefly narrated the story of the unratified claims convention, ending in Monroe's diplomatic misfortunes, and announced that the Spaniards showed every intention of advancing from Texas, until they should be repressed by force.

" Considering that Congress alone is constitutionally invested with the power of changing our condition from peace to war, I have thought it my duty to await their authority for using force in any degree which could be avoided. I have barely instructed the officers stationed in the neighborhood of the aggressions to protect our citizens from violence, to patrol within the borders actually delivered to us, and not to go out of them but when necessary to repel an inroad or to rescue a citizen or his property."

Passing next to the conduct of Napoleon, the Message mentioned the decided part taken by France

---

[1] Jefferson to Monroe, May 4, 1806; Writings, v. 9.

[2] State Papers, ii. 613.

against the United States on every point of the Spanish dispute, —

" her silence as to the Western boundary leaving us
to infer her opinion might be against Spain in that
quarter.   Whatever direction she might mean to give to
these differences, it does not appear that she has con-
templated their proceeding to actual rupture, or that at
the date of our last advices from Paris her Government
had any suspicion of the hostile attitude Spain had taken
here.   On the contrary, we have reason to believe that
she was disposed to effect a settlement on a plan analo-
gous to what our ministers had proposed, and so com-
prehensive as to remove as far as possible the grounds of
future collision and controversy on the eastern as well as
western side of the Mississippi.   The present crisis in
Europe is favorable for pressing such a settlement, and
not a moment should be lost in availing ourselves of it.
Should it pass unimproved, our situation would become
much more difficult.   Formal war is not necessary, it is
not probable it will follow ; but the protection of our
citizens, the spirit and honor of our country, require that
force should be interposed to a certain degree.   It will
probably contribute to advance the object of peace.   But
the course to be pursued will require the command of
means which it belongs to Congress exclusively to yield
or to deny.   To them I communicate every fact material
for their information, and the documents necessary to
enable them to judge for themselves.   To their wisdom,
then, I look for the course I am to pursue, and will pursue with sincere zeal that which they shall approve."

After the reading of this Message the House was
more perplexed than ever.   The few Federalists

sneered. The warlike tone of the Annual Message, contradicting their theory of Jefferson's character, had already ended, as they believed, in surrender. John Randolph was angry. He felt that the President had assumed, for Madison's political profit, the tone of public bravado toward England and Spain, while Congress was required to overrule Madison's bold policy and to impose on the country what would seem a crouching cowardice of its own. The Message was at once referred to a special committee of seven members, with Randolph at its head, his friend Nicholson second in the number, John Cotton Smith, a vigorous Federalist, coming third ; while, whether the Speaker intended it or not, the only person in the committee on whom the President could depend for useful service was Barnabas Bidwell, the new member from Massachusetts. Bidwell's conversion from Federalism was but recent, and neither his Federalism nor his democracy was of a kind that Randolph loved.

To this point the Louisiana precedent was closely followed, and Randolph seemed to have no excuse for refusing to do in 1805 what he had done in 1802 ; yet nothing could be surer than that the Randolph of 1805 was a very different man from the Randolph of three years before, as the Republican party of 1805 widely differed from the party which first elected Jefferson to the Presidency. No double-dealing, hesitation, or concealment was charged against Randolph. According to his own story, he called upon the President immediately, and learned, not without some surprise, that an appropriation of two millions was wanted to purchase Florida. He told the President without reserve "that he would never agree to such a measure, because the money had not been asked for in the Message; that he could not consent to shift upon his own shoulders or those of the House the proper responsibility of the Executive; but that even if the money had been explicitly demanded, he should have been averse to granting it, because, after the total failure of every attempt at negotiation, such a step would disgrace us forever," — with much more to the same effect, which was mildly combated by Jefferson.[1]

The next day, December 7, the committee met, and Randolph, as he probably expected, found that Bidwell alone intended to support the Administration. Bidwell did not venture to act as the direct mouthpiece of the President, but undertook on his own authority to construe the Message as a demand for money, and proposed a grant to that effect. The rest of the committee gravely followed Randolph in professing to find no such meaning in the Message; Bidwell's motion had no supporter, and was promptly overruled. Jefferson's labored Resolutions, which Nicholson carried in his pocket for the committee to adopt, were suppressed; Nicholson returned them the next day

[1] First Letter of Decius, in the "Richmond Enquirer," August, 1806.

to Gallatín, with a brief expression of his own decided disapproval.[1]

The committee separated, not to meet again for a fortnight; but during the following week Randolph had several interviews with the President and Secretary of State. Madison told him "that France would not permit Spain to adjust her differences with us; that France wanted money, and that we must give it to her, or have a Spanish and French war."[2]   If Madison said this he told the truth. Randolph made an unfair use of the confidential words; for he proclaimed them as his excuse for declaring a public and personal war on the Secretary of State, which he waged thenceforward in a temper and by means so revolting as in the end to throw the sympathies of every unprejudiced man on the side of his victim.

"From the moment I heard that declaration," said Randolph afterward, "all the objections I originally had to the procedure were aggravated to the highest possible degree. I considered it a base prostration of the national character to excite one nation by money to bully another nation out of its property; and from that moment, and to the last moment of my life, my confidence in the principles of the man entertaining those sentiments died, never to live again."

These words would have carried more conviction had Randolph's quarrel with Madison not been of

[1] Nicholson to Gallatin, Dec. 8, 1805 ; Gallatin MSS.
[2] Decius, No. 1; Randolph's speech of April 5, 1806 ; Annals of Congress, 1805–1806, pp. 984–985.

much older date. In truth he wanted a means to break down the secretary's chance of election as President, and he thought to find it here. As he said openly in Congress and in the press, " his confidence in the Secretary of State had never been very high, but now it was gone forever." [1]

The serious charge against Madison was one which Madison alone could reveal. Down to October 23 he had held Randolph's view and had protested against turning the Spanish negotiation into a French job. He could hardly blame Randolph for adhering to an opinion which had been held by President and Cabinet until within a few weeks, when they had abandoned it without explanation or excuse.

Stubbornly refusing to act, Randolph, December 14, mounted his horse and rode to Baltimore, leaving the President for the moment helpless. Every hour's delay shook party discipline, and imperilled Armstrong's success. The President appealed to Nicholson; but Nicholson also disliked the intended policy, and could be persuaded to use his influence only so far as would enable the committee to act, with the understanding that its action would be adverse to the President's wishes. Although the situation was still secret, it threatened to become scandalous, and soon became so altogether.

December 21 Randolph returned. As he dismounted at the Capitol, he was received by Nicholson, who told him of the irritation which his delay had

[1] Decius, No. 1.

caused. The committee was instantly called together. As Randolph went to the committee-room he was met by Gallatin, who put into his hands a paper headed, " Provision for the purchase of Florida." Although Gallatin's relations with Randolph were friendly, they did not save the Secretary of the Treasury from a sharp rebuff. Randolph broke out roughly : he would not vote a shilling for the purchase of Florida ; the President should not be allowed to throw upon Congress the odium " of delivering the public purse to the first cut-throat that demanded it ; " on the record the Executive would appear as recommending manly and vigorous measures, while Congress would appear as having forced him to abandon them, when in fact it was acting all the while at Executive instigation ; " I do not understand this double set of opinions and principles, — the one ostensible, the other real : I hold true wisdom and cunning to be utterly incompatible." With this sweeping censure of President, Cabinet, and party, Randolph turned his back on Gallatin and walked to the committee-room. There he had no trouble in carrying matters with a high hand. Instead of recommending an appropriation, the committee instructed Randolph to write to the Secretary of War asking his opinion what force was needed to protect the Southern frontier.

Christmas was then at hand, and not a step had yet been taken. Unless the spirit of faction could be crushed, not only was the fate of Madison sealed, but the career of Jefferson himself must end in failure. Nothing could be done with Randolph, who in a final interview at the White House, flatly declared "that he too had a character to support and principles to maintain," and avowed his determined opposition to the whole scheme of buying Florida of France. Jefferson, little as he liked to quarrel, accepted the challenge. Negotiations then ceased, and a party schism began.

If Randolph could not be overcome in debate, he might at least be overborne by numbers; if the best part of the old Republican party went with him, the rank and file of Northern and Western democrats would remain to support the Administration. Once more the committee was called together. Bidwell moved to appropriate two millions for foreign relations; the majority rejected his motion and adopted a report echoing the warlike tone of the President's public message, and closing with a Resolution to raise troops for the defence of the Southern frontier "from Spanish inroad and insult, and to chastise the same." This report was laid before the House by Randolph Jan. 3, 1806, when two additional Resolutions were immediately moved, — one appropriating money for extraordinary expenses in foreign intercourse, the other continuing the Mediterranean Fund for a new term of years; and the three Resolutions were referred to the House in Committee of the Whole, with closed doors.

Monday, Jan. 6, 1806, the debate began; and throughout the following week the House sat in secret session, while Randolph strained every nerve to break the phalanx of democrats which threatened to overwhelm him. Perpetually on the floor, he declaimed against the proposed negotiation at Paris ; while Nicholson, unwillingly consenting to vote for the two millions, said openly that he hoped in God the negotiation would fail. When at length a vote could be reached, the Administration carried its point, — seventy-two members supporting the President, against a minority of fifty-eight ; but in this minority was included no small number of the most respectable Republicans. Twelve of the twenty-two Virginia members broke away from the President ; and for the first time in a struggle vital to Jefferson's credit, more than half the majority consisted of Northern men.

The House having recovered control of the matter, thrust Randolph aside, rapidly passed a Bill appropriating two million dollars for extraordinary expenses in foreign relations, and Jan. 16, 1806, sent it to the Senate by a vote of seventy-six to fifty-four. It was accompanied by a secret message explaining that the money was intended for the purchase of Spanish territory east of the Mississippi. The Senate closed its doors, and with the least possible debate, Feb. 7, 1806, passed the bill, which, February 13, received the President's approval. Not until March 13,[1] six months after Armstrong's despatch had been

[1] Madison to Armstrong and Bowdoin, March 13, 1806 ; State Papers, iii. **539**.

written, did Madison at length send to Paris a public authority for Armstrong to offer France five million dollars for Florida and Texas to the Colorado, — an authority which should have been secret and prompt, to be worth sending at all.

Jefferson carried his point; he won a victory over Randolph, and silenced open resistance within the party; but his success was gained at a cost hitherto unknown in his experience. The men who were most obedient in public to his will growled in private almost as fiercely as Randolph himself. Senator Bradley made no secret of his disgust. Senator Anderson of Tennessee frankly said that he wished the Devil had the Bill; that the opposition did not half know how bad it was; that it was the most pernicious measure Jefferson had ever taken; "but so it was, so he would have it, and so it must be!"[1] Three Republican Senators — Bradley, Logan, and Mitchill — absented themselves at the final vote; four more — Adair, Gilman, Stone, and Sumter — voted against the Bill, which on its third reading obtained only seventeen voices in its favor against eleven in opposition. Worse than this, the malcontents felt that for the first time in the history of their party the whip of Executive power had been snapped over their heads; and, worst of all, the New England Federalists took for granted that Jefferson had become a creature of Napoleon. Of all political ideas that could gain a lodgment in the public mind, this last was the most fatal!

[1] Diary of J. Q. Adams (Feb. 8, 1806), i. 405.

That either Jefferson or Madison was led by French sympathies has been shown to be untrue. Both of them submitted to the violence of all the belligerents alike, and their eagerness for Florida caused them by turns to flatter and to threaten Spain, France, and England; but not even for the sake of Florida would they have taken either a direct or an indirect part with France. Their unwillingness to offend Napoleon rose not from sympathy with him, but from the conviction that he alone could give Florida to the United States without the expense and losses inevitable in a war. Unhappily the public knew little of what President Jefferson had done or was doing; and another piece of legislation, carried through Congress at the same moment with the " Two-million Act," went far to fix the Federalists in their belief that the Administration obeyed the beck and call of the French Emperor.

The Annual Message made no allusion to St. Domingo; no public announcement had been given that the Executive wished for further legislation in regard to its trade, when, Dec. 18, 1805, Senator Logan of Pennsylvania brought forward a Bill to prohibit the trade altogether. That he acted without concert with Madison was not to be conceived. Logan privately admitted as his only object the wish of enabling Madison to tell the French government that the trade was forbidden, and that the merchants who carried it on did so at their own peril.[1] The Federalist senators opposed the Bill, and were joined by several Republi-

[1] Diary of J. Q. Adams (Jan. 15, 1806), i. 383.

cans. General Smith and Dr. Mitchill spoke against it. The opposition showed that the measure would sacrifice several hundred thousand dollars of revenue; that it would close the last opening which the new British policy left for American commerce with the West Indies; that it would throw the commerce with St. Domingo wholly into British hands; that it was an attempt to carry out French objects by American legislation, which would endanger the property and lives of American citizens in the island; and finally, that it was done in obedience to Napoleon's orders. December 27 the Senate called for the diplomatic correspondence on the subject, and the President communicated the extraordinary notes in which Talleyrand and Turreau declared that the commerce " must " not continue. The Senate received this mandate without protest or remonstrance; and after a long debate passed the Bill, Feb. 20, 1806, by a party vote of twenty-one to eight. Of the twenty-seven Republican senators, Stone of North Carolina alone voted against it. Amid execrations against the Haytian negroes, the Bill was next forced through the House almost without debate, and Feb. 28, 1806, received the President's signature.

This law,[1] limited to one year, declared that any American vessel " which shall be voluntarily carried, or shall be destined to proceed " to St. Domingo should be wholly forfeited, ship and cargo. Passed

[1] Act of Feb. 28, 1806; Annals of Congress, 1805–1806, p. 1228.

in consequence of Napoleon's positive order, communicated by the President to Congress as though to overawe objection, the Act violated the principles of international law, sacrificed the interests of Northern commerce, strained the powers of the Constitution as formerly construed by the party of State-rights, and, taken in all its relations, might claim distinction among the most disgraceful statutes ever enacted by the United States government. Nevertheless, this measure, which bore on its face the birth-mark of Napoleonic features, did in fact owe its existence chiefly to a different parentage. In truth, the Southern States dreaded the rebel negroes of Hayti more than they feared Napoleon. Fear often made them blind to their own attitudes; in this instance it made them indifferent to the charge of servility to France. The opportunity to declare the negroes of Hayti enemies of the human race was too tempting to be rejected; and not only did the Southern Republicans eagerly seize it, but they persuaded their Northern allies to support them. John Randolph himself, though then wearying the House day after day with cries that Madison had sold the honor of the United States to France, never alluded to this act of subservience, which would have made any other Administration infamous, and quietly absented himself at the vote, that he might seem neither to obey Bonaparte's mandate nor to oppose the Bill. Of the twenty-six voices against it, nearly all were Federalists; yet in this curious list, side by side with Josiah Quincy, Samuel

Dana, and John Cotton Smith, stood the names of Jacob Crowninshield and Matthew Lyon, democrats of the deepest dye and objects of John Randolph's bitterest sneers.

The "Two-million Act" and the Act forbidding commerce with St. Domingo were measures equally necessary for the success of the Florida purchase. Without conciliating Napoleon at St. Domingo, Jefferson could not expect his help at Paris. These measures, together with some appearance of military activity, completed the Executive scheme of foreign policy in regard to France and Spain; the more difficult task remained of dealing with England.

When the first news of Sir William Scott's decision in the case of the "Essex" arrived in America, the merchants were indignant; and their anger steadily rose as the confiscation of American ships became more general, until at length, in December, 1805, Stephen's pamphlet, "War in Disguise," arrived, and was reprinted in the newspapers. By the close of the year 1805 no one could longer doubt that Great Britain had, so far as suited her purposes, declared war against the United States.

The issue was simple. The United States might make war in return, or submit. Any measure short of open hostilities had unquestionably been taken into Pitt's account, and would produce no effect on his policy. War alone could move him from his purpose; but war would destroy American commerce and ruin Federalist resources, while any retaliation

short of war would not only prove ineffective, but
would injure the American merchants alone. Their
dilemma was so unavoidable that they could not fail
to be caught in it. George Cabot saw their danger
from the first. Much against his will the merchants
of Boston placed him upon a committee to draw a
remonstrance to Congress against the British doctrine
of neutral trade. " Our friend Cabot," wrote Fisher
Ames,[1] " is much, too much, mortified that he is one
of them. He hates hypocrisy, and respects principles; and he dreads lest the popular feeling should
impel the committee to deny what he believes to be
true, or to ask for what he knows to be mischievous." The Boston " Memorial,"[2] drawn by James
Lloyd, was as cautious as popular feeling would tolerate, and asked no action from Government except
the appointment of a special mission to strengthen
the hands of Monroe at London; but Cabot signed it
with extreme reluctance, and only with the understanding that it did not represent his personal views.
The Philadelphia " Memorial " closed with stronger
language, suggesting that war must be the result
if Great Britain refused redress. The Baltimore
" Memorial," drawn by William Pinkney, spoke in
strong tones, but offered no advice. Toward the middle of January, 1806, these memorials, together with

[1] Ames to Pickering; Ames's Works, i. 342. Cf. Lodge's
Cabot, p. 315.

[2] Boston Memorial; Annals of Congress, 1806-1809, Appendix, p. 890.

others, were sent to Congress by the President, with a Message inviting the Legislature to take the matter in hand, but offering no opinion as to the proper course to pursue.[1]

The fears of George Cabot were quickly justified. He chiefly dreaded the theories of the Republican party, which in his opinion were more destructive to American commerce than the British doctrines themselves or the demands of James Stephen. Jefferson and Madison were bent on testing the theory of the first Inaugural Address, — that commerce was the handmaid of agriculture; but in the harshest application of the slave-code of South Carolina or Georgia such treatment as agriculture proposed to her handmaid would have been rejected as inhuman, for it was a slow torture.

The theory of peaceable coercion, on which Jefferson relied, had often been explained as a duel in which either side counted upon exhausting its opponent by injuring itself. As Madison once said of the British manufacturers: "There are three hundred thousand souls who live by our custom: let them be driven to poverty and despair, and what will be the consequence?" The question was more easily asked than answered, for in the actual condition of Europe economical laws were so violently disturbed that no man could venture to guess what fresh extravagance might result from new delirium; but while the three hundred thousand Englishmen

[1] Message of Jan. 17, 1806; State Papers, ii. 727.

were starving, three hundred thousand Americans
would lose the profit on their crops, and would idly
look at empty warehouses and rotting ships.   English laborers had for many generations been obliged
to submit to occasional suffering; Americans were
untrained to submission.   Granting that the Boston
merchant, like the injured Brahmin, should seat himself at the door of the British offender, and slowly
fast to death in order that his blood might stain
the conscience of Pitt, he could not be certain that
Pitt's conscience would be stimulated by the sacrifice,
for the conscience of British Tories as regarded the
United States had been ever languid.   Cabot saw no
real alternative between submission to Great Britain
and the entire sacrifice of American commerce.   He
preferred submission.

The subject in all its bearings quickly came before
Congress.   Jan. 15, 1806, the Senate referred to a
special committee that part of the President's Message which related to the British seizures.   February
5, General Smith reported on behalf of the committee a series of Resolutions denouncing these seizures
as an encroachment on national independence, and
recommending the prohibition of British woollens,
linens, silks, glass-wares, and a long list of other
articles.   On this Resolution the debate began, and
soon waxed hot.

CHAPTER VII.

NOTHING in Jefferson's life was stranger to modern ideas of politics than the secrecy which as President he succeeded in preserving. For two months the people of the United States saw their representatives go day after day into secret session, but heard not a whisper of what passed in conclave. Angry as Randolph was, and eager as the Federalists were to make mischief, they revealed not even to the senators or the foreign ministers what was passing in the House; and the public at large, under their democratic government, knew no more than Frenchmen of their destinies of war and peace. Such a state of things was contrary to the best traditions of the Republican party: it could not last, but it could end only in explosion.

When the debate on Smith's non-importation Resolutions began in the Senate February 12, the previous struggle which had taken place over the Spanish policy and the "Two-million Act" was still a secret; Randolph's schism was unknown beyond the walls of the Capitol; the President's scheme of buying West Florida from France after having, as he maintained, bought it once already, was kept, as he wished, untold. The world knew only that some mysterious

business was afoot; and when Senator Samuel Smith's
attack on trade began, the public naturally supposed
it to be in some way connected with the measures so
long discussed in secret session.

The President's attitude became more and more
uneasy. Jefferson disliked and dreaded the point in
dispute with England. The Spanish policy was his
own creation, and he looked upon it with such regard
as men commonly bestow upon unappreciated inven-
tions, — he depended on its success to retrieve defeats
elsewhere ; but for the very reason that he exhausted
his personal influence to carry the Spanish policy
against opposition, he left British questions to Congress and his party. Where England was to be dealt
with, Madison took the lead which Jefferson declined.
For many years past Madison had been regarded as
the representative of a policy of commercial restriction against Great Britain. To revive his influence,
his speeches and resolutions of 1794 [1] were reprinted
in the "National Intelligencer" as a guide for Congress ; his pamphlet against the British doctrines of
neutral trade was made a political text-book ; while
his friends took the lead in denouncing England and
in calling for retaliation. He himself lost no chance
of pressing his views, even upon political opponents.
"I had considerable conversation with Mr. Madison,"
wrote one of them February 13, " on the subjects now
most important to the public. His system of proceeding toward Great Britain is to establish permanent

[1] Annals of Congress, 1793–1795, p. 155.

commercial distinctions between her and other nations, — a retaliating navigation act, and aggravated duties on articles imported from her." [1] By his own choice, and in a manner almost defiant of failure, Madison's political fortunes were united with the policy of coercing England through restrictions of trade.

At first much was said of an embargo. Senator Jackson of Georgia, Dec. 20, 1805, declared with his usual vehemence in favor of this measure. " Not a nation," said he, " exists which has West Indian colonies but is more or less dependent on us, and cannot do without us ; they must come to our terms, or starve. On with your embargo, and in nine months they must lie at your feet ! " John Randolph, sure to oppose whatever Madison wished, also looked with favor on this course. " I would (if anything) have laid an embargo," he said. [2] The embargo party at best was small, and became smaller when toward the close of December, 1805, news arrived that Admiral Nelson had fought a great naval battle, October 21, against the combined French and Spanish fleets, off Cape Trafalgar, ending in a victory so complete as to leave England supreme upon the ocean. The moral effect of Nelson's triumph was great. Embargo was the last step before war, and few Americans cared to risk war with England under any

[1] Diary of J. Q. Adams (Feb. 13, 1806), i. 408.
[2] Randolph's Speech of March 5, 1805 ; Annals of Congress, 1805–1806, p. 571.

circumstances ; with harbors undefended and without an ally on the ocean, war was rashness which no one would face. Madison's more gentle plan of partial restrictions in trade became the Republican policy.

Even before Senator Samuel Smith reported his Resolutions, February 5, to the Senate, the British minister Merry wrote to his Government that the members most opposed to commercial restrictions, despairing of effectual resistance, would endeavor only to limit the number of articles to be prohibited, and to postpone the date on which the law should take effect, in order to send a special mission to England and negotiate an amicable arrangement. Merry added that a special mission had been under discussion from the first : —

" But I now learn that it has been, and continues to be, opposed by the President, who wishes that Mr. Monroe . . . should continue to carry on the negotiation alone. Matters, however, being now brought to a disagreeable crisis by the clamor of the nation and the instigation of the Administration, some of the members of the Senate are, I find, endeavoring to engage the rest of their body to join them in exercising their constitutional privilege of advising the President on the occasion ; and that their advice to him will be to suspend any step that can have a hostile tendency until the experiment has been tried of an extraordinary mission." [1]

Merry was exactly informed as to the fate of General Smith's Resolutions even before they had

[1] Merry to Mulgrave, Feb. 2, 1806 ; MSS. British Archives.

been reported to the Senate. They were three in number; but only the third, which recommended non-importation, was drawn by Smith. The first and second, the work of Senator Adams of Massachusetts, were not wholly welcome either to the Administration or to the minority. The first declared the British seizures "an unprovoked aggression," a "violation of neutral rights," and an "encroachment upon national independence." The second requested the President to "demand and insist upon" indemnity, and to make some arrangement about impressments. The first Resolution, although fatal to future Federalist consistency, was unanimously adopted by the Senate, February 12, almost without debate, — even Timothy Pickering recording his opinion that the British government had encroached upon national independence. The second Resolution was criticised as an attempt at dictation to the Executive, which would give just cause of offence to the President. By this argument the Senate was induced to strike out the words " and insist;" but although the Resolution, thus altered, was weak, seven Republican senators voted against it as too strong.

The reason of this halting movement had been explained by Merry to Lord Mulgrave nearly two weeks before. The Senate stumbled over the important personality of James Monroe. The next Presidential election, some three years distant, warped the national policy in regard to a foreign encroachment. Senator Samuel Smith, ambitious to distinguish himself in diplomacy, having failed to obtain the mission to Paris, wished the dignity of a special envoy to London, and was supported by Wilson Cary Nicholas. The friends of Madison were willing to depress Monroe, whom John Randolph was trying to elevate. Even Mrs, Madison, in the excitement of electioneering, allowed herself to talk in general society very slightingly of Monroe; [1] and there were reasons which made interference from Mrs. Madison peculiarly irritating to Monroe's friends.[2] Dr. Logan, the senator from Pennsylvania, while helping Madison to satisfy Napoleon in regard to St. Domingo, was prominent in suggesting that it would be well to set Monroe gently aside.[3] This coalition of Madison, Smith, Logan, and Wilson Cary Nicholas was so strong as to control the Senate.

The second Resolution was adopted Feb. 14, 1806; and a week afterward, General Smith and Dr. Mitchill were appointed a committee to carry the two Resolutions to the White House. Two years later, in response to Monroe's complaints, President Jefferson explained how these senators managed to impose on the Executive a policy of their own.

" After delivering the Resolutions," said Jefferson [4] in an aggrieved tone, " the committee entered into free conversation, and observed that although the Senate could

[1] Diary of J. Q. Adams (March 13, 1806), i. 420.
[2] Adams's Randolph, p. 203.
[3] Diary of J. Q. Adams (Feb. 1, 1806), i. 395.
[4] Jefferson to Monroe, March 10, 1808; Works, v. 253.

not in form recommend any extraordinary mission, yet that as individuals there was but one sentiment among them on the measure, and they pressed it. I was so much averse to it, and gave them so hard an answer, that they felt it and spoke of it. But it did not end here. The members of the other House took up the subject and set upon me individually, and these the best friends to you as well as myself, and represented the responsibility which a failure to obtain redress would throw on us both, pursuing a conduct in opposition to the opinion of nearly every member of the Legislature. I found it necessary at length to yield my own opinion to the general voice of the national council, and it really seemed to produce a jubilee among them."

Jefferson saw his most devoted followers waver in their allegiance, and was reduced to temporize in order to avoid worse evils. General Smith in the Senate seemed interested in embarrassing him. If Smith could not be minister to England, he was bent upon becoming minister to France. Armstrong had challenged attack by his management of American claims before the French commission, and had written to the French government an indiscreet letter against a certain claim made by a firm of Nicklin & Griffith, of Philadelphia. When the President nominated him as special minister, with Bowdoin, to conduct the new Florida negotiation, a strong opposition appeared in the Senate, at the head of which was General Smith. March 17 the vote was taken ; the Senate was equally divided, fifteen to fifteen, and Vice-President Clinton's voice alone saved Armstrong from rejection. Had the Senate been left to follow out its own aims, the President's authority might perhaps have been shaken, and a period of faction might have followed; but fortunately for the President and for the Secretary of State, among the enemies with whom they had to deal was one whose temper passed the bounds of common-sense.

Until the month of March, 1806, Randolph's opposition was confined to Spanish affairs in secret session. The House was even slower than the Senate to take up the matter of British relations. Dec. 4, 1805, the subject was referred to the Committee of Ways and Means. Jan. 17, 1806, another message was sent to the same committee; but day after day passed without bringing a report from Randolph, until Smilie of Pennsylvania moved to discharge the Committee of Ways and Means in order to bring the subject before the House in Committee of the Whole. Randolph was ill and absent when the House, Jan. 29, 1806, decided to take the matter from his hands.

On the same day Andrew Gregg, a member from Pennsylvania, moved a Resolution forbidding the importation of all goods the growth or product or manufacture of Great Britain. Still the House left the subject without decision or discussion. February 10 Joseph Nicholson introduced another Resolution, which came probably from Gallatin. Gregg's non-importation measure would cost the Treasury five million dollars a year, and Gallatin preferred a less sweeping prohibition. Even Senator Smith's scheme was too strong for Nicholson, who pointed out that coarse woollens, Jamaica rum, Birmingham hardware, and salt were necessities with which America could not supply herself, nor could any nation except England supply her. Nicholson's Resolution prohibited only such British goods as might be replaced by other nations than England, or might be produced at home, — manufactures of leather, tin, brass, hemp, flax, silk ; high-priced woollens ; woollen hosiery ; glass, silver, and plated ware, paper, pictures, prints, — a formidable list of articles, which if not, like Jamaica rum, necessary to America, were essentials to civilized existence.

Other Resolutions were introduced, but those of Gregg and Nicholson by common consent maintained pre-eminence ; and between the policies marked by them as complete or partial non-importation Congress had to decide. Although the subject was before the House, the month of February passed without debate. Not until March 5, 1806, did Gregg call up his Resolution. In doing so, he made a speech studiously moderate. He seemed disinclined to defend the carrying-trade, and abstained from treating the British seizures as cause for war, but rather threw the weight of his argument on the manifest outrage of impressments ; yet even this he treated as though it were a question of unfriendly fiscal regulation.

" I have no apprehension whatever of a war," he said, " Great Britain is too well versed in the business of calculation, and too well acquainted with her own interest, to persevere in this lawless system at the hazard of losing customers whose annual purchases of her manufactures and other merchandise exceeds, I believe, thirty millions of dollars."

Gregg would not endanger peace, but he would say to Great Britain, —

" in this mild and moderate, though manly and firm, language : ' You have insulted the dignity of our country by impressing our seamen and compelling them to fight your battles against a Power with whom we are at peace ; you have plundered us of much property by that predatory war which you authorize to be carried on against our commerce. To these injuries, insults, and oppression we will submit no longer. . . . If you persist in your hostile measures, if you absolutely refuse acceding to any propositions of compromise, we must slacken those bonds of friendship by which we have been connected. You must not expect hereafter to find us in your market purchasing your manufactures to so large an amount.' This is their vulnerable part ; by attacking them in their warehouses and workshops, we can reach their vitals."

If Pitt should retaliate, Gregg would go further ; he would confiscate all the private property belonging to British subjects on which he could lay his hands, treaty stipulations to the contrary notwithstanding.

The Pennsylvanian contented himself with pacific measures, and his oratory had the merit of consistency with his party doctrines and principles ; but the democracy of Massachusetts, which would never understand or obey the theories of Virginia and Pennsylvania, could not rest content with Gregg's Quaker ideas.

"After the course we are now taking," said Crowninshield, "should Britain persist in her captures and in her oppressive treatment of our seamen, and refuse to give them up, I would not hesitate to meet her in war. But, as I observed before, I do not believe Great Britain will go to war. Our trade is too valuable to her. She knows, too, that in such an event she will lose her eastern provinces; the States of Vermont and Massachusetts will ask no other assistance than their own militia to take Canada and Nova Scotia. Some of her West Indian islands will also fall. She knows also other things. Her subjects own sixteen millions of the old public debt of the United States, eight millions of the Louisiana stock, and three or four millions bank stock, and have private debts to the amount of ten or twelve millions, — amounting in the whole to nearly forty millions of dollars. Will Great Britain, by going to war, risk her provinces and this large amount of property? I think she will not put so much to hazard."

When Crowninshield sat down, John Randolph took the floor. In Randolph's long career of oratorical triumphs, no such moment had offered itself before, or was to occur again. Still in Virginian eyes the truest and ablest Republican in Congress, the representative of power and principle, the man of the future, Randolph stood with the halo of youth, courage, and genius round his head, — a sort of Virginian Saint Michael, almost terrible in his contempt for whatever seemed to him base or untrue.

He began by saying that he entered on the subject "manacled, handcuffed, and tongue-tied;" his lips were sealed; he could but "hobble over the subject as well as his fettered limbs and palsied tongue would enable him to do it;" and with this preamble he fell upon Gregg and Crowninshield:[1] —

"It is mere waste of time to reason with such persons; they do not deserve anything like serious refutation. The proper arguments for such statesmen are a strait-waist-coat, a dark room, water-gruel, and depletion."

The proposed confiscation of British property called out a sneer at Crowninshield: —

"God help you if these are your ways and means for carrying on war! if your finances are in the hands of such a chancellor of the exchequer! Because a man can take an observation and keep a log-book and a reckoning, can navigate a cock-boat to the West Indies or the East, shall he aspire to navigate the great vessel of State, to stand at the helm of public councils? *Ne sutor ultra crepidam!*"

Again and again he turned aside to express contempt for the Northern democrats: —

"Shall this great mammoth of the American forest leave his native element and plunge into the water in a mad contest with the shark? Let him stay on shore, and not be excited by the muscles and periwinkles on the strand!"

On the point of policy Randolph took ground which, if not warlike, was at least consistent, — the ground which all Southern Republicans of the Jeffer-

[1] Annals of Congress, 1805–1806, p. 555.

son school would have taken, if shame had not
withheld them.   Even if determined in the end to
submit, the President and Secretary wished to keep
up the form of resistance.   Randolph declared that
the form was absurd ; he would do nothing to protect
" this mushroom, this fungus of war," — a carrying-
trade which at the first moment of peace would no
longer exist : —

" I will never consent to go to war for that which I
cannot protect.   I deem it no sacrifice of dignity to say
to the Leviathan of the deep : We are unable to contend
with you in your own element; but if you come within
our actual limits, we will shed our last drop of blood in
their defence."

Had Randolph contented himself with taking this
position, he could not have been overthrown, for he
carried with him the secret sympathy of the Southern
Republicans ; but he had not the self-control that was
needed in the face of an opponent so pliant and conciliatory as Jefferson.   Randolph took rare pleasure
in making enemies, while Jefferson never made one
enemy except to gain two friends.   Not satisfied with
attacking Crowninshield and Gregg, Randolph gave
full play to his anger against the whole House, and
even assailed the Executive : —

" I have before protested, and I again protest, against
secret, irresponsible, overruling influence.   The first question I asked when I saw the gentleman's Resolution was,
Is this a measure of the Cabinet?   Not of an open declared Cabinet, but of an invisible, inscrutable, unconsti-

tutional Cabinet, without responsibility, unknown to the
Constitution.   I speak of back-stairs influence, — of men
who bring messages to this House, which, although they
do not appear on the Journals, govern its decisions.   Sir,
the first question that I asked on the subject of British
relations was, What is the opinion of the Cabinet;
what measures will they recommend to Congress? — well
knowing that whatever measures we might take they
must execute them, and therefore that we should have
their opinion on the subject.   My answer was (and
from a Cabinet minister too), '*There is no longer any
Cabinet!*'"

Though forbidden to mention what had occurred
in secret session, "manacled, handcuffed, and tongue-
tied" as he was, Randolph dragged the Spanish secret
to light : —

"Like true political quacks, you deal only in handbills
and nostrums.   Sir, I blush to see the record of our proceedings ; they resemble nothing but the advertisements
of patent medicines.   Here you have 'the worm-destroy-
ing lozenges;' there 'Church's cough-drops;' and to
crown the whole, 'Sloan's vegetable specific,' — an infallible remedy for all nervous disorders and vertigoes of
brainsick politicians. . . . And where are you going to
send your political panacea, resolutions and handbills
excepted; your sole arcanum of government, your King
Cure-all?   To Madrid?   No! you are not such quacks as
not to know where the shoe pinches.   To Paris.!   You
know at least where the disease lies, and there you apply
your remedy.   When the nation anxiously demands the
result of your deliberations, you hang your head and
blush to tell.   You are afraid to tell!"

Randolph next attacked Madison. He took up the secretary's late pamphlet and overwhelmed its argument with contempt. He declared that France was the real enemy of America; that England was acting under the dictates of necessity; that the situation of Europe had completely changed since 1793, and that England occupied the place which France then held: "she is the sole bulwark of the human race against universal dominion, — no thanks to her for it!" As for a policy, he proposed to abandon commerce and to amputate mercantile interests: —

"I can readily tell gentlemen what I will not do. I will not propitiate any foreign nation with money. I will not launch into a naval war with Great Britain. . . . I will send her money on no pretext whatever; much less on pretence of buying Labrador or Botany Bay, when my real object was to secure limits which she formally acknowledged at the Peace of 1783. I go further: I would, if anything, have laid an embargo; this would have got our own property home, and our adversary's into our power. If there is any wisdom left among us, the first step toward hostility will always be an embargo. In six months all your mercantile megrims would vanish. As to us, although it would cut deep, we can stand it."

Before closing this desultory harangue, the orator once more turned to taunt the President: —

"Until I came into the House this morning, I had been stretched on a sick bed; but when I behold the affairs of this nation — instead of being where I hoped, and the people believed they were, in the hands of responsible men — committed to Tom, Dick, and Harry, to the refuse of the retail trade of politics, I do feel, I cannot help feeling, the most deep and serious concern. . . . I know, sir, that we may say, and do say, that we are independent (would it were true!), as free to give a direction to the Executive as to receive it from him; but do what you will, foreign relations, every measure short of war, and even the course of hostilities, depends upon him. He stands at the helm, and must guide the vessel of State. You give him money to buy Florida, and he purchases Louisiana. You may furnish means; the application of those means rests with him. Let not the master and mate go below when the ship is in distress, and throw the responsibility upon the cook and the cabin-boy! I said so when your doors were shut; I scorn to say less now they are open. Gentlemen may say what they please; they may put an insignificant individual to the ban of the republic: I shall not alter my course."

That such a speech from a man so necessary to the Government should throw consternation among the majority, was a matter of course. No such event had ever happened in Congress as the public rebellion of a great party leader. The Federalists had quarrelled as bitterly, but had made no such scandal. Yet serious as Randolph's defection might be, it would have done little harm had it not been that in denouncing the course taken by Jefferson and Madison he had much secret sympathy. Nay, as regarded Gregg's Resolution, he expressed the feelings of the President himself and of the Cabinet. The so-called resistance to England, like the resistance to Spain, was a sham, and all parties agreed with Randolph in opposing serious retaliation.

Nothing was needed but that Randolph should keep his temper in order to win a triumph. Napoleon could be trusted to give Jefferson no more provinces at any price, for within a few days after Randolph's outbreak news arrived that the battle of Austerlitz had been fought, and the Treaty of Pressburg signed. Jefferson himself could be trusted to prevent Gregg's Resolution from passing, for the news that Pitt was dead and Fox in power arrived almost at the same moment with that of Austerlitz. The entire situation had changed; an entirely new policy must be invented, and this could hardly fail to follow Randolph's ideas. He had only to wait; but meanwhile he was consumed by a fever of rage and arrogance. Thinking that the time had come to destroy the Secretary of State, he set himself vigorously to the task. Day after day he occupied the floor, attacking Madison with more and more virulence. He insisted that " the business from first to last had been managed in the most imbecile manner."

"I do not speak of the negotiator [Monroe] — God forbid! — but of those who drew the instruction of the man who negotiated. We bought Louisiana from France under the terms of the Treaty of San Ildefonso. According to the Executive understanding, that country extended to the Perdido and the River Bravo. We immediately legislated on our first claim and passed a law erecting the bay and shores of the Mobile into a revenue district.

What was the fact? That we were legislating without information. We had never been told that Laussat had been directed to receive the country only to the Iberville and the Lakes. We consequently legislated in error, for want of Executive information. This was the beginning." [1]

At length, April 7, Randolph committed his last and fatal blunder by going formally into opposition.

" I came here," he said, " prepared to co-operate with the Government in all its measures. I told them so. But I soon found there was no choice left, and that to co-operate in them would be to destroy the national character. I found I might co-operate, or be an honest man. I have therefore opposed, and will oppose them."

Such tactics, in the face of a man so supple as President Jefferson, invited failure. With every weapon of offence in his hand, and with the assurance of triumph, Randolph threw his chances away and found himself within a few weeks delivered to the mercy of Secretary Madison and the Northern democrats. Jefferson's strong qualities were called into play by Randolph's method of attack. Jefferson was not apt to be violent, nor was he despotic in temper ; but he was, within certain limits, very tenacious of his purpose, and he had to a certain degree the habits of a paternal despot. Randolph's sudden assault, carrying with it some twenty-five or thirty of the ablest and best Republicans in Congress, greatly

[1] Annals of Congress, 1805–1806, p. 961.

alarmed the President, who set himself quietly and earnestly to the task of restoring order to his shattered columns. The Northern democrats were easily held firm, for they hated Randolph and had little love for Virginia. As for the rebellious cohort of "old Republicans," Jefferson exhausted his resources in coaxing them to desert their leader.

March 13 the House laid Gregg's Resolution aside; Nicholson's was then taken up, adopted March 17, and sent to a special committee to be framed as a Bill. Meanwhile the President busily conciliated opposition; and his first thought was of Monroe in London, certain to become the centre of intrigue. March 16 Jefferson wrote to warn his old friend against the danger of making common cause with Randolph. The task was difficult, because it was necessary at the same time to break the news that Monroe must submit to the implied censure of a special mission.

"Some of your new friends," wrote Jefferson,[1] " are attacking your old ones, out of friendship for you, but in a way to render you great injury. . . . Mr. Nicholson's Resolutions will be passed this week, probably by a majority of one hundred Republicans against fifteen Republicans and twenty-seven Federalists. When passed, I shall join Mr. Pinkney of Maryland as your associate for settling our differences with Great Britain. He will depart on a fortnight's notice, and will be authorized to take your place whenever you think yourself obliged to return."

[1] Jefferson to Monroe, March 16, 1806; Jefferson MSS.

Two days later he wrote again.[1] In the interval Nicholson's Resolution had been adopted by a vote of eighty-seven to thirty-five, and Randolph's minority of Republican members had been reduced, beyond the President's hope, to a mere half-dozen grumblers.

"Mr. R. withdrew before the question was put," wrote Jefferson. "I have never seen a House of Representatives more solidly united in doing what they believe to be the best for the public interest. There can be no better proof than the fact that so eminent a leader should at once, and almost unanimously, be abandoned."

At the same moment Randolph wrote to Monroe that the Republican party was broken in pieces, and that the "old Republicans" were united in the support of Monroe against Madison for the Presidency.[2] Randolph complained bitterly of the atmosphere of intrigue which surrounded the Administration ; but as regarded him at least, Jefferson's retort was plausible that he had never found fault with intrigue so long as he had a share in it. After challenging the contest with Madison, he had only himself to blame if the President, who was a master of intrigue, used the weapon freely to defend his favorite and himself.

To detach Randolph's friends from their leader was an object which the President pursued with zeal and success. He was a little disposed to overawe Monroe ; but he was glad to conciliate Joseph Nicholson, next to Randolph the most formidable "old Republican"

[1] Jefferson to Monroe, March 18, 1806; Jefferson MSS.
[2] Adams's Randolph, p. 199–202.

in public life. Nicholson was torn by conflicting sympathies; he loved Randolph, and he did not love Madison. On the other hand he was attached to Gallatin by marriage and respect. A poor man, with a large family, Nicholson found the life of a Congressman unprofitable; and when he was offered a seat on the Bench as Judge of the Sixth Maryland Circuit, he accepted the appointment. April 9, 1806, his letter of resignation was read to the House, and the democrats knew that Randolph had lost his strongest friend.

The Speaker remained to be dealt with. To overawe Macon was impossible; to buy him was out of the question; to crush him was only a last resort; no other resource was left than to coax him.

"Some enemy, whom we know not, is sowing tares between us," wrote the President to the Speaker, at the moment when he was warning Monroe and lifting Nicholson to the Bench.[1] "Between you and myself nothing but opportunities of explanation can be necessary to defeat these endeavors. At least, on my part, my confidence in you is so unqualified that nothing further is necessary for my satisfaction."

Jefferson never was more sincere than in making this advance to a friend from whom the course of events threatened to part him: but unfortunately the point of doubt was not so much Jefferson's confidence in Macon as it was Macon's confidence in Jefferson. At bottom remained the unpleasant thought

[1] Jefferson to Macon, March 22, 1806; Jefferson MSS.

that Jefferson had ceased to be either a Virginian or a Republican; had chosen other friends and advisers than Macon, other objects and ambitions than Macon pursued.

Even Randolph was treated with delicacy. Jefferson would gladly have won him back, had Randolph admitted a hope that he would accept Madison's candidacy; but on that point no compromise could be conceived. Madison's fate was trembling in the balance. Sacrifice of Madison was impossible to the President, and nothing short of sacrifice would satisfy Randolph. The " old Republican " schism must therefore be left to itself; the schismatics were too honest and respectable to be dealt with. The President exhausted his power when he won back the wavering, fixed Gallatin in allegiance to Madison, and carried Nicholson out of the arena; but although gentle and forbearing in regard to these honest, and as he thought, misguided men, Jefferson did not think it necessary to show equal deference to the merely selfish interests which had made use of this moment of confusion in order to exact terms from the Government. He showed that he could punish, by making an example of General and Senator Samuel Smith.

Robert Smith in the Cabinet was so near to his brother Samuel in the Senate that Jefferson could no longer trust his secrets to the Cabinet itself. After crushing in the House Randolph's opposition to the Spanish policy, and after yielding to Smith and the Senate in regard to a special English mission, the

President was required to make certain appointments, one of which was that of a new minister to aid and succeed Monroe in London, whence it was supposed that Monroe wished to return. General Smith's wider plan assumed that Monroe was on his way home, and would be succeeded by a regular minister, assisted, for commercial negotiations, by a special envoy. The special envoy was to be himself; the permanent minister was to be his brother-in-law Wilson Cary Nicholas. He had even written to assure Nicholas of the appointment, when his project was defeated by the secret and unexpected interference of the President.

April 1, 1806, Samuel Smith wrote to his brother-in-law an account of his hopes and disappointment: [1]

" Monroe had written that he would leave Great Britain in November; therefore a mission of two, — one to remain as minister, the other a merchant of some distinction and of general information to go as envoy extraordinary, — was desired by all ; and here, this proposal generally — I may say universally — meant S. S. Two only exceptions : As Monroe will remain until the whole business shall be settled, many wish now an able merchant to join him ; in either case to make a commercial treaty with Great Britain. To such a treaty there is a rooted aversion in the mind of the President and Mr. Madison. I ought to apologize for leading you into error. I still do believe that you were originally intended for London. A good Federalist is to succeed Monroe,

[1] Samuel Smith to W. C. Nicholas, April 1, 1806; Nicholas MSS.

and has been privately written to by the President without the knowledge of any of his Cabinet; they appeared astonished when he mentioned what he had done."

The good Federalist thus put over Smith's head was William Pinkney, a prominent lawyer of Smith's city of Baltimore. Such a step without consulting the Smiths, and against their personal interests, was a strong measure on the part of Jefferson, quite out of keeping with his ordinary practice. Offence of tried friends in order to conciliate Federalists was little to his taste; but General Smith's conduct had become so factious as to warrant reproof. Smith was reduced to submission. He had not shared in Randolph's bitterness against the Spanish policy, but he had attempted to make use of the old Republican schism for his personal objects; and after Randolph's overthrow, Smith could no longer venture upon open opposition. Though beaten by only one vote in his attack on Armstrong's nomination, Smith felt that his defeat was made final by the collapse of Randolph's rebellion. He admitted to Nicholas that no effective resistance could be made to the Florida purchase, and that nothing remained but obedience to the President's will: —

"The question was simply, Buy or fight! Both Houses by great majorities said, Buy! The manner of buying appears a little disagreeable. Politicians will believe it perfectly honest to induce France 'by money' to coerce Spain to sell that which she has absolutely declared was her own property, and from which she would not part. Mr. Randolph expects that this public explosion of our views and plans will render abortive this negotiation, and make the Executive and poor little Madison unpopular. Against this last he vents his spleen. However, he spares nobody, and by this conduct has compelled *all* to rally round the Executive for *their own preservation*. From the Potomac north and east, the members adhere to the President; south they fall daily from their allegiance."

Thus, after four months of confusion, victory declared itself on the President's side. Randolph's violence, even more than Jefferson's dexterity, was fatal to the old Republican uprising. As early as April 1 discipline was restored, with Madison stronger than ever before. The few remaining days of the session only confirmed the result.

CHAPTER VIII.

THE President's triumph was decided as early as March 17, for on that day General Smith's assault upon Armstrong was defeated in the Senate by Vice-President Clinton's casting vote; and in the House, Randolph's resistance to the non-importation policy against England ended in his discomfiture and withdrawal; but although even at that early moment no one could doubt Jefferson's irresistible strength, yet no one who knew John Randolph could suppose that either the President or his Secretary of State was in future to sleep on roses.

The session ended April 21; and during the few weeks that intervened between Randolph's defeat, March 17, and the adjournment, the exasperated Virginian developed a strange and unequalled genius. His position was new. The alternation of threat and entreaty, of lofty menace and reluctant obedience, which marked the conduct of the State Department in its dealings with France and England, had no real admirer in the United States. When Randolph denounced the change in Spanish policy, not a voice was raised in its defence, and the public wondered that so powerful a President should be left an unprotected

victim to assaults so furious. In truth Madison himself must have been tongue-tied; no resource of logic
could excuse his sudden abandonment of the determination " to extinguish in the French government
every hope of turning our controversy with Spain into
a French job, public or private." Even had he succeeded in excusing himself, his success must have
proved that Randolph's crime consisted in maintaining the ground which had been taken and held by
President, secretary, and plenipotentiaries down to
the moment, Oct. 23, 1805, when without explanation
the ground was abandoned. Silence and numbers
were the only arguments in defence of such a change,
and to these forms of logic the followers of the
Administration at first resorted. " It is a matter
of great astonishment to me," wrote Wilson Cary
Nicholas to Jefferson April 2, " that such a philippic
as we have seen could have been uttered in Congress, and not one word said in justification of the
Administration." [1] Toward the end of the session
this silence ceased; the majority made great efforts
to answer Randolph; but the answers were weaker
than the silence.

Besides this difficulty in the nature of the case, the
majority felt more than ever the advantage enjoyed
by Randolph in his vigor and quickness of mind.
For two months he controlled the House by audacity
and energy of will. The Crowninshields, Varnums,
and Bidwells of New England, the Sloans, Smilies,

[1] W. C. Nicholas to Jefferson, April 2, 1806; Jefferson MSS.

and Findleys of the Middle States, could do nothing with him; but by the time he had done with them they were bruised and sore, mortified, angry, and ridiculous. The consciousness of this superiority, heightened to extreme arrogance by the need of brushing away every moment a swarm of flies which seemed never to know they were crushed, excited Randolph to madness. He set no bounds to the expression of his scorn not only for the Northern democrats, but for the House itself and for the whole government. At one member he shook his fist, and imperiously bade him sit down or to go down the back-stairs; another member he called an old toothless driveller, superannuated, and mumbling in second dotage.[1] He flung Madison's pamphlet with violent contempt on the floor of the House; and he told the House itself that it could not maintain a decision two hours together against the Yazoo lobby.

Sloan of New Jersey, a sort of butt in the party, who could not forgive Randolph's allusion to the "vegetable specific," retorted that Randolph behaved like "a maniac in a strait-jacket accidentally broke out of his cell." No doubt his conduct was open to the charge; but none the less the maniac gave great trouble and caused extreme confusion. Even after three fourths of the House came to share Sloan's opinion, and began the attempt to control Randolph by every means in their power, they found the task beyond them.

[1] Annals of Congress, 1805-1806, p. 1107.

The Non-importation Bill, framed on Nicholson's Resolution, was quickly reported, and March 25 the House agreed to fix November 15 as the date on which the Act should go into operation. Randolph could not prevent its passage, but he could make it contemptible, if it was not so already; and he could encourage the Government and people of England to treat it with derision.

"Never in the course of my life," he cried,[1] "have I witnessed such a scene of indignity and inefficiency as this measure holds forth to the world. What is it? A milk-and-water Bill! A dose of chicken-broth to be taken nine months hence! . . . It is too contemptible to be the object of consideration, or to excite the feelings of the pettiest State in Europe."

The Bill immediately passed by a vote of ninety-three to thirty-two; but every man on the floor felt that Randolph was right, and every foreign minister at Washington adopted his tone.

Two days afterward he called up certain Resolutions denouncing as unconstitutional the union of civil and military authority in the same person, and declaring that a contractor under Government was a civil offi-cer, and as such incapable of holding a seat in the House. These Resolutions struck in every direction; they were a reproof to the House, to the President, and to individual members like Matthew Lyon, who had taken mail contracts, or John Smith, the senator from Ohio, who was a large contractor for army sup-

[1] Annals of Congress, March 26, 1806, p. 851.

plies. General Wilkinson at St. Louis held civil and military powers; the new territory about to be organized under the name of Michigan was to have a governor of the same sort. A vote against Randolph's Resolutions contravened one of the cardinal principles of the Republican party; a vote for them censured the party itself and embarrassed Government. Beaten by very large majorities on these two declaratory points, Randolph succeeded in carrying through the House a Bill that rendered military and naval officers incapable of holding also any civil office. This measure slept quietly on the table of the Senate.

Hardly a day passed without bringing the House into some similar dilemma. March 29 the Senate sent down a Bill for settling the Yazoo claims; it had passed the Senate by a vote of nineteen to eleven soon after the death of its hottest opponent, Senator James Jackson of Georgia. Randolph exultingly seized upon the Bill in order to plaster it, like the hue-and-cry after a runaway thief, against the very doors of the White House: —

"This Bill may be called the Omega, the last letter of the political alphabet; but with me it is the Alpha. It is the head of the divisions among the Republican party; it is the secret and covert cause of the whole. . . . The whole weight of the Executive government presses it on. We cannot bear up against it. The whole Executive government has had a bias to the Yazoo interest ever since I had a seat here. This is the original sin which has created all the mischiefs which gentlemen pretend to throw on the impressment of our seamen, and God knows what. This is the cause of those mischiefs which existed years ago."

The Yazoo sin, he said, had been one principal cause of his failure in the impeachment of Justice Chase; the secret mechanism of Government would be so powerfully brought to bear on members that if the Bill were postponed over Sunday he would not give a farthing for the issue; gentlemen would come in with speeches ready cut-and-dried until a majority dwindled to nothing. Exasperating and insulting as this language was, the House did not resent it; and a motion that the Bill be rejected passed by a vote of sixty-two to fifty-four, while Randolph exulted over its fate.

March 31 Randolph, aided by the Federalists and some thirty Republicans, succeeded in removing the injunction of secrecy from the Spanish proceedings. No sooner was the Journal published, and he found that it did not contain the President's secret message of Dec. 6, 1805, than he seized this chance to make public all that had occurred in secret session. April 5, after moving that the injunction of secrecy should be taken from the Message, he entered into the history of his own relations with the President and Secretary of State in the tangled thread of Spanish negotiations. His remarks that day, though severe, were comparatively temperate; but when the debate was renewed April 7, he announced that he meant to oppose the Government, because he had to choose between opposition and dishonesty. He charged that Madison had tried to get money from the Treasury for this negotiation without waiting for a vote of Congress ; and he declared that the documents, " if published, would fix a stain upon some men in the government and high in office which all the waters in the ocean would not wash out." His denunciations began to rouse passion ; if his opponents could not equal him in debate, they could in violence of temper. Madison's brother-in-law, John G. Jackson of Virginia, took up his charges in a high tone, and several expressions passed which foreshadowed a duel. On the vote Randolph was beaten by a majority of seventy-four to forty-four ; but he had published the secrets of Madison's friends, and their refusal to print the Message showed the want of courage with which they were chiefly charged.

On every point of real importance Randolph's authority overawed the House. The President in his Annual Message had talked much of defences, and had even hinted his readiness to build seventy-fours. A committee of the House reported Resolutions advising that the sum of one hundred and fifty thousand dollars should be spent in fortifying harbors ; that two hundred and fifty thousand dollars should be appropriated to build fifty gunboats ; and that six hundred and sixty thousand dollars should be voted toward building six line-of-battle ships. When these Resolutions were brought up March 25, only thirty members could be found to vote for the seventy-fours.

April 15 the subject came up again in connection with the Bill for fortifying harbors and building gunboats. Josiah Quincy made a strong argument, warning Congress that in the sacrifice of commercial interests which lay at the bottom of its policy, there was danger not only to the prosperity but to the permanence of the Union. He remarked that while seventeen millions had been voted to buy Louisiana and Florida for the sake of securing the South and West; while in this single session four hundred and fifty thousand dollars must be voted for Indian lands, — yet the entire sum expended since the foundation of the government in fortifications for the nine capital harbors of the Union was only seven hundred and twenty-four thousand dollars. The city of New York, with at least one hundred million dollars of capital in deposit, might at any moment be laid under contribution by two line-of-battle ships. Quincy begged the House to bear in mind that the ocean could not be abandoned for the land by the people of New England, of whom thousands would rather see a boat-hook than all the sheep-crooks in the world : —

"Concerning the land of which the gentleman from Virginia [Randolph] and the one from North Carolina [Macon] think so much, they think very little. It is in fact to them only a shelter from the storm, a perch on which they build their eyrie and hide their mate and their young while they skim the surface or hunt in the deep."

Quincy's speech was far superior to the ordinary level of Congressional harangues, and its argument was warmly supported by a democrat as extreme as Matthew Lyon; but barely thirty votes could be mustered against Randolph's economy; and although the New England democrats joined hands with the New England Federalists in supporting an appropriation for building two new frigates in place of others which had been lost or condemned, they could muster only forty-three votes against Randolph's phalanx.

Probably no small part of Randolph's hostility to the navy was due to his personal dislike for Robert Smith the secretary, and for his brother Samuel the senator. This enmity already showed signs of serious trouble in store. Gallatin struggled in vain with Robert Smith's loose habit of accounts. Joseph Nicholson, closely allied to Gallatin, naturally drew away from the Smiths, whose authority in Maryland roused ill-feeling. Randolph took sides with Gallatin and Nicholson, the more because Samuel Smith had undertaken to act an independent part in the politics of the session, and had too plainly betrayed selfish motives. When Randolph, after delaying the navy estimates as long as he could, moved the appropriations April 10, he took the opportunity to be more than usually offensive. He said that an Appropriation Bill was a mere matter of form; that the items might as well be lumped together; that the secretary would spend twice the amount if he chose, as he had done the year before, and that the House would have to make up the deficiency. " A spendthrift," said he, " can never be supplied with money fast enough to anticipate his wants."

The Bill passed, of course; but the navy was reduced to the lowest possible point, and fifty gunboats were alone provided in response to the President's strong recommendations. Randolph and his friends believed only in defence on land, and their theory was no doubt as sound as such theories could ever be; but it was the curse of " old Republican " principles that they could never be relaxed without suicide, and never enforced without factiousness. For defence on land nothing was so vital as good roads. A million dollars appropriated for roads to Sackett's Harbor, Erie, Detroit, St. Louis, and New Orleans would have been, as a measure of land defence, worth more than all the gunboats and forts that could be crowded along the Atlantic; but when the Senate sent down a Bill creating commissioners to lay out the Cumberland road to the State of Ohio, although this road was the result of a contract to which Congress had pledged its faith, so many Republicans opposed it under one pretext or another, with John Randolph among them, that a change of four votes would have defeated the Bill. No more was done for national defence by land than by water, although the echo of Nelson's guns at Trafalgar was as loud as the complaints of plundered American merchants, and of native American seamen condemned to the tyranny and the lash of British boatswains.

The drift of Randolph's opposition was easily seen; he wanted to cover the Administration with shame for having taken a warlike tone which it never meant to support. His tactics were calculated to make Madison contemptible at home and abroad by inviting upon him the worst outrages of foreign governments. That he succeeded so far as foreign governments were concerned was almost a matter of course, since even without his aid Spain, France, and England could hardly invent an outrage which they had not already inflicted; but at home Randolph's scheme failed, because Madison could be degraded only by making the American people share in his humiliation. The old Republicans relieved Madison of responsibility for national disgrace, and made Congress itself answerable for whatever disasters might follow, — a result made clear by Randolph's last and most mischievous assault. To meet the five millions required for the purchase of Florida, at a moment when the Non-importation Act threatened to cut down the revenue, Gallatin needed all the existing taxes, including the Mediterranean Fund, which ceased by law after the peace with Tripoli. April 14 Randolph suddenly, without the knowledge or consent of Gallatin, moved to repeal the duty on salt. This heavy and unpopular tax produced about half a million dollars, and its repeal was so popular that no one dared oppose it. The next day Randolph brought in a Bill repealing the salt tax and continuing the Mediterranean Fund. By that time members had become aware of his factious motives, and denounced them; but so far from disavowing his purpose, the chairman of the Committee of Ways and Means proclaimed that since he could not force the Government to keep within the limit of specific appropriations he meant to sequester the revenue so as to leave but a scanty surplus. After his speech the Bill was engrossed without opposition, the Federalists being pleased to embarrass Government, and the Republicans afraid of sacrificing popularity. April 17 the Bill passed by a vote of eighty-four to eleven and was sent to the Senate. The part which related to the salt tax was there struck out; but when, April 21, the last day of the session, the Bill so mutilated came again before the House, Randolph exerted to the utmost his powers of mischief, not so much in order to repeal the salt tax as to destroy the Senate Bill, and so deprive Government of its still greater resource, the Mediterranean Fund, which produced nearly a million. He induced the House to insist upon its own Bill. A committee of conference was appointed; the Senate would not recede; Randolph moved that the House adhere. Angry words passed; ill-temper began to prevail; and when at last Randolph was beaten by the narrow vote of forty-seven to forty, his relative Thomas Mann Randolph, the President's son-in-law, suddenly rose and spoke of his namesake in terms intended for a challenge; while Sloan of New Jersey occupied part of the night with a long diatribe against the chairman of the Ways and Means Committee.

Never had worse temper been seen at Washington than in the last weeks of this session. Madison's friends, conscious that their attitude was undignified, became irritable, and longed for a chance to prove their courage. Randolph was not the only enemy who devoted the energy of personal hatred to the task of ruining the Secretary of State. In the case of Randolph Madison was not to blame, and neither challenged nor wished a contest. Even the policy which Randolph so violently assailed was less the policy of the secretary than of the President. Madison did nothing to invite the storm, and could have done nothing to escape it; but another tempest raged, to which he voluntarily exposed himself.

The Marquis of Casa Yrujo passed the autumn of 1805 in Philadelphia, and in obedience to instructions tried to renew friendly relations with the Secretary of State. During Madison's stay in the city Yrujo induced the secretary to accept an invitation to dinner to meet Governor McKean, Yrujo's father-in-law. The marquis paid no attention to the hints sent him from the President that he would confer a favor on the United States government by returning to Spain without delay. He was well aware that he had nothing to gain by conferring more favors on Jefferson; and the conduct of Turreau and Merry was not such as to deter a Spanish minister from defying to his heart's content the authority of the President.

On the appearance of the Annual Message, which

contained a general and loose statement of grievances against Spain, Yrujo wrote Dec. 6, 1805, a keen note to the Secretary of State, criticising, not without justice, the assertions made by the President. To Yrujo's note, as to the St. Domingo note of Turreau, the secretary made no reply. He held that the contents of an Executive communication to Congress were not open to diplomatic discussion, — a doctrine doubtless correct in theory and convenient to the Executive, but offering the disadvantage that if foreign governments or their envoys chose to disregard it, the Secretary of State must either enforce discipline or submit to mortification. Madison accepted the challenge; he meant to enforce discipline, and aimed at expelling Yrujo from the country. The Cabinet decided that Yrujo, pending the request for his recall, should receive no answer to his letters, and should not be permitted to remain in Washington.

Backed by the President's authority and by the power of the government, Madison might reasonably expect an easy victory over the Spaniard, and he acted as though it were a matter of course that Yrujo should accept his fate; but Yrujo seemed unconscious of peril. Athough the Spanish minister's presence at the capital was well known not to be desired by the President, the society of Washington was startled Jan. 15, 1806, by learning that the marquis had arrived. The same evening Yrujo, dining with General Turreau, received a formal note which roused him to passion only equalled by the temper of John Randolph. The exasperating letter, signed by Madison, said that as the President had requested Yrujo's recall, and as Cevallos had intimated that the marquis wished to return to Spain on leave, it had been supposed that the departure would have taken place at once, and therefore his appearance at Washington was a matter of surprise : —

" Under these circumstances the President has charged me to signify to you that your remaining at this place is dissatisfactory to him ; and that although he cannot permit himself to insist on your departure from the United States during an inclement season, he expects it will not be unnecessarily postponed after this obstacle has ceased."

A routine diplomatist would have protested and obeyed ; but Yrujo was not a routine diplomatist. Not in order to learn correct deportment had he read the " Aurora " or studied the etiquette of Jefferson's *pêle-mêle*. Minister and marquis as he was, he had that democratic instinct which always marked the Spanish race and made even the beggars proud ; while his love of a fray shocked Turreau and caused Merry to look upon his Spanish colleague as a madman. At that moment Madison was little esteemed or feared by any one ; the recoil of his foreign policy had prostrated him, and Randolph was every day, in secret session, overwhelming him with contempt. Yrujo had no reason to fear the result of a contest ; but even had there been cause for fear, he was not a man to regard it.

Turreau in vain attempted to restrain him; nothing would satisfy Yrujo but defiance. January 16, the day after receiving Madison's letter, the Spanish minister answered it.

"As the object of my journey is not with a view to hatch plots," said he, with a side-blow at Madison which the secretary soon understood, "my arrival here is an innocent and legal act, which leaves me in the full enjoyment of all my rights and privileges, both as a public character or a private individual. Making use therefore of these rights and privileges, I intend remaining in the city, four miles square, in which the Government resides, as long as it may suit the interest of the King my master or my own personal convenience. I must at the same time add that I shall not lose sight of these two circumstances as respects the period and season in which our mutual desires for my departure from the United States are to be accomplished."

Having thus retaliated Madison's insult, Yrujo next made his revenge public. January 19 he sent to the Department a formal protest, couched in language still more offensive than that of his letter: —

"Having gone through the personal explanations which for just motives I was compelled to enter into in my first answer to your letter of the 15th inst., I must now inform you, sir, what otherwise would then have constituted my sole reply; namely, that the envoy extraordinary and minister plenipotentiary of his Catholic Majesty near the United States receives no orders except from his sovereign. I must also declare to you, sir, that I consider both the style and tenor of your letter as indecorous, and its object an infraction of the privileges attached to my public character."

Finally he sent to his colleagues copies of this correspondence, which soon afterward was printed in every Federalist newspaper, together with the note criticising the Annual Message, the reception of which had never been acknowledged by the Secretary of State.

Thus far Madison gained no credit in the scuffle, but merely called upon his own head one more intolerable insult. Perhaps in Yrujo's apparent madness some share of method might be detected; for he knew the character of Madison, — his willingness to irritate and his reluctance to strike. At all events, the Spaniard remained at Washington and defied the Government to do its worst. The Cabinet consulted, examined into the law, inquired for precedents, and at last decided that the Government could not expel him. Merry took Yrujo's part, and Turreau had much to do with moderating the President's measures and with checking interference from Congress.[1]   The Government in all its branches was overawed, and even the senators were alarmed. "The marquis's letters last published seem to have frightened many of them so that probably nothing will be done."[2] So wrote a member of the Senate who alone exerted himself to strengthen the President's hands. Yrujo remained a fortnight or more at Washington, and

[1] Diary of J. Q. Adams (Feb. 15, 1806), i. 410.
[2] Diary of J. Q. Adams (Feb. 20, 1806), i. 414.

after carrying his point returned at his leisure to Philadelphia. The only measure which Madison ventured to take was that of refusing to hold any communication with him or to receive his letters; but even this defence was turned by Yrujo into a vantage-ground of attack.

Among other adventurers then floating about the world was one Francesco de Miranda, a native of Caraccas, who for twenty years had been possessed by a passion for revolutionizing his native province, and for becoming the Washington of Spanish America. Failing to obtain in England the aid he needed, he came to New York in November, 1805, with excellent letters of introduction. Miranda had a high reputation; he was plausible and enthusiastic; above all, he was supposed to represent a strong patriot party in Spanish America. War with Spain was imminent; the President's Annual Message seemed almost to declare its existence. In New York Miranda instantly became a hero, and attracted about him every ruined adventurer in society, among the rest a number of Aaron Burr's friends. Burr himself was jealous, and spoke with contempt of him; but Burr's chief ally Dayton, the late Federalist senator from New Jersey, was in Miranda's confidence. So was John Swartwout the marshal, Burr's devoted follower; so was William Steuben Smith, surveyor of the port, one of the few Federalists still left in office. These, as well as a swarm of smaller men, clustered round the Spanish American patriot, either to help his plans or to further

their own. By Smith's advice Miranda hired the ship
"Leander," owned by one Ogden and commanded by a
Captain Lewis ; with Smith's active aid Miranda next
bought arms and supplies, and enlisted men.

Meanwhile Miranda went to Washington. Arriving
there in the first days of the session, before the
pacific secret message and its sudden change of policy
toward Spain were publicly known, he called upon the
Secretary of State. December 11 he was received by
the secretary at the Department ; then invited to
dine ; then he put off his departure in order to dine
with the President at the White House, — at a time
when he was engaged, in conjunction with the surveyor of the port of New York, in fitting out a
warlike expedition against Spanish territory. What
passed between him and Madison became matter
of dispute. The secretary afterward admitted that
Miranda told of his negotiations with the British
government, and made no secret of his hopes to
revolutionize Colombia; to which Madison had replied
that the government of the United States could not
aid or countenance any secret enterprise, and was
determined to interfere in case of any infraction of
the law. Miranda's account of the secretary's conversation was very different ; he wrote to Smith, from
Washington, letters representing Madison to be fully
aware of the expedition then fitting out, and to be
willing that Smith should join it. He made a parade
of social relations with the President and secretary,
and on returning to New York was open in his allu-

sions to the complicity of Government. Doubtless his statements were false, and those of Madison were alone worthy of belief; but the Secretary of State was not the less compromised in the opinion of his enemies.

Miranda quickly returned to New York; and when about a month later the "Leander" was ready to sail, he wrote a letter to Madison announcing his intended departure, and taking a sort of formal and official leave, as though he were a confidential emissary of the President. He had the assurance to add that "the important matters" which he had communicated "will remain, I doubt not, in the deepest secret until the final result of this delicate affair. I have acted here on that supposition, conforming myself in everything to the intentions of the Government, which I hope I have seized and observed with exactitude and discretion." [1]

Ten days afterward the "Leander" sailed with a party of filibusters for the Spanish main, and the Secretary of State awoke to the consciousness that he had been deceived and betrayed. Fortunately for Madison, Miranda had not left behind him a copy of this letter, but had merely told his friends its purport. The letter itself remained unseen; but the original still exists among the Archives of the State Department, bearing an explanatory note in Madison's handwriting, that Miranda's "important" communications related to "what passed with the British gov-

[1] Miranda to Madison, Jan. 22, 1806; Madison MSS.

ernment," and that in saying he had conformed in New York to the President's intentions, Miranda said what was not true.

Then Madison, after receiving and entertaining Miranda at Washington while a high government official was openly enlisting troops for him at New York, ordered the Spanish minister to leave the Federal city, and refused to receive the minister's communications on any subject whatever. He had driven Casa Calvo and Morales from Louisiana, and at the same time allowed a notorious Spanish rebel to organize in New York a warlike expedition against Spanish territory.

Madison could hardly suppose that Yrujo would fail to make him pay the uttermost penalty for a mistake so glaring. Never before had the Spaniard enjoyed such an opportunity. After defying the secretary at Washington, Yrujo returned to Philadelphia, where he arrived on the evening of February 4. As he stepped from his carriage letters were put into his hand. Three of these letters were from the Spanish consul at New York, and contained only the notice that the "Leander" was about to sail.[1] Serious as this news was, it did not compare in importance with information furnished by Jonathan Dayton. For reasons of his own Dayton kept Yrujo informed of events unknown even to Merry and Turreau, and unsuspected by the President or his Cabinet. In some cases he probably tried to work on Yrujo's credulity.

[1] Yrujo to Cevallos, Feb. 12, 1806; MSS. Spanish Archives.

" The Secretary of State," according to Dayton's story, " with whom Miranda had two conferences, doubtless suspecting the origin of this mission, had at first treated him with reserve ; but at last had opened himself so far as to say that he did not know whether the United States would or would not declare war against Spain, because this step must depend on Congress ; that in this uncertainty he could not permit himself to offer Miranda the aid asked ; but that if private citizens in the United States chose to advance their funds for the undertaking, as Miranda had suggested, the Government would shut its eyes to their conduct, provided that Miranda took his measures in such a way as not to compromise the Government. At the same time the secretary coincided in Miranda's idea that in case the United States should determine upon war with Spain, this undertaking would prove to be a diversion favorable to the views of the American government."

This had been told to Yrujo, and reported by him to his Government before the visit to the capital. In the excitement caused by Madison's order to leave Washington, Yrujo confided in General Turreau, and went so far as to hint to Madison himself his knowledge that Madison was engaged in " hatching plots" against Spain. Dayton's latest information was still more serious. Besides exact details in regard to the force and destination of Miranda, Dayton said it had been agreed between Madison and Miranda that the Government should use the pretext of asking Yrujo's recall in order to refuse to receive communications from him, and thus prevent

him from claiming official interference against the
" Leander."

No sooner did the idea of a profound intrigue effect
a lodgment in the Spaniard's mind, than he turned
it into a means of wounding the Secretary of State.
After writing letters the whole night, and sending off
swift-sailing pilot-boats to warn the Spanish authorities of Miranda's plans, the marquis turned his attention to the secretary.   He sent a letter to the
Department, complaining that the "Leander" had
been allowed to sail; but knowing that the Department would decline to receive his letter, he took
another measure which secured with certainty a hearing.   He wrote a similar letter to Turreau, begging
his interference.[1]

Turreau could not refuse.   No sooner did he receive
Yrujo's letter, February 7, than he went to the Department and had an interview with the secretary,
which he reported to Yrujo on the same day:[2] —

" I was this morning with Madison.   I imparted to him
my suspicions and yours.   I sought his eyes, and, what
is rather rare, I met them.   He was in a state of extraordinary prostration while I was demanding from him a
positive explanation on the proceedings in question.   It
was with an effort that he broke silence, and at length
answered me that the President had already anticipated
my representations by ordering measures to be taken
against the accomplices who remained in the country and

[1] Yrujo to Turreau, Feb. 4, 1806; MSS. Spanish Archives.
[2] Turreau to Yrujo, Feb. 7, 1806; MSS. Spanish Archives,

against the culprits who should return. I leave you to judge whether I was satisfied by this answer, and I quitted him somewhat abruptly in order to address him in writing. I am occupied in doing so."

Madison might well show disturbance. To conciliate Turreau and Napoleon had been the chief object of his policy since the preceding October. For this he had endured arrogance such as no other American secretary ever tolerated. The Florida negotiation had not yet begun; John Randolph had delayed it and declaimed against it until Madison's reputation was involved in its success. Turreau held its fate in his hand; and suddenly Turreau appeared, demanding that Madison should prove himself innocent of charges that involved a quarrel with France as the ally and protector of Spain, while Madison had in his desk the parting letter from Miranda which if published would have proved the truth of these charges to the mind of every diplomatist and political authority in Europe.

Before many days had passed, Yrujo set the Federalist press at work. The President removed Smith from his office of surveyor, and caused both Smith and Ogden to be indicted. Indignant at being, as they believed, sacrificed to save Madison, Smith and Ogden sent memorials to Congress, which were presented by Josiah Quincy, April 21, the last day of the session, when the House was already irritable and the endurance of Madison's friends was exhausted by the vexatious attacks to which they had been for so many months exposed without capacity to reply or power to prevent them. John G. Jackson of Virginia, who had already invited a duel with Randolph, broke into a furious tirade against Quincy. " I say it is a base calumny of which the gentleman has made himself the organ ; and in saying so I hold myself responsible in any place the gentleman pleases." The House voted by an immense majority to return the memorials to the men from whom they came. The charges against the secretary were hustled aside, and Congress adjourned with what little dignity was left it; but Yrujo won his victory, and gave to the Secretary of State the fullest equivalent for the secretary's assault. For another year he defied his enemy by remaining as Spanish minister in America ; but he held no more relations with Government, and at his own request was then sent to represent Don Carlos IV. at the Court of Eugène Beauharnais at Milan.

Thus the first session of the Ninth Congress closed, April 21, 1806, leaving the Administration master of the field, but strong in numbers alone. How long a government could maintain its authority by mere momentum of inert mass had become a serious question to Jefferson and his successor.

CHAPTER IX.

As the members of Congress, after their wrangles, at last, April 22, wandered homeward, and John Randolph's long, lean figure disappeared on horseback beyond the Potomac, both the President and the Secretary of State drew a sigh of relief; for never before in the history of the Government had a President been obliged to endure such public insults and outrages at the hands of friend and enemy alike. The Federalists had quarrelled with each other as bitterly as the Republicans were quarrelling, but in Congress at least they had held their peace. Under their sway neither Spain, France, nor England insulted them or their Presidents with impunity. Sanguine as Jefferson was, he could not but feel that during two sessions he had been treated with growing disrespect both in Congress and abroad; and that should the contempt for his authority increase, his retirement would offer melancholy proof that the world no longer valued his services. So clearly did he see the danger that, as has been shown, he would gladly have changed the external appearance of his policy. February 18, 1806, he wrote his letter declaring himself convinced that Europe must be taught to know her error in supposing his Government to be "entirely in Quaker principles;"[1] and that unless this idea could be corrected, the United States would become the plunder of all nations. The attempt to teach Europe her error made his position worse. A month later, after the President had done all that he dared to do toward alarming the fears of Europe, the British minister at Washington wrote that both the American government and the American people, so far from meaning to use force, were trembling lest Great Britain should declare war:[2]

"The fear and apprehension of such a crisis is manifestly so great that I think I may venture to say that should his Majesty's government, in consequence of the menace insinuated in the President's Message, have thought proper to make any demonstration of their determination to resist whatever measures might be adopted here, by sending a reinforcement to the British squadron on the American station sufficiently great to be noticed, such a measure on their part would have the salutary effect of putting a stop at once to all the hostile proceedings of this Government."

In view of speeches like those of Gregg, Crowninshield, and Randolph, with their running commentary on the President's policy, such a conclusion as that which Merry had reached could not be called unjust. A few weeks afterward the British minister found

[1] See p. 111.
[2] Merry to Lord Mulgrave, March 19, 1806 ; MSS. British Archives.

his theory put to a severe test. April 25, 1806, soon
after the adjournment of Congress, an event occurred
which seemed calculated to bring the two nations
into collision. The " Leander," the " Cambrian,"
and the " Driver," blockading the port of New York,
were in the habit of firing shot across the bows of
merchant vessels in order to bring them to. According to the British account, — which was of course as
favorable to the frigate as possible, — a shot fired by
the " Leander " to stop a passing vessel happened
by an unlucky chance to be in line with a coasting
sloop far beyond, and killed one John Pierce, brother
of the coaster's captain. Making his way to the city
with the mangled body of his brother, the captain
roused New York to excitement over the outrage. A
meeting of citizens was held at the Tontine Coffee-
house ; but the Republicans allowed the Federalist
leaders to conduct it. Rufus King, Oliver Wolcott,
and other well-known enemies of President Jefferson
reported a series of resolutions censuring the Government for permitting the seizures, impressments, and
murders which were a consequence of the blockade,
recommending that all intercourse with the block-
ading squadron should be stopped, and advising that
John Pierce should be buried with a public funeral.
Meanwhile the people took the law into their own
hands, intercepting supplies for the squadron, and
compelling the few British officers on shore to hide
themselves. Pierce's funeral was turned into a popular
demonstration. Captain Whitby of the " Leander "

was indicted for murder by the grand jury; and the mayor despatched to Washington the necessary affidavits, on which the President might rest such further action as should seem fit.

Jefferson was greatly annoyed at this new misfortune, which allowed his Federalist enemies to charge upon him responsibility for British aggressions. In truth the Federalist merchants were the chief opponents of war with England; and their patriotic feeling was for the most part a sham. Yet the matter could not be ignored; and accordingly, May 3, the President issued a proclamation closing the ports and harbors of America forever to the three British frigates and to their commanders, and ordering all officers of the United States to arrest Captain Whitby wherever he might be found within American jurisdiction. This manner of redressing his own wrongs placed Jefferson at a disadvantage in asking for redress from Fox, who might naturally reply that if the United States government chose to make its appeal to municipal law, it could not expect the Government of Great Britain to offer further satisfaction; but popular excitement was for the moment more important than diplomatic forms.

Jacob Crowninshield, returning from Washington to Massachusetts after the adjournment of Congress, happened to be in New York at the time of Pierce's funeral, and wrote to the President on the subject. The President, May 13, answered his letter at some length.

" Although the scenes which were acted on shore," he said,[1] " were overdone with electioneering views, yet the act of the British officer was an atrocious violation of our territorial rights. The question what should be done was a difficult one. The sending three frigates was one suggestion. . . . While we were thus unable to present a force of that kind at New York, we received from Mr. Merry the most solemn assurances that the meeting of the three British vessels at New York was entirely accidental, from different quarters, and that they were not to remain. We concluded, therefore, that it was best to do what you have seen in the proclamation, and to make a proper use of the outrage and of our forbearance at St. James's to obtain better provisions for the future."

This was not all. Jefferson avowed himself in favor of a navy. His fifty new gunboats would, he thought, put New Orleans and New York in safety :

" But the building some ships of the line, instead of our most indifferent frigates, is not to be lost sight of. That we should have a squadron properly composed to prevent the blockading our ports is indispensable. The Atlantic frontier, from numbers, wealth, and exposure to potent enemies, has a proportionate right to be defended with the western frontier, for whom we keep up three thousand men. Bringing forward the measure, therefore, in a moderate form, placing it on the ground of comparative right, our nation, which is a just one, will come into it, notwithstanding the repugnance of some on the subject when first presented."

That Jefferson should repeat the opinions and echo the arguments of the Federalist Presidents was an

[1] Jefferson to Crowninshield, May 13, 1806 ; Jefferson MSS.

experience worth noting; but as a matter of statesmanship, there was reason to fear that the change came too late. The theory of peaceable coercion had been made the base of Jefferson's foreign policy; and upon it his fortunes must stand or fall. Merry, though willing to quiet President Jefferson's fears so far as concerned the accident of Pierce's death, was little affected by the outcry of New York, for he saw that the United States government could not change its pacific system. He wrote to Fox an urgent remonstrance against concession to American demands : [1]

" I consider it my duty to accompany this statement with a conviction on my part, from what is evident of the division of parties throughout the United States, from the weakness of the Government, from the prominent passion of avarice which prevails among every class of the community, and their intolerance under internal taxes, which must be imposed in the event of a war with any Power, that should his Majesty's government consider the pretensions that are asserted from hence as unjust, and be therefore disposed to resist them, such a resistance would only be attended with the salutary effect of commanding from this Government that respect which they have recently lost toward Great Britain."

Within the last year England had seized a large portion of American shipping and commerce; hundreds of American citizens had been taken by force from under the American flag, some of whom were already lying beneath the waters off Cape Trafalgar;

[1] Merry to C. J. Fox, May 4, 1806 ; MSS. British Archives.

the port of New York had been blockaded by a British squadron, which drew its supplies from the city, and lay habitually within its waters, except when engaged in stopping and searching vessels beyond the three-mile line; and at last an American citizen was killed within American jurisdiction by the guns of the block-ading squadron. In return the United States govern-ment had threatened to buy no more fine woollens and silks from England; and had stopped the fresh meat and vegetables which the officers of the " Cam-brian " and " Leander " were in the habit of procur-ing in the New York market. That Merry should still complain, that he should wish to stifle even this whisper of protest, and should talk of the American government in the same breath as trembling with fear and as having lost respect toward England, showed that he had a memory better than his pow-ers of observation. He was still brooding over Jeffer-son's *péle-méle* and his heelless slippers.

For that offence, committed in the heyday of diplo-matic triumph, the President had bitterly atoned. As Jefferson twisted and twined along a course daily becoming more tortuous, he found that public disaster was followed by social trials; on all sides he felt the reaction of his diplomatic failures. This kind of an-noyance left little trace in history, and was commonly forgotten or ignored by the people; but Jefferson was more than commonly sensitive to social influences, and if it annoyed him to be slandered, it annoyed him still more to be laughed at. He could not retaliate, and the more he exerted himself to appear above his vexations, the more he exposed himself to ridicule.

General Turreau, with grim amusement, reported faithfully what he saw and heard. At one moment Jefferson, trying to discover some plan for checking British authority, broached to the minister of Napoleon a scheme for uniting all Christian Powers in a novel alliance against each other's aggressions.

" Your Excellency will of course understand," wrote the sardonic Turreau to the saturnine Talleyrand,[1] " that it is not a system of armed neutrality which Mr. Jefferson would like to see established. Everything which tends to war is too far removed from his philanthropic principles, as it is from the interests of his country and the predominant opinion. The guaranty of neutrals would repose on the inert force of all the Powers against the one that should violate the neutral compact, and whose vessels would then find all foreign ports shut to them."

Turreau was amused by the incongruity of inviting Napoleon Bonaparte not only to protect neutral rights, but to do so by peaceful methods, and to join with Great Britain in a Christian confederation which should have for its main object the protection of American commerce, in order to save President Jefferson the expense of protecting it himself; but the humor of the scheme was not to be compared with its rashness. Had Jefferson foreseen the future, he

[1] Turreau to Talleyrand, Jan. 15, 1806 ; Archives des Aff. Étr., MSS.

would have abstained from suggesting ideas to a despot of Napoleon's genius.

Turreau entertained at heart a liking for Jefferson ; and indeed no one could come within the President's kindly influence without admitting its charm. " There is something voluptuous in meaning well." There was something voluptuous in Jefferson's way of meaning well; and if the quality increased the anger of the New England Puritans, who saw in it only hypocrisy, or if it drove John Randolph nearly to frenzy, it softened the hearts of bystanders like Turreau, who atoned for their weakness toward the President by contempt for his favorite the Secretary of State. May 10 Turreau wrote to Talleyrand :

" This infatuation of Mr. Jefferson for a commonplace man, whose political opinions are becoming every day more and more an object of suspicion to the leaders of the dominant party, will not surprise those who know the actual chief of the Federal government. Mr Jefferson as a private man joins to estimable qualities an uncommon degree of instruction ; he cultivates successfully philosophy, the sciences, and the arts ; he knows well the true interests of his country ; and if he seems sometimes to sacrifice them, or at least to offend them, when they do not accord with his extreme popularity, this is not with him the result of matured reflection, but only of a kindly sentiment, the impulse of which he blindly follows. But in my opinion Mr. Jefferson lacks the first of the qualities which make a statesman ; he has little energy, and still less of that audacity which is indispensable in a place so eminent, whatever may be the form of government. The slightest event makes him lose his balance, and he does not even know how to disguise the impression he receives. Although the last session was quite stormy, it was easy to foresee that everything would end in propositions of agreement, because no one wished war; and yet Mr. Jefferson has worried himself so much with the movements of Congress that he has made himself ill, and has grown ten years older. Not that he has yet reached the point of repenting having begun a second term. What has further contributed to render his position disagreeable is the drawing off of a part of his friends, and even of the diplomatic corps, who, with the exception of the French minister, no longer visit the President. This isolation renders him the more sensible to the reiterated outrages he receives in Congress even in open session. I have certain information that he has been extremely affected by it." [1]

Neither these annoyances nor the unlucky accident of Pierce's death, following so long a series of political misfortunes, could prevent the skies from clearing with the coming spring. If the Southern Republicans for a time seemed, as General Smith said, to be falling away daily from the Administration, the President could still congratulate himself on the steadiness of the Northern democrats, who asked for no better fortune than to be rid forever of John Randolph's tyranny. On the whole, Jefferson was well pleased with the behavior of his majority. His chief care was to find a parliamentary leader who could

[1] Turreau to Talleyrand, May 10, 1806 ; Archives des Aff. Étr., MSS.

take Randolph's place; and he was willing that this leadership should pass out of Virginia hands, even though it should fall into the hands of Massachusetts. He wrote to Barnabas Bidwell, urging him to take the vacant position : [1] —

"The last session of Congress was indeed an uneasy one for a time ; but as soon as the members penetrated into the views of those who were taking a new course, they rallied in as solid a phalanx as I have ever seen act together. They want only a man of business and in whom they can confide to conduct things in the House, and they are as much disposed to support him as can be wished. It is only speaking a truth to say that all eyes look to you."

Jefferson's great hope seemed likely soon to be realized beyond his own anticipations, when New England should not only accept democratic principles, but should also control the party which Virginia had brought into power. In the April election of 1806 Massachusetts chose a democratic legislature ; the Federalist Governor Strong was re-elected by only a few hundred votes, while a democrat was actually elected for lieutenant-governor. The conduct of England, which caused Jefferson his most serious difficulties abroad, worked in his favor among the people of America, who were more patriotic than their leaders, and felt by instinct that whatever mistakes in policy their Government might commit, support was the alternative to anarchy.

[1] Jefferson to Bidwell, July 5, 1806; Works, v. 14; Jefferson MSS.

The factions in New York and Pennsylvania fought their tedious and meaningless battles, which had no longer a national interest. The newspapers continued to find in personal abuse the most lively amusement they could furnish to their readers. The acts of Jefferson and Madison were extolled or vilified according to the partisan division of the press; and material for attack and defence was never lacking. During the summer of 1806 Miranda's expedition and the trial of Smith and Ogden, which resulted from it, filled many columns of the papers. Conviction of these two men for violating the neutrality laws seemed to be the President's earnest wish; yet when members of the Administration were subpœnaed for the defence, Jefferson ordered them to disobey the summons, alleging that their attendance in court would interfere with their performance of official duties. The question whether this rule was proper in practice or correct in law came soon afterward before the Supreme Court, and received elaborate discussion; but in the case of Smith and Ogden, the refusal of Madison to obey the subpœna was a political necessity. Had he been forced into the witness-box, he must have produced Miranda's letter; and in the face of evidence so compromising to the superior officers of government, no jury would have convicted a subordinate.

Before the trial began, the President removed Smith from his office of surveyor of the port of New York; and after its close he removed Swartwout from the

post of marshal. The reasons for punishing Swartwout were given in a Cabinet memorandum written
by Jefferson : —-

"Swartwout the marshal, to whom in his duel with
Clinton Smith was second, summoned a panel of jurors
the greater part of which were of the bitterest Federalists. His letter, too, covering to a friend a copy
of 'Aristides,' and affirming that every fact in it was
true as Holy Writ. Determined unanimously that he
be removed."

Thanks to Swartwout's jury and to Madison's share
in Miranda's confidence, Smith was acquitted. As in
many other government cases, the prosecution ended
in a failure of justice.

The Spaniards easily defeated Miranda, and captured or drove away his forces. Events followed
with such rapidity that this episode was soon forgotten. Yrujo did his utmost to keep it alive. The
Federalist newspapers printed more than one attack
on Madison evidently from Yrujo's pen, which annoyed the secretary and his friends ; while Yrujo remained in the country only by way of bravado, to
prove the indifference of his Government to the good-
will of the United States. On the Texan frontier the
Spaniards showed themselves in increasing numbers,
until a collision seemed imminent. Wilkinson, on his
side, could collect at Natchitoches no force capable
of holding the Red River against a serious attack.
Whether Wilkinson himself were not more dangerous
than the Spaniards to the government of the United

States was a question which disturbed men like John Randolph more than it seemed to interest Jefferson.

Fortunately the Treasury was as strong as the Army and the Foreign Department were weak. Gallatin made no mistakes; from the first he had carried the Administration on his shoulders, and had defied attack. Duane hated him, for Gallatin's influence held Duane in check, and seemed the chief support of Governor McKean in Pennsylvania; but Duane's malignity could find no weak point in the Treasury. The revenue reached $14,500,000 for 1806, and after providing the two millions appropriated for the Florida purchase, left a balance for the year of four hundred thousand dollars beyond all current demands. The Treasury held a surplus of at least four millions. The national debt was reduced to less than $57,500,000; and this sum included the Louisiana stock of $11,250,000, which could not be paid before the year 1818. After the year 1808, Gallatin promised an annual surplus of five or six millions, ready for any purpose to which Congress might choose to apply it. Even the Federalists gave up the attempt to attack the management of the Treasury; and if they sometimes seemed to wish for a foreign war, it was chiefly because they felt that only a war could shake the authority and success of Gallatin. "For many years past," wrote Timothy Pickering in 1814,[1] "I have said, 'Let the ship run

[1] Pickering to Gouverneur Morris, Oct. 21, 1814; Lodge's Cabot, p. 535.

aground! The shock will throw the present pilots overboard; and then competent navigators will get her once more afloat, and conduct her safely into port.'" Only war with England, by breaking down the Treasury, could effect Pickering's purpose.

Of such a war, in spite of the Rule of 1756, the blockade of New York, the impressment of seamen, and the slaughter of Pierce, there was no immediate prospect. The death of William Pitt and the accession of Charles James Fox to power quieted fear. The American people were deliberately resolved not to join in the outburst of passion which Pierce's death caused in New York. Little sense was felt of a common interest between agriculture and shipping; so that even the outrage of Pierce passed without stirring men who followed the plough and swung the scythe. New York was but a seaport, half foreign in population and interests, an object of jealousy to good citizens, who looked askance at manufactures and middlemen. The accidental death of a seaman was no matter of alarm. Every patriotic American wanted peace with England, and was glad to be told that Fox had promised pleasant things to Monroe.

Although the merchants had been robbed, the people at large were more prosperous and contented than ever. The summer of 1806 was one of quiet and rapid progress. While Europe tossed on her bed of pain, and while Russia built up the fourth coalition against Napoleon, only to drench with blood the battle-fields of Jena, Eylau, and Friedland, the United States moved steadily toward their separate objects, caring little for any politics except their own. In foreign affairs their government, after threatening to break through the bounds it had set to its own action and to punish the offenders of its dignity, ended by returning to its old ground and by avowing, as in 1801, that war was not one of its weapons. In domestic matters no serious division of opinion existed. The American people went to their daily tasks without much competition or mental effort, and had no more wish to wrangle about problems of the future than to turn back on their path and face Old-World issues. Every day a million men went to their work, every evening they came home with some work accomplished; but the result was matter for a census rather than for history. The acres brought into cultivation, the cattle bred, the houses built, proved no doubt that human beings, like ants and bees, could indefinitely multiply their numbers, and could lay up stores of food; but these statistics offered no evidence that the human being, any more than the ant and bee, was conscious of a higher destiny, or was even mechanically developing into a more efficient animal. As far as politics proved anything, the evidence seemed to show that the American tended already to become narrow in his views and timid in his methods. The great issues of 1776 and of 1787 had dwindled into disputes whether robbery and violence should be punished by refusing to buy millinery and

hardware from the robbers, and whether an unsuc-
cessful attempt to purloin foreign territory should be
redeemed by bribing a more powerful nation to purloin it at second hand. The great issues of democracy
and republicanism were still alive, but their very
success removed these subjects for the moment from
the field of politics. That a democracy could for so
long a time maintain itself above Old-World miseries
was a triumph; but thus far the democracy had been
favored by constant good fortune, and even in these
five years conservatives thought they felt a steady decline of moral tone. What would happen when society should be put to some violent test?

In politics nothing that proved progress could be
seen. In other directions little positive result had
been reached.

Far in the wilderness a few men, in the pay of the
United States government, were toiling for the ad-
vancement of knowledge. In the summer of 1805
General Wilkinson ordered Lieutenant Pike, a young
officer in the first infantry, to take a sergeant, a
corporal, and seventeen privates, and ascertain the
true sources of the Mississippi. For scientific purposes such a party of explorers could do little of
permanent value, but as a military reconnoissance
it might have uses. Lieutenant Pike worked his way
up the stream from St. Louis. October 16, 1805,
he reached a point two hundred and thirty-three miles
above the Falls of St. Anthony, and there stopped to
establish a winter station. December 10 he started

again with a part of his men and went northward with sleds until, Jan. 8, 1806, he reached a British trading-station on Sandy Lake, from which he struggled to Leech Lake, where another British establishment existed. His visit was rather an act of formal authority than a voyage of exploration; but he notified both the British and the Indian occupants of the territory that they were under the rule of the United States government. After accomplishing this object he began his return march February 18, and reached St. Louis April 30, 1806, having shown such energy and perseverance in this winter journey as few men could have surpassed.

General Wilkinson was so well pleased with the success of the expedition that he immediately ordered Pike upon another. This time the headwaters of the Arkansas and Red rivers were to be explored as far as the Spanish settlements of New Mexico. July 15, 1806, with about the same number of men as before, Pike left St. Louis, and September 1 reached the Osage towns on the Missouri River. Striking across the prairie, he marched through a country filled with jealous Pawnee Indians, till he reached the Arkansas River, and ascending its branches, left a permanent monument to his visit by giving his name to Pike's Peak in Colorado. Turning toward the southwest, he entangled himself in the mountains; and after suffering terribly in snow and ice, at last, Feb. 26, 1807, was stopped by the Spanish authorities at Santa Fé, who sent him to Chihuahua, and thence allowed him to return through Texas to the United States.

Both these expeditions were subordinate to the larger exploration of Lewis and Clark, which President Jefferson himself organized, and in which he took deep interest. After passing the winter at the Mandan village, as has been already told, Lewis with thirty-two men set out April 7 in boats and canoes for the headwaters of the Missouri. The journey proved to be full of labor, but remarkably free from danger; the worst perils encountered were from rattlesnakes and bears. The murderous Sioux were not seen; and when, August 11, Lewis reached the end of river navigation, and found himself at the base of the mountains that divided the waters of the Missouri from those of the Columbia, his greatest anxiety was to meet the Indians who occupied the line of passage. His troubles rose from the poverty, rather than from the hostility, of these tribes. They supplied him with horses and with such provisions as they had, and he made his way peacefully down the western slope until he could again take canoes. November 7 the explorers reached the mouth of the Columbia River, and saw at last the ocean which bounded American ambition. There they were forced to pass the winter in extreme discomfort, among thievish and flea-bitten Indians, until March 26, 1807, they could retrace their steps.

Creditable as these expeditions were to American energy and enterprise, they added little to the stock

of science or wealth.   Many years must elapse before
the vast region west of the Mississippi could be
brought within reach of civilization.   The crossing
of the continent was a great feat, but was nothing
more.   The French explorers had performed feats
almost as remarkable long before ; but, in 1805, the
country they explored was still a wilderness.   Great
gains to civilization could be made only on the Atlantic coast under the protection of civilized life.   For
many years to come progress must still centre in the
old thirteen States of the Union.   The expeditions of
Lewis and Pike returned no immediate profits ; but in
the city of New York men were actively engaged
in doing what Lewis could not do, — bringing the
headwaters of the western rivers within reach of
private enterprise and industry.   While Lewis slowly
toiled up the Missouri River, thinking himself fortunate if he gained twenty miles a day against the
stream, the engine which Robert Fulton had ordered
from the works of Watt and Bolton in England had
been made, and Fulton returned to New York to
superintend its use.   With the money of Chancellor
Livingston he began to construct the hull of his new
steamboat and adjust it to the engine.

The greatest steps in progress were often unconsciously taken, and Fulton's steamboat was an example of this rule.   Neither in private talk nor in the
newspapers did his coming experiment rouse much
notice.   To the public, Fulton's idea, though vision-
ary, was not new.   Indeed Fulton stood in immi-

nent danger of being forestalled by rivals. In 1804
Oliver Evans experimented with a stern-wheel steamboat on the Delaware River, while at the same time
John C. Stevens was experimenting with a screw-
propeller on the Hudson. Nothing practical had as
yet come from these attempts. The public seemed to
regard them as matters which did not concern it,
and the few thousand dollars needed to pay for a
proper engine and hull could with difficulty be wrung
from capitalists, who were derided for their folly.
Fulton worked with better support than his predecessors had enjoyed, but with little encouragement or
show of interest from the press or the public.

So far as concerned activity of mind, politics still
engrossed public attention. The summer of 1806,
quiet and prosperous as it seemed, betrayed uneasiness, — a mysterious political activity, connected with
no legitimate purpose of party. Except in Connecticut and Massachusetts, the Federalists, as an organized body, could hardly be said to exist. Democrats,
Republicans, and Federalists were divided for the
moment rather by social distinctions than by principle; but the division was not the less real. Every
year added strength to the national instinct; but
every year brought also a nearer certainty that the
denationalizing forces, whether in New England under
Timothy Pickering, or in Virginia under John Randolph, or in Louisiana under some adventurer, would
make an effort to break the chain that hampered
local interests and fettered private ambition. Under

a Virginia President and a slave-owning majority of Congress, the old anti-national instinct of Virginia was paralyzed, and the dangers to rise from it were postponed; but the freer play was given to the passions of Boston and New Orleans, — to the respectable seditiousness of Timothy Pickering and the veneered profligacy of Aaron Burr. The time had come when Burr was to bring his conspiracy to the test of action, and to try the strength of a true democracy. During the autumn of 1806 Burr's projects and movements roused a sudden panic, less surprising than the tolerance with which his conspiracy had been so long treated by the President and the press.

CHAPTER X.

WHEN Burr ceased to be Vice-President of the United States, March 4, 1805, he had already made himself intimate with every element of conspiracy that could be drawn within his reach. The list of his connections might have startled Jefferson, if the President's easy optimism had not been proof to fears. In London, Burr's friend Colonel Williamson confided his plans to Pitt and Lord Melville. At Washington the British minister, Merry, wrote to Lord Mulgrave in support of Williamson's negotiation. The creole deputies from New Orleans were Burr's friends, and Derbigny was acquainted with " certain projects " he entertained. General Wilkinson, governor of the Louisiana Territory, whose headquarters were at St. Louis, closely attached to Burr almost from childhood, stood ready for any scheme that promised to gratify inordinate ambition. James Brown, Secretary of the Territory, was Burr's creature. Judge Prevost, of the Superior Court at New Orleans, was Burr's stepson. Jonathan Dayton, whose term as senator ended the same day with Burr's vice-presidency, shared and perhaps suggested the " projects." John Smith, the senator from Ohio, was

under the influence of Burr and Dayton.   John Adair
of Kentucky was in Wilkinson's confidence.   The
Swartwouts in New York, with the "little band" who
made Burr their idol, stood ready to follow him wherever he might lead.   In South Carolina Joseph Allston,
the husband of Theodosia Burr, might be induced
to aid his father-in-law ; and Allston was supposed to
be the richest planter in the South, worth a million of
dollars in slaves and plantations.   The task of uniting
these influences and at a given moment raising the
standard of a new empire in the Mississippi Valley
seemed to an intriguer of Burr's metal not only feasi-
ble, but certain of success.

After the parting interview with Merry in March,
1805, when they arranged terms to be asked of the
British government, Burr went to Philadelphia, and
in April crossed the mountains to Pittsburg, on his
way to New Orleans.   Wilkinson was to have joined
him ; but finding that Wilkinson had been delayed,
Burr went on alone.   Floating down the Ohio, his
ark lashed to that of Matthew Lyon, he first stopped
a few hours at an island about two miles below
Parkersburg, where an Irish gentleman named Blennerhassett lived, and where he had spent a sum,
for that day considerable, in buildings and improvements.   The owner was absent ; but Mrs. Blennerhassett was at home, and invited Burr to dinner.
The acquaintance thus begun proved useful to him.
Passing to Cincinnati, he became, May 11, 1805, a
guest in the house of Senator Smith.   Dayton was

already there; but Wilkinson arrived a few days later, after Burr had gone on by land to Nashville. Wilkinson publicly talked much of a canal around the Falls of the Ohio River, to explain the community of interest which seemed to unite himself with Burr, Dayton, and Senator Smith; but privately he wrote, May 28, to John Adair, soon to be Breckenridge's successor as senator from Kentucky : " I was to have introduced my friend Burr to you; but in this I failed by accident. He understands your merits, and reckons on you. Prepare to visit me, and I will tell you all. We must have a peep at the unknown world beyond me."

Meanwhile Burr reached Nashville in Tennessee, where he was received with enthusiastic hospitality. Every one at or near the town seemed to contend for the honor of best treating or serving him.[1] Dinners were given, toasts were drunk; the newspapers were filled with his doings. No one equalled Andrew Jackson in warmth of devotion to Colonel Burr. At all times of his life Jackson felt sympathy with a duellist who had killed his man; but if his support was enlisted for the duellist who had killed Hamilton, his passions were excited in favor of the man who should drive the Spaniards from America; and Burr announced that this was to be the mission of his life. As major-general of the Tennessee militia, Jackson looked forward to sharing this exploit.

[1] Deposition of Matthew Lyon; Wilkinson's Memoirs, ii. Appendix, lxviii.

After spending a week or more at Nashville, Burr descended in one of General Jackson's boats to the mouth of the Cumberland, where his ark was waiting; and June 6 he joined General Wilkinson at Fort Massac, — a military post on the north shore of the Ohio River, a few miles above its junction with the Mississippi. The two men remained together at Massac four days, and Burr wrote to his daughter, Mrs. Allston: "The General and his officers fitted me out with an elegant barge, — sails, colors, and ten oars, — with a sergeant and ten able, faithful hands. Thus equipped, I left Massac on the 10th June." Wilkinson supplied him also with a letter of introduction to Daniel Clark, the richest and most prominent American in New Orleans. Dated June 9, 1805, it announced that the bearer would carry secrets. "To him I refer you for many things improper to letter, and which he will not say to any other."

While Burr went down the river to New Orleans, Wilkinson turned northward to St. Louis, where he arrived July 2. He was in high spirits and indiscreet. Two of his subordinate officers, Major Hunt and Major Bruff, afterward told how he sounded them, — and Major Bruff's evidence left no doubt that Wilkinson shared in the ideas of Burr and Dayton; that he looked forward to a period of anarchy and confusion in the Eastern States, as the result of democracy; and that he intended to set up a military empire in Louisiana. Already, June 24, he signed Lieutenant Pike's instructions to explore the headwaters of the Arkansas River. Adair, certainly in the secret, believed the object of this expedition to be the opening of a road to Santa Fé and to the mines of Mexico.[1] Every recorded letter or expression of Wilkinson during the spring and summer of 1805 showed that he was in the confidence of Burr and Dayton; that he gave them active aid in their scheme for severing the Union; and that they in their turn embraced his project of Mexican conquest.

Burr reached New Orleans June 25, 1805, and remained a fortnight, entertained by the enemies of Governor Claiborne and of the Spaniards. Conspiracies were commonly most active and most dangerous when most secret; and the mark of secrecy, almost wholly wanting to this conspiracy in the Northern States, was never removed, by any public inquiry or admission, from its doings at New Orleans. According to the story afterward told by Wilkinson on the evidence of Lieutenant Spence, Burr on his arrival in Louisiana became acquainted with the so-called Mexican Association, — a body of some three hundred men, leagued together for the emancipation of Mexico from Spanish rule.[2] Of this league Daniel Clark afterward declared that he was not a member; but if his safety as a merchant required him to keep aloof, his sympathies were wholly with the Association. After Burr's arrival, and under his influ-

[1] Adair to Wilkinson, Jan. 27, 1806; Wilkinson's Memoirs, ii. Appendix, lxxvii.

[2] Wilkinson's Memoirs, ii. 283.

ence, the scheme of disunion was made a part of the Mexican plan; and these projects soon became so well known in New Orleans as to reach the ears of the Spanish agents and excite their suspicions, until Clark two months later complained to Wilkinson that Burr's indiscretion was bringing them all into danger.[1] Clark's letter was written as though he were an innocent bystander annoyed at finding himself included in an imaginary conspiracy against the Spanish government. In truth it seemed also to be written as a warning to Burr against trusting a certain " Minor of Natchez " : —

" Were I sufficiently intimate with Mr. Burr, and knew where to direct a line to him, I should take the liberty of writing to him. Perhaps, finding Minor in his way, he was endeavoring to extract something from him, — he has amused himself at the blockhead's expense, — and then Minor has retailed the news to his employers. Inquire of Mr. Burr about this and let me know on my return [from Vera Cruz], which will be in three or four months. The tale is a horrid one if well told. Kentucky, Tennessee, the State of Ohio, the four territories on the Mississippi and Ohio, with part of Georgia and Carolina, are to be bribed with the plunder of the Spanish countries west of us to separate from the Union."

This letter, written by Clark, Sept. 7, 1805, showed that Burr's plans were notorious at New Orleans, and that his indiscretion greatly annoyed his friends.

[1] Daniel Clark to Wilkinson, Sept. 7, 1805 ; Wilkinson's Memoirs, ii. Appendix, xxxiii.

Two years afterward, Wilkinson reminded Clark of the letter.[1]

"You will recollect," wrote Wilkinson, "you desired me to write Burr on the subject, which I did, and also gave his brother-in-law, Dr. Brown, an extract of your letter to transmit him."

Burr's reply has been preserved: —

"Your letter of November," he wrote to Wilkinson,[2] Jan. 6, 1806, "which came, I believe, through J. Smith, has been received and answered. Your friend [Clark] suspects without reason the person [Minor] named in his letter to you. I love the society of that person; but surely I could never be guilty of the folly of confiding to one of his levity anything which I wished not to be repeated. Pray do not disturb yourself with such nonsense."

Daniel Clark and Wilkinson were therefore assured, not that the tale was untrue, but that Burr had not confided to Minor, or "to one of his levity" anything which Burr "wished not to be repeated." Nevertheless Clark, whose abilities were far greater than those of Burr, and whose motives for secrecy were stronger, knew that Burr must have talked with extreme indiscretion, for his plans had already come to the ears of the Spanish agents in Louisiana. Many residents of New Orleans knew of the scheme, — "many absurd and wild reports are circulated here,"

[1] Wilkinson to Clark, Oct. 12, 1807; Clark's Proofs, p. 154.
[2] Wilkinson's Memoirs, ii. Appendix, lxxxvi.

wrote Clark ; and whether they shared it or not, they certainly did not denounce it.

No plea of ignorance could avail any of Burr's friends. His schemes were no secret. As early as Aug. 4, 1805, more than a month before Daniel Clark sent his warning to General Wilkinson, the British minister was so much alarmed at the publicity already given to the plot that he wrote to Lord Mulgrave a panic-stricken letter, evidently supposing that the scheme was ruined by Burr's indiscretion : [1] —

" He or some of his agents have either been indiscreet in their communications, or have been betrayed by some person in whom they considered that they had reason to confide ; for the object of his journey has now begun to be noticed in the public prints, where it is said that a convention is to be called immediately from the States bordering on the Ohio and Mississippi for the purpose of forming a separate government. It is, however, possible that the business may be so far advanced as, from the nature of it, to render any further secrecy impossible."

The French minister was hardly less well informed. Feb. 13, 1806, Turreau wrote to his government,[2] mentioning Miranda's departure, and adding, —

" The project of effecting a separation between the Western and Atlantic States marches abreast with this one. Burr, though displeased at first by the arrival of Miranda, who might reduce him to a secondary *rôle*, has

[1] Merry to Mulgrave, Aug. 4, 1805 ; MSS British Archives.

[2] Turreau to Talleyrand, Feb. 13, 1806 ; Archives des Aff. Étr., MSS.

set off again for the South, after having had several conferences with the British minister.   It seems to me that
the Government does not penetrate Burr's views, and
that the difficult circumstances in which it finds itself,
and where it has placed itself, force it to dissimulate.
This division of the confederated States appears to me
inevitable, and perhaps less remote than is commonly
supposed; but would this event, which England seems
to favor, be really contrary to the interests of France?
And, assuming it to take place, should we not have a
better chance to withdraw, if not both confederations, at
least one of them, from the yoke of England?"

That Burr should have concealed from his principal allies — the creoles of New Orleans — plans which
he communicated so freely elsewhere, was not to be
imagined.   Burr remained only about a fortnight at
New Orleans; then returned on horseback through
Natchez to Nashville, where he became again the
guest of Andrew Jackson.   He passed the month of
August in Tennessee and Kentucky; then struck
into the wilderness across the Indiana Territory to
St. Louis in order to pass a week more with General Wilkinson and Secretary Brown.   He found
Wilkinson discouraged by the rebuffs he had met in
attempting to seduce his subordinate officers and the
people of the territory into the scheme.   Although
Wilkinson afterward swore solemnly that he had no
part or parcel in Burr's disunion project, his own
evidence proved that the subject had been discussed
between them, and that his fears of failure had at

the time of their meeting at St. Louis checked his enthusiasm : [1] —

" Mr. Burr, speaking of the imbecility of the government, said it would moulder to pieces, die a natural death, — or words to that effect; adding that the people of the Western country were ready to revolt. To this I recollect replying that if he had not profited more by his journey in other respects, he had better have remained at Washington or Philadelphia; for ' surely,' said I, ' my friend, no person was ever more mistaken. The Western people disaffected to the government! They are bigoted to Jefferson and democracy.' "

Wilkinson afterward claimed to have written at that time a letter to the Secretary of the Navy warning him against Burr; but the letter never reached its supposed address. He certainly gave to Burr a letter of introduction to Governor Harrison, of the Indiana Territory, which suggested decline of sympathy with the conspiracy; for it urged Harrison to return the bearer as the Territorial delegate to Congress, — a boon on which the Union " may much depend." [2]

Burr reached St. Louis Sept. 11, 1805; he left it September 19, for Vincennes and the East. Two months afterward he arrived at Washington and hurried to the British legation. His friend Dayton, who had been detained by a long illness in the West,

[1] Wilkinson's Evidence, Burr's Trial; Annals of Congress, 1807–1808, p. 611.

[2] Wilkinson's Memoirs, ii. 303.

arrived and made his report to Merry only two days
before.

The conspiracy counted on the aid of Great Britain, which was to be the pivot of the scheme; but
Burr's hopes were blasted by learning from Merry
that no answer had been received from the British
government in reply to the request for money and
ships. Merry explained that an accident had happened to the packet-boat, but both had reason to
know that hope of aid from the British government
had vanished.

"These disappointments gave him, he [Burr] said,[1]
the deepest concern, because his journey through the
Western country and Louisiana as far as New Orleans,
as well as through a part of West Florida, had been attended with so much more success than he had even
looked for, that everything was in fact completely prepared in every quarter for the execution of his plan; and
because he had therefore been induced to enter into an
engagement with his associates and friends to return to
them in the month of March next, in order to commence
the operations. He had been encouraged, he said, to go
such lengths by the communications he had received from
Colonel Williamson, which gave him some room to hope
and expect that his Majesty's government were disposed
to afford him their assistance. . . . He was sensible that
no complete understanding on the subject could well take
place without verbal communication; but he flattered
himself that enough might be explained in this way to

[1] Merry to Lord Mulgrave, Nov. 25, 1805; MSS. British
Archives.

give a commencement to the business, and that any ulterior arrangements might safely be left till the personal interviews he should have with the persons properly authorized for the purpose, whom he recommended to be sent with the ships of war, which it was necessary should cruise off the mouth of the Mississippi at the latest by the 10th of April next, and to continue there until the commanding officer should receive information from him or from Mr. Daniel Clark of the country having declared itself independent. He wished the naval force in question to consist of two or three ships of the line, the same number of frigates, and a proportionable number of smaller vessels."

The British minister was curious to know precisely the result of the Western tour ; but on this subject Burr talked vaguely, and, contrary to his usual custom, mentioned few names.

"Throughout the Western country persons of the greatest property and influence had engaged themselves to contribute very largely toward the expense of the enterprise ; at New Orleans he represented the inhabitants to be so firmly resolved upon separating themselves from their union with the United States, and every way to be so completely prepared, that he was sure the revolution there would be accomplished without a drop of blood being shed, the American force in that country (should it not, as he had good reason to believe, enlist with him) not being sufficiently strong to make any opposition. It was accordingly there that the revolution would commence, at the end of April or the beginning of May, provided his Majesty's government should consent to lend their assistance toward it, and the answer, together with the pecuniary aid which would be wanted, arrived in time to enable him to set out the beginning of March."

From Pitt, besides the naval force, Burr wanted a credit for one hundred and ten thousand pounds, to be given in the names of John Barclay of Philadelphia, and Daniel Clark of New Orleans. In his report to Merry on the results of the Western tour he said no more than he had a right to say, without violent exaggeration. He barely hinted at complicity on the part of Wilkinson, Smith, Adair, and Andrew Jackson. He gave Merry clearly to understand that the heart of his plot was not in the Ohio Valley, but at New Orleans. He laid little weight on the action of Kentucky or Tennessee; with him, the point of control was among the creoles.

"Mr. Burr stated to me — what I have reason to believe to be true from the information I have received from other quarters — that when he reached Louisiana he found the inhabitants so impatient under the American government that they had actually prepared a representation of their grievances, and that it was in agitation to send deputies with it to Paris. The hope, however, of becoming completely independent, and of forming a much more beneficial connection with Great Britain, having been pointed out to them, and this having already prevailed among many of the principal people who are become his associates, they had found means to obtain a suspension of the plan of having recourse to France."

Burr impressed Merry with the idea that West Florida was also to be taken within the scope of his scheme. " The overture which had been made to him at New Orleans from a person of the greatest influence in East and West Florida, and the information he had otherwise acquired respecting the state of those countries," were among the reasons which he pressed upon the British government as motives for aiding the conspiracy with a naval force. England was then at war with Spain.

One more argument was pressed by Burr, for no one knew better than he the use to which New England might be put.

" He observed — what I readily conceive may happen — that when once Louisiana and the Western country became independent, the Eastern States will separate themselves immediately from the Southern ; and that thus the immense power which is now risen up with so much rapidity in the western hemisphere will, by such a division, be rendered at once informidable."

Whatever may have been Merry's sympathies or wishes, he could do no more than report Burr's conversation to Lord Mulgrave with as much approval as he dared give it. Meanwhile Burr was thrown into extreme embarrassment by the silence of Mulgrave. Burr's report showed that the creoles in New Orleans, with Daniel Clark as their financial ally, were induced to countenance the conspiracy only because they believed it to be supported by England. Without that support, Burr could not depend on creole assistance. Had he been wise, he would have waited ; and perhaps he might in the end have brought the British

government to accept his terms.   If Pitt intended to
plunder American commerce and to kidnap American
citizens, he must be prepared to do more ; and Burr
might calculate on seeing the British Tories placed
by their own acts in a position where they could not
afford to neglect his offers.

Burr stayed a week in Washington ; and although
the object of his Western journey was so notorious
that even the newspapers talked about it, his reception at the White House and at the departments
was as cordial as usual.   About Dec. 1, 1805, he returned to Philadelphia, where he began the effort
to raise from new sources the money which till
then he hoped to provide by drafts on the British
treasury.   The conspirators were driven to extraordinary shifts.   Burr undertook the task of drawing
men like Blennerhassett into his toils, and induced
Dayton to try an experiment, resembling the plot
of a comic opera rather than the seriousness of
historical drama.

Dec. 5, 1805, as Miranda was leaving New York to
entrap Madison, three days after Burr had returned
to Philadelphia from his unsatisfactory interview with
Merry, the Marquis of Casa Yrujo, as yet innocent of
conspiracy, and even flattering himself upon having
restored friendly relations with the Government, received a secret visit at his house in Philadelphia from
Jonathan Dayton, whom he had known at Washington
as the Federalist senator from New Jersey.   Dayton,
in a mysterious manner, gave him to understand that

the Spanish government would do well to pay thirty
or forty thousand dollars for certain secrets; and
finding the marquis disposed to listen, Dayton recited
a curious tale.

" This secret," said he,[1] " is known at the present
moment to only three persons in this country. I am one
of them; and I will tell you that toward the end of the
last session and near the end of last March Colonel Burr
had various very secret conferences with the British minister, to whom he proposed a plan not only for taking the
Floridas, but also for effecting the separation and independence of the Western States, — a part of this plan
being that the Floridas should be associated in this new
federative republic; England to receive as the price of
her services a decisive preference in matters of commerce
and navigation, and to secure these advantages by means
of a treaty to be made as soon as she should recognize
this new republic. This plan obtained the approval of
the British minister, who sent it and recommended it to
his Court. Meanwhile Colonel Burr has been in New
Orleans, in the Mississippi Territory, in the States of
Tennessee, Kentucky, and Ohio, to sound and prepare
their minds for this revolution. In all these States he
has found the most favorable disposition, not only for
this emancipation, which the Western States evidently
desire, but also for making an expedition against the
kingdom of Mexico. This is an idea that occurred to us
after sending the first plan to London; and having given
greater extension to the project, Colonel Burr sent to
London a despatch with his new ideas to Colonel Williamson, — an English officer who has been many years

[1] Yrujo to Cevallos, Dec. 5, 1805 ; MSS. Spanish Archives.

in this country, and whose return he expects within a month or six weeks. The first project was very well received by the English Cabinet, and more particularly by Mr. Dundas, or Lord Melville, who was the person charged with this correspondence; but as he had reason to fear dismission from office for causes well known through the debates of Parliament, this plan has suffered some delay; but Mr. Pitt has again turned his attention to it."

On the strength of this information Dayton seriously proposed to terrify Yrujo and Don Carlos IV. into paying the expenses of Burr's expedition. An idea so fantastic could have sprung from no mind except Burr's; but, fantastic as it was, he pursued it obstinately, although by doing so he betrayed to Spain the followers whom he was striving to inveigle into an imaginary assault on Spanish empire. Dayton asserted that the revolution would begin on the appearance of the British squadron off the coast of West Florida in February or March, 1806; that to make this revolution more popular, after the Floridas were taken, the expedition against Mexico would be attempted; that they feared no opposition from a government so weak as the Federal; that the United States troops were all in the West, and that Colonel Burr had caused them to be sounded in regard to the expedition against Mexico; that they were all ready to follow him, and he did not doubt that there existed in them the same disposition to sustain the rights of the Western States, in which they lived, against the impotent forces of the Federal government; that Mexico was to be assailed, in co-operation with the English fleet, by troops to be disembarked at Tampico or thereabout; and that the revolutionized Spanish possessions would be made republics.

To reveal such a plan was to destroy its chance of success; and in thus presenting himself before the Spanish minister Dayton appeared as a traitor not only to the Union, but also to the conspirators with whom he was engaged. Such a character was not likely to create confidence. Yrujo instantly saw that Burr stood behind Dayton; that England could not have encouraged the conspiracy, for, had she done so, the conspirators would never come to beg a few thousand dollars from Spain; and that the Mexican scheme, if it ever existed, must have been already abandoned, or it would not have been revealed. Dismissing the ex-senator with civility and a promise to talk with him further, Yrujo wrote to his Government a long account of the interview. He pointed at once to Clark as the person through whom Burr drew his information about Mexico. Yrujo was perplexed only by Jefferson's apparent blindness to the doings in the West. The marquis was a Spaniard; and for twenty years the people of the United States had talked of Spaniards with contempt. Even Jefferson freely assumed their faithlessness and paltriness; but surely if Yrujo had cared to concentrate in a few words his opinion of American political character, no American could have wondered if these few words, like a flash of lightning, left no living thing where they struck.

" I am sure," he wrote to Cevallos, " that the Administration will not let itself be deceived by Colonel Burr's wiles ; but I know that the President, although penetrating and detesting as well as fearing him, and for this reason, not only invites him to his table, but only about five days ago had a secret conference with him which lasted more than two hours, and in which I am confident there was as little good faith on the one side as there was on the other."

The assertion could not be denied. The White House rarely saw, within a few days' interval, two less creditable guests than Aaron Burr, fresh from confiding his plans to Anthony Merry, and Francesco de Miranda, openly engaged in a military attack from the port of New York upon the dominions of Spain.

Yrujo was at first inclined to distrust Dayton ; but Miranda's undertaking, which crossed Burr's plans, gave to the ex-senator the means of proving his good faith. Indeed, in a few days more, Dayton made a clean breast, admitting that England had disappointed Burr's expectations, and that Burr had authorized the offer to sell his services to Spain.

" I have had with him two very long conferences," wrote Yrujo three weeks later,[1] " in which he has told me that Colonel Burr will not treat with Miranda, whom he considers imprudent, and wanting in many qualities necessary for an undertaking of such magnitude as he

[1] Yrujo to Cevallos, Jan. 1, 1806 ; MSS. Spanish Archives.

has on hand.   Miranda has returned to New York, much piqued at finding that Colonel Burr was very determined to have nothing to do with him.   He also told me that Colonel Williamson, who was sent to London with the plan for the British ministry, not finding Mr. Pitt so warm as Lord Melville for the project of raising the Western States, had turned to plans in that capital, and showed, by the want of exactness in his correspondence, that he was not following up the object with the same zeal as at first he undertook it; that in consequence they were disposed to despatch to London a New York gentleman named Warton, well known for his intimacy with Burr, but that on the verge of his departure another plan suggested itself to Burr, which he seems rather inclined to execute.   This plan, excepting the attack on the Floridas, has the same object, which he, as well as his chief friends, hope may be put in execution even without foreign aid.   For one who does not know the country, its constitution, and, above all, certain localities, this plan would appear almost insane; but I confess, for my part, that in view of all the circumstances it seems to me easy to execute, although it will irritate the Atlantic States, especially those called central, — that is, Virginia, Maryland, Delaware, Pennsylvania, New Jersey, and New York.   It is beyond question that there exists in this country an infinite number of adventurers, without property, full of ambition, and ready to unite at once under the standard of a revolution which promises to better their lot.   Equally certain is it that Burr and his friends, without discovering their true object, have succeeded in getting the good-will of these men, and inspiring the greatest confidence among them in favor of Burr."

The "almost insane" plan which Dayton unfolded to the Spanish minister was nothing less than to introduce by degrees into the city of Washington a certain number of men in disguise, well armed, who, at a signal from Burr, were to seize the President, Vice-President, and the President of the Senate, — the substitute always named at the beginning of each session, in case of the death, illness, or absence of the two first. Having thus secured the heads of government, the conspirators were to seize the public money deposited in the Washington and Georgetown banks, and to take possession of the arsenal on the Eastern Branch. Burr hoped by this blow to delay or paralyze opposition, and perhaps to negotiate with the individual States an arrangement favorable to himself; but in the more probable case that he could not maintain himself at Washington, he would burn all the national vessels at the Navy Yard, except the two or three which were ready for service, and embarking on these with his followers and the treasure, he would sail for New Orleans and proclaim the emancipation of Louisiana and the Western States.

Wild as this scheme was, it occupied Burr's mind for the rest of the winter, and he made many efforts to draw discontented officers of the government into it. He sounded Commodore Truxton, without revealing his whole object; but to William Eaton, the hero of Derne, he opened himself with as much confidence as to Merry and Yrujo. Eaton was at Washington in January and February, 1806, sore at the manner in which his claims were treated by Congress, and extravagant in ideas of his own importance. To him Burr laid open the whole secret, even in regard to the plan for attacking Washington. The story was the same which had been told to Merry and Yrujo.[1] He spoke of Wilkinson as his second in command; of his son-in-law, Allston, as engaged in the enterprise; and of New Orleans as the capital of his Western empire, whence an expedition would be sent for the conquest of Mexico. The line of demarcation was to be the Alleghany Mountains; and although he expressed some doubts about Ohio, he declared himself certain of Kentucky and Tennessee.

" If he could gain over the marine corps and secure to his interests the naval commanders Truxton, Preble, Decatur, and others, he would turn Congress neck and heels out of doors, assassinate the President (or what amounted to that), and declare himself the protector of an energetic government."

The scheme of attacking Washington was merely an episode due to Burr's despair of British or Spanish aid. Burr was reduced to many devices in order to keep his conspiracy alive. December 12, immediately after the disappointing interview with Merry, and Dayton's first advance to Casa Yrujo, Burr wrote to Wilkinson a letter evidently intended to conceal his diplomatic disaster and to deceive his friend. He said that there would be no war with Spain, and fore-

[1] Deposition of General Eaton ; Life of William Eaton, p. 396.

told the peaceful course of Government.[1] " In case
of such warfare, Lee would have been commander-
in-chief. Truth, I assure you. He must you know
come from Virginia." As to the conspiracy, he reserved it for a few short lines, intelligible enough to
those who knew that New Orleans was to declare
its independence on the arrival of a British squadron in February, and that the revolutionary government would at once send a delegation to Natchez
or St. Louis to make a formal tender of military
command to General Wilkinson.

" On the subject of a certain speculation it is not
deemed material to write till the whole can be communicated. The circumstance referred to in a letter from
Ohio remains in suspense. The auspices, however, are
favorable, and it is believed that Wilkinson will give
audience to a delegation, composed of Adair and Dayton,
in February."

Meanwhile the Government asked no questions.
Denunciation of Burr and Wilkinson was dangerous ;
it was tried again and again with disastrous results.
Major Bruff, at St. Louis, who suspected the truth,
dared not bring such a charge against his superior
officer : [2] but a certain Judge Easton, to whom Burr
confided at St. Louis, ventured to write a letter to
a senator of the United States charging Wilkinson

[1] Burr to Wilkinson, Dec. 12, 1806 ; Wilkinson's Memoirs,
ii. Appendix, lxxxiv.

[2] Evidence of Major Bruff, Burr's Trial ; Annals of Congress,
1807–1808, p. 597.

with being concerned in Miranda's expedition; and was told in reply that the letter was burned, and that the writer should mind his own business, and take care how he meddled with men high in power and office. So thick an atmosphere of intrigue, especially in Spanish matters, was supposed to pervade the White House; men's minds were so befogged with public messages about a Spanish war and secret messages about peace, with private encouragement to Miranda and public punishment of Miranda's friends, with John Randolph's furious charges of duplicity and Madison's helpless silence under these charges,— that until the President himself should say the word, Burr, Wilkinson, Dayton, and their associates were safe, and might hatch treason in the face of all the world.

President Jefferson had already too many feuds on his hands, and Burr had still too many friends, to warrant rousing fresh reprisals at a time when the difficulties of the Administration were extreme. The President continued to countenance Burr in public, alleging in private that the people could be trusted to defeat his schemes. Doubtless the people could be trusted for that purpose, but they had instituted a government in order to provide themselves with proper machinery for such emergencies, and the President alone could set it in action. General Eaton made an attempt to put the President on his guard. He first consulted two leading Federalist Congressmen,— John Cotton Smith and Samuel Dana,— who advised him to hold his tongue, for his solitary word would not avail against the weight of Burr's character.[1] Nevertheless, in March, 1806, he called at the White House and saw the President.

" After a desultory conversation, in which I aimed to draw his attention to the West, I took the liberty of suggesting to the President that I thought Colonel Burr ought to be removed from the country, because I considered him dangerous in it. The President asked where he should send him. I said to England or Madrid. . . . The President, without any positive expression, in such a matter of delicacy, seemed to think the trust too important, and expressed something like a doubt about the integrity of Mr. Burr. I frankly told the President that perhaps no person had stronger grounds to suspect that integrity than I had ; but that I believed his pride of ambition had so predominated over his other passions that when placed on an eminence and put on his honor, a respect to himself would secure his fidelity. I perceived that the subject was disagreeable to the President ; and to bring him to my point in the shortest mode, and in a manner which would point to the danger, I said to him, if Colonel Burr was not disposed of, we should in eighteen months have an insurrection, if not a revolution, on the waters of the Mississippi. The President said he had too much confidence in the information, the integrity, and attachment of the people of that country to the Union, to admit any apprehensions of that kind."

If the President had confidence in the people of New Orleans, he had not shown it in framing a form

[1] Evidence of William Eaton, Burr's Trial; Annals of Congress, 1807–1808, pp. 511, 512.

of government for them; and if he admitted no apprehensions in March, 1806, he admitted many before
the year closed. In truth, he deceived himself. That
he was afraid of Burr and of the sympathy which
Burr's career had excited, was the belief of Burr himself, who responded to Jefferson's caution by a contempt so impudent as to seem even then almost in-
credible. Believing that the President dared not
touch him, Burr never cared to throw even a veil over
his treason. He used the President's name and the
names of his Cabinet officers as freely as though he
were President himself; and no one contradicted or
disavowed him. So matters remained at Washington
down to the close of the session.

"I detailed," said Eaton,[1] "the whole projects of Mr.
Burr to certain members of Congress. They believed
Colonel Burr capable of anything, and agreed that the
fellow ought to be hanged, but thought his projects too
chimerical, and his circumstances too desperate, to give
the subject the merit of serious consideration."

[1] Deposition of Jan. 26, 1807 ; Life of Eaton, p. 401.

CHAPTER XI.

THE death of Pitt destroyed all immediate possibility of drawing England into conspiracy with Burr, — if indeed a possibility had ever existed. The attempt to obtain money from Spain was equally hopeless. Except for Madison's conduct in receiving Miranda and refusing to receive Yrujo, Dayton would probably have obtained nothing from Spain; but the information he was able to give Yrujo in regard to Miranda's plans and proceedings deserved reward, and Dayton received at different times sums of money, amounting in all to about three thousand dollars, from the Spanish treasury. Dayton's private necessities required much larger sums.

Burr was also ruined. He could not return to New York, where an indictment hung over his head. Conspiracy was easier than poverty; but conspiracy without foreign aid was too wild a scheme for other men to join. Jefferson might at that moment have stopped Burr's activity by sending word privately to him and his friends that their projects must be dropped; but Jefferson, while closing every other path, left that of conspiracy open to Burr, who followed it only with much difficulty. In order to retain any friends or followers he was obliged to deceive them all, and entangle himself and them in an elaborate network of falsehood. Dayton alone knew the truth, and helped him to deceive.

April 16, 1806, a few days before the adjournment of Congress, Burr wrote to Wilkinson a letter implying that Wilkinson had required certain conditions and an enlargement of the scheme; Burr assured him that his requirements, which probably concerned aid from Truxton, Preble, Eaton, and Decatur, had been fully satisfied : —

" The execution of our project is postponed till December. Want of water in Ohio rendered movement impracticable; other reasons rendered delay expedient. The association is enlarged, and comprises all that Wilkinson could wish. Confidence limited to a few. Though this delay is irksome, it will enable us to move with more certainty and dignity. Burr will be throughout the United States this summer. Administration is damned which Randolph aids. Burr wrote you a long letter last December, replying to a short one deemed very silly. Nothing has been heard from the Brigadier since October. Is Cushing and Porter right? Address Burr at Washington." [1]

Burr's letters to Wilkinson were always in cipher, and mysteriously worded; but in this despatch nothing was unintelligible. Wilkinson afterward explained that he was himself the " Brigadier," and the two names were those of officers under his command.

[1] Wilkinson's Memoirs, ii. Appendix, lxxxiii.

The same western mail which carried this letter to Wilkinson carried another to Blennerhassett, inviting him to join in a " speculation," which would " not be commenced before December, if ever." Probably Burr made many other efforts to obtain money from petty sources; he certainly exerted himself to delude the Spanish government into lending him assistance. Hitherto he had left this task to Dayton, his secretary of state, but May 14, 1806, the Spanish minister wrote to Don Pedro Cevallos,[1] —

" The principal [Burr] has opened himself to me ; and the communications I have had with him confirm me in the idea, not only of the probability, but even of the facility, of his success, under certain circumstances. To insure it, some pecuniary aid on our part and on that of France is wanted. I have been careful to be very circumspect in my answers, and have not compromised myself in any manner; but when I return to Spain next spring I shall be bearer of the whole plan, with the details that may be wanted. There will also arrive in Spain before long, more or less simultaneously with me though by different ways, two or three very respectable persons, both from Louisiana and from Kentucky and Tennessee, with the same object. They all consider the interests of these countries as united and in conformity with those of Spain and France ; but the principal, or more correctly the principals, here do not wish to open themselves to the Emperor Napoleon's minister [Turreau], as they lack confidence in him. Consequently, it will be proper either not to communicate the matter at all

[1] Yrujo to Cevallos, May 14, 1806; MSS. Spanish Archives.

to that government, or to do it with the intimation that
its representative here shall not have the least notice of
it; for, I repeat, they have no confidence in him, and
this has been a condition imposed on me in the communications I have received."

Finding Yrujo obstinate in refusing to advance
money, Burr tried to alarm him by pretending to
take up again the scheme of attacking Florida and
Mexico. June 9, 1806, Yrujo wrote another long
despatch on the subject. Burr, he said, had suddenly
ceased to visit him as frequently as usual, and Dayton
had explained the coldness as due to Burr's belief
that the new Administration in England would be
more liberal and zealous than that of Pitt. Dayton
added that Burr was drawing up new instructions
for Williamson; that he had even decided to send
Bollman to London to invite co-operation from the
British government in an attack on the Spanish possessions. Dayton professed to have acted as the protector of Spain from Burr's unprincipled ambition.

"Dayton told me [1] he had observed to Burr that although he (Burr) was assuredly the principal, yet a plan
of this nature ought to be put in deliberation in the cabinet council which certain chiefs are to hold in New Orleans in the month of December next, and that for his
own part he thought this idea unjust and impolitic; to
which Burr answered that they would always be able to
alter the plan as circumstances should require, and that
in fact this point, or at least the direction to be given to
it, would be determined in New Orleans. Dayton told

[1] Yrujo to Cevallos, June 9, 1806; MSS. Spanish Archives.

me that he would oppose with all his strength measures of this nature, and that he knew General Wilkinson, who was to be a member of the Congress, would make the same opposition; and that in order to drive the idea of such a temptation out of Burr's head, and of other people's also, it would be well for us to reinforce our garrisons at Pensacola and Mobile, and that then the circumstance of our respectable condition of defence might be used as a weighty argument for abandoning such a project. After holding this conference with me, Dayton returned to his residence; and before starting, wrote me a note to say that the night before Burr had read him the instructions to be given to Bollman, and that they were of the tenor indicated to me."

Godoy and Cevallos were hardly so imbecile as to pay for creating at New Orleans a new American empire more dangerous to Spanish possessions than the peaceful republic over which Jefferson presided at Washington. Don Pedro Cevallos read Yrujo's despatches with great interest. At first he even hinted that if the United States were bent on forcing a war with Spain, these adventurers, in case of actual hostilities, might be made useful;[1] but this suggestion was accompanied by many warnings to Yrujo not to commit himself or to contribute money, and at last by a flat announcement that the King would not in any way encourage Burr's designs.[2]

[1] Cevallos to Casa Yrujo, March 28, 1806; MSS. Spanish Archives.

[2] Cevallos to Casa Yrujo, July 12, 1806; MSS. Spanish Archives.

The conspirators were in a worse position as regarded England. By a fatal stroke of ill-luck, Merry's despatch of Nov. 25, 1805, written to be read in secrecy by the Tory Lord Mulgrave, was received at the Foreign Office Feb. 2, 1806, ten days after Pitt's death, and was probably opened by Charles James Fox, — almost the last man in England to whom Merry would have willingly shown it. The only answer received by Merry reached Washington about June 1, 1806, and consisted in the dry announcement that his Majesty had been pleased to listen favorably to Mr. Merry's request for a recall, and had appointed the Hon. David Montague Erskine as his successor.

Merry complained piteously that he had never suggested a wish to be recalled, that he had indeed the strongest desire to remain, and felt himself greatly aggrieved at his treatment; but Fox was remorseless, and Merry could only prepare for Erskine's arrival. Smarting under this sudden reproof, Merry held his parting interview with Burr. Doubtless it was as little cheerful on one side as on the other; but Merry did not think himself required to give an immediate or a minute account of it to Fox. He waited until Erskine's arrival, and then, in one of his last despatches, Nov. 2, 1806, after Burr had begun his operations in the West, Merry wrote,[1] —

"I saw this gentleman [Burr] for the last time at this place [Washington] in the month of June last, when he

[1] Merry to C. J. Fox, June 1, 1806; MSS. British Archives.

made particular inquiry whether I had received any answer from my Government to the propositions he had requested me to transmit to them, and lamented exceedingly that I had not, because he, and the persons connected with him at New Orleans, would now, though very reluctantly, be under the necessity of addressing themselves to the French and Spanish governments. He added, however, that the disposition of the inhabitants of the Western country, and particularly Louisiana, to separate themselves from the American Union was so strong that the attempt might be made with every prospect of success without any foreign assistance whatever; and his last words to me were that, with or without such support, it certainly would be made very shortly."

After receiving this rebuff from England, Burr and Dayton needed singular impudence to threaten Yrujo with the terror of Charles James Fox; but impudence had become their only resource. Every step taken thenceforward by the conspirators was taken by means of a new imposture; until at last they became petty swindlers who lived from day to day by cheating each other. How flagrant their imposture was, has been partly shown in their attempt to deceive Yrujo; but their treatment of Wilkinson was far more dishonest.

Toward the end of July, 1806, Burr had accomplished all that could be done in the East, and prepared to begin his campaign to New Orleans. By strenuous efforts money had been raised to set the subordinate adventurers in motion. Among these were Erick Bollman, famous for an attempt to rescue

Lafayette from confinement at Olmütz; a French
officer named De Pestre, or Dupiester; Samuel Swartwout, a younger brother of Robert; and finally young
Peter V. Ogden, a nephew of Dayton. The time had
come when each actor must take his place, and must
receive orders as to the *rôle* he was to play.

Of all Burr's intimates, Wilkinson was not only the
most important, but also the most doubtful. He had
hung back and had made conditions. Since October,
1805, nothing had been heard from him, and his last
letter had contained objections " deemed very silly."
At last a letter, dated May 13, arrived. This letter
never saw the light; afterward, at the trial, Wilkinson challenged its production, and accused Burr of
falsehood in asserting that it had been destroyed at
Wilkinson's request or with his knowledge. Only
one conclusion might be taken as certain in regard
to its contents, — they did not suit the situation of
Dayton and Burr.

Dayton's reply was dated July 24, 1806, and was
sent by his nephew, Peter V. Ogden, to Wilkinson.

" It is now well ascertained that you are to be dis-
placed in next session," wrote Dayton, working on his
old friend's pride and fears. " Jefferson will affect to
yield reluctantly to the public sentiment, but yield he
will. Prepare yourself, therefore, for it. You know the
rest. You are not a man to despair, or even despond,
especially when such prospects offer in another quarter.
Are you ready? Are your numerous associates ready?
Wealth and glory! Louisiana and Mexico!"

Together with this exhortation from Dayton, Burr sent a cipher despatch, afterward famous as the key to the whole conspiracy. Published at different times with varying versions, as suited Wilkinson's momentary objects, the correct reading probably ran very nearly as follows : —

" July 29, 1806. Your letter, postmarked 13th May, is received. At length I have obtained funds, and have actually commenced. The Eastern detachments, from different points and under different pretences, will rendezvous on the Ohio 1st of November. Everything internal and external favors our views. Naval protection of England is secured. Truxton is going to Jamaica to arrange with the admiral on that station. It will meet us at the Mississippi. England, a navy of the United States, are ready to join, and final orders are given to my friends and followers. It will be a host of choice spirits. Wilkinson shall be second to Burr only ; Wilkinson shall dictate the rank and promotion of his officers. Burr will proceed westward 1st August, never to return. With him goes his daughter ; the husband will follow in October, with a corps of worthies. Send forthwith an intelligent and confidential friend with whom Burr may confer ; he shall return immediately with further interesting details ; this is essential to concert and harmony of movement. Send a list of all persons known to Wilkinson west of the mountains who could be useful, with a note delineating their characters. By your messenger send me four or five commissions of your officers, which you can borrow under any pretence you please ; they shall be returned faithfully. Already are orders given to the contractor to forward six months' provisions to points

Wilkinson may name; this shall not be used until the last moment, and then under proper injunctions. Our object, my dear friend, is brought to a point so long desired. Burr guarantees the result with his life and honor, with the lives and honor and the fortunes of hundreds, the best blood of our country. Burr's plan of operation is to move down rapidly from the Falls, on the 15th of November, with the first five hundred or a thousand men, in light boats now constructing for that purpose; to be at Natchez between the 5th and 15th of December, there to meet you; there to determine whether it will be expedient in the first instance to seize on or pass by Baton Rouge. On receipt of this, send Burr an answer. Draw on Burr for all expenses, etc. The people of the country to which we are going are prepared to receive us; their agents, now with Burr, say that if we will protect their religion, and will not subject them to a foreign Power, that in three weeks all will be settled. The gods invite us to glory and fortune; it remains to be seen whether we deserve the boon. The bearer of this goes express to you. He is a man of inviolable honor and perfect discretion, formed to execute rather than project, capable of relating facts with fidelity, and incapable of relating them otherwise; he is thoroughly informed of the plans and intentions of Burr, and will disclose to you as far as you require, and no further. He has imbibed a reverence for your character, and may be embarrassed in your presence; put him at ease, and he will satisfy you."

Had Burr and Dayton not felt strong reason to doubt Wilkinson's course, they would not have invented a tissue of falsehoods such as these letters contained. So far as concerned Wilkinson's future conduct, no one could deny that this gross deception set him free from any ties that might have previously bound him to Dayton or Burr.

Furnished with these and other letters almost equally compromising, Ogden and Swartwout, at the end of July, started on their way. Swartwout was directed to see Adair in Kentucky, and to deliver to him despatches, the contents of which have never been made known, but were doubtless identical with the letters to Wilkinson. At the same time Erick Bollman started by sea with similar despatches for New Orleans.

Early in August Burr followed, taking with him his daughter Mrs. Allston, and his chief of staff Colonel De Pestre. After crossing the mountains he threw aside ordinary caution. At Canonsburg, about fifteen miles beyond Pittsburg, he stopped at the house of an old friend, Colonel Morgan, and there so freely asserted the imbecility of the Federal government and the certainty of a speedy separation of the Western States from the Eastern, that Morgan thought himself bound to give President Jefferson a warning.

The conversation at Canonsburg took place in the afternoon and evening of August 22. A few days afterward Burr arrived at Blennerhassett's island, where he found the owner waiting with enthusiasm to receive him. Of all the eager dupes with whom Burr had to deal, this intelligent and accomplished Irish gentleman was the most simple. After wasting

half his property on his island, he discovered that he
had left himself not more than thirty or forty thousand dollars to live upon; and this small property
was invested in funds which produced so little as to
leave him always embarrassed. He wished ardently
to make his fortune by some bold speculation; and
Burr had no more pressing necessity than to obtain
the funds which Blennerhassett burned to invest.
Burr said to Blennerhassett in effect what he said to
Wilkinson; but Blennerhassett was less able than
Wilkinson to detect falsehood. The actual speculation which was to make Blennerhassett's fortune
seemed certain of success. Burr had invented more
than one way of getting money; and among his
various expedients none was more ingenious than that
of buying a certain Spanish claim, known as the
Bastrop grant, covering an immense district on the
Red River, and supposed to be owned in part by one
Lynch in Kentucky. Burr had undertaken to buy
Lynch's interest for forty thousand dollars, of which
only four thousand or five thousand dollars need be
paid in money; and he persuaded Blennerhassett
that on the most moderate estimate, they could reap
from it the profit of a million. Blennerhassett was
assured that before the end of the year Louisiana
would be independent, with Burr for its ruler, under
the protection of England. Wilkinson and the United
States army were pledged to accept the revolution
and to support Burr. Tennessee was secured; and
though Kentucky and Ohio were doubtful, they would

end by following Tennessee. The government at Washington would fall to pieces, and the new empire under a stronger government, would rise at once to power. Then Bastrop's grant would take character; its actual cheapness was due to doubts as to its validity: but the moment its validity was decided by the new government, all whose members would be interested in it, the value of the grant would become enormous; emigration would be directed to the spot, and Blennerhassett's fortune would be vast. He would, meanwhile, go at once as minister to England, with Erick Bollman for secretary of legation.[1]

In an incredibly short time Blennerhasset's head was turned. Unluckily for him, his wife's head was turned even more easily than his own; and the charms of Theodosia Allston, who became a guest at the island, dazzled the eyes of both. Before Burr had been two days in the house, Blennerhassett was so enthusiastic a supporter of the scheme that he set himself to work, under Burr's eye, to publish a series of essays in order to show the State of Ohio that disunion was an infallible cure for all its natural or acquired ills. The first of these essays was quickly finished, taken to Marietta, and printed in the "Ohio Gazette" of September 4 under the signature "Querist."

September 2, before the "Querist" appeared, Burr continued his journey down the river to Cincinnati, where he arrived September 4, and remained a few

[1] Blennerhassett Papers, p. 351.

days with Senator Smith, talking freely about the impotence of the government, the rights and wrongs of the Western people, and their inducements to set up a separate empire. September 10 he crossed the river to Lexington in Kentucky, and shortly afterward went to Nashville in Tennessee.

Owing chiefly to the friendship of Andrew Jackson, the town of Nashville was strongly attached to Burr, and was supposed to favor the disunion scheme. Tennessee was the only State which Burr always claimed positively as his own. Whether he had better grounds for his confidence in Jackson than for his faith in Wilkinson and Daniel Clark might be doubted; but Tennessee was at least vehement in hatred of the Spaniards. The Spaniards were pressing close against Wilkinson's little force at Natchitoches, and Burr made use of the threatened war in order to cover his own scheme. September 27 a public dinner was given to him at Nashville, and Jackson offered as a toast the old sentiment of 1798: "Millions for defence; not a cent for tribute." A few days later Burr returned to Kentucky; and within a week suddenly appeared in the newspaper at Nashville a strange proclamation signed "Andrew Jackson, Major-General Second Division," and dated Oct. 4, 1806, in which the brigade commanders were ordered to place their brigades at once on such a footing as would enable them on the shortest notice to supply their quotas "when the government and constituted authorities of our country" should require them to march. This unauthorized step was commonly supposed to be taken in the interest of Burr's conspiracy, and compromised Jackson gravely in the eyes of the Government at Washington.

Meanwhile Theodosia Allston and her husband had been left in charge of the Blennerhassetts, while Blennerhassett himself behaved as though he were a village school-boy playing the part of chieftain in an imaginary feudal castle. He went about the country raising recruits and buying supplies, chattering to every young and active man he met about the expedition which was to make their fortunes. He confided in his gardener, a simple, straightforward fellow named Peter Taylor, "that Colonel Burr would be king of Mexico, and that Mrs. Allston would be queen of Mexico whenever Colonel Burr died." He added that Burr " had a great many friends in the Spanish territory ; two thousand Roman Catholic priests were enlisted in his corps ; that those priests and the societies which belonged to them were a strong party ; that the Spaniards, like the French, had got tired of their government and wanted to swap it ; that the British were also friends to this expedition ; and that he was the very man who was to go to England on this piece of business for Colonel Burr." When at the subsequent trial Taylor told this tale, the world was incredulous, and insisted upon disbelieving his story ; but Blennerhassett's papers proved the extent of his delusion. By common consent the Blennerhassetts and Allstons agreed that Theodosia was to inherit the

empire from her father; but doubts existed whether
Allston could take the crown as Theodosia's husband.
"I will win it by a better title," he cried, — "by my
deeds in council and in field!"[1]   Mrs. Blennerhassett was impatient to exchange her solitary island for
the court of her young empress; and Blennerhassett
longed to set sail as minister for England with Erick
Bollman for secretary of legation.   Under the influence of this intoxication, Blennerhassett offered to
advance money to the extent of all his property for
Burr's use if Allston would give him a written and
sealed guaranty to a certain amount; which Allston
did.[2]

Leaving his wife at the island, while fifteen boats
were building at Marietta and kilns for baking bread
were constructed on the island itself, Blennerhassett
went with the Allstons down the river to Lexington,
and there rejoined Burr on his return from Nashville,
about October 1.   No time had been lost.   The boats
building at Marietta would carry about five hundred
men; others to be built elsewhere would carry five
hundred more.   Recruiting went rapidly forward.
Finally, the purchase-money for Lynch's interest in
Bastrop's grant, about four or five thousand dollars,
was paid; and Blennerhassett congratulated himself
on owning a share in four hundred thousand acres
of land in the heart of Louisiana.

[1] Blennerhassett Papers, p. 333; Blennerhassett to Allston,
March 2, 1811.

[2] Blennerhassett Papers, pp. 397, 535.

To communicate with his friends in New York and Philadelphia, Burr sent De Pestre October 25, with directions to report the movements of the Western conspirators to the Marquis of Casa Yrujo, as well as to Swartwout and Dayton. Burr gave De Pestre to understand that one object of his mission was to blind the Spanish minister in regard to the schemes against Mexico and Florida; in reality De Pestre's mission was probably for the purpose of raising money. Yrujo was already well informed from other sources. November 10, before De Pestre's arrival, the Marquis wrote to his Government that some five hundred men were collecting on the upper Ohio to move down the river in squads : [1] —

" Colonel Burr will go down with them under pretext of establishing them on a great land-purchase he is supposed to have made. In passing Cincinnati they expect to get possession of five thousand stand of arms which the government deposited there at the time of its differences with us about the navigation of the Mississippi. After thus dropping the mask, this armed troop will follow down the course of the Mississippi. Colonel Burr will stop at Natchez, where he will wait until the Assembly of New Orleans has met, which will happen at once ; and in this meeting (*junta*) they will declare the independence of the Western States, and will invite Burr meanwhile to place himself at the head of their government. He will accept the offer, will descend to New Orleans, and will set to work, clothed in a character which the people will have given him. I understand

[1] Yrujo to Cevallos, Nov. 10. 1806 ; MSS. Spanish Archives.

that Colonel Burr has already written the declaration of independence, and that it is couched in the same terms that the States adopted in theirs against Great Britain. This circumstance is the more notable inasmuch as the actual President was the person who drew it up in 1776. When Burr made the project of acting in agreement with England and seizing the Floridas, he expected to master them with troops that should accompany him from Baton Rouge. Although I am assured that this project is abandoned, and that on the contrary he wishes to live on good terms with Spain, I have written to Governor Folch of West Florida to be on his guard; and although I am persuaded that by means of Governor Folch's connection with General Wilkinson, he must be perfectly informed of the state of things and of Burr's intentions, I shall write to-day or to-morrow another letter to the Governor of Baton Rouge to be on the alert."

Yrujo believed that Wilkinson, the General in command of the American army, then supposed to be on the point of attacking the Spanish force in his front, was secretly and regularly communicating with the Spanish Governor of West Florida.

Burr was engaged in deceiving every one; but his attempt to deceive Yrujo, if seriously meant, was the least comprehensible of all his manœuvres. December 4 the Spanish minister wrote to his Government another despatch which betrayed his perplexity at Burr's conduct: —

"I am positively assured," he said, "that from one day to another will embark from New York for New Orleans, to join Colonel Burr in Louisiana, three of his intimate friends, depositaries of his whole confidence; namely, Mr. Swartwout, lately marshal of the district of New York, a certain Dr. Erwin, and the famous Colonel Smith, the same who was implicated in the business of Miranda, and whose son went out as an aide-de-camp of that adventurer. Accordingly I wrote to the governors of both Floridas and to the Viceroy of Mexico, giving them a general idea of this affair, and recommending them to watch the movements of Colonel Burr and of his adventurers. This is an excess of precaution, since by this time they must not only know through the New Orleans and Natchez newspapers of the projects attributed to Colonel Burr, but also through the confidential channel of the No. 13 of the Marquis of Casa Calvo's cipher with the Prince of Peace, who is one of the conspirators, and who is to contribute very efficaciously to the execution of the scheme in case it shall be carried into effect."

The person designated as No. 13 in the cipher used between Casa Calvo and Godoy was the general-in-chief of the American forces, Wilkinson. The Marquis's despatch next mentioned the arrival of De Pestre, who appeared about November 27 at Yrujo's house : —

"About a week ago a former French officer came to see me, one of Burr's partisans, who came from Kentucky in search of various articles for the execution of his undertaking. . . . This officer handed me a letter from Colonel Burr, in which, after recommending him to me, the writer said simply that as this person had lately visited those States, he could give me information about them worthy of my curiosity. The date of this letter was Lexington, October 25."

De Pestre gave to Yrujo the assurance that all was going well with the undertaking; but the special message he was charged to deliver seemed to be the following: —

" He also told me, on the part of the Colonel, that I should soon hear that he meant to attack Mexico, but that I was not to believe such rumors; that on the contrary his plans were limited to the emancipation of the Western States, and that it was necessary to circulate this rumor in order to hide the true design of his armaments and of the assemblages of men which could no longer be kept secret; that Upper and Lower Louisiana, the States of Tennessee and Ohio, stood ready and ripe for his plans, but that the State of Kentucky was much divided; and as this is the most important in numbers and population, an armed force must be procured strong enough to control the party there which should be disposed to offer resistance. He added, on Burr's part, that as soon as the revolution should be complete, he should treat with Spain in regard to boundaries, and would conclude this affair to the entire satisfaction of Spain; meanwhile he wished me to write to the Governor of West Florida to diminish the burdens on Americans who navigate the Mobile River, and ask him, when the explosion should take place, to stop the courier or couriers who might be despatched by the friends of Government from New Orleans."

Burr's message caused Yrujo to warn all the Spanish officials in Florida, Texas, and Mexico that " although

No. 13 seems to have acted in good faith hitherto, his fidelity could not be depended upon if he had a greater interest in violating it, and that therefore they must be cautious in listening to him and be very vigilant in regard to events that would probably happen in their neighborhood." De Pestre's mission made Yrujo more suspicious than ever, and he spared no precaution to render impossible the success of any attack on Florida or Mexico.

After De Pestre had visited New York, he returned to Philadelphia, and December 13 again called upon Yrujo.

"He told me," reported Yrujo,[1] "that he had seen Mr. Swartwout in New York, whom he had informed of Burr's wish that he, as well as Dr. Erwin, Colonel Smith, and Captain Lewis, who was captain of the merchant ship 'Emperor' and brother of the captain of Miranda's vessel the 'Leander,' should set out as soon as possible for New Orleans. Likewise he instructed him, on the part of the colonel, that the youths enlisted to serve as officers should set out as soon as possible for their posts. These, my informant told me, are different. Some two or three of them, the quickest and keenest, go to Washington to observe the movements of Government, to keep their friends in good disposition, and to despatch expresses with news of any important disposition or occurrence. Three go to Norfolk to make some despatch of provisions. A good number of them will go direct to Charleston to take command as officers, and see to the embarkation of the numerous

[1] Yrujo to Cevallos, Dec. 16, 1806; MSS. Spanish Archives.

recruits whom Colonel Burr's son-in-law has raised in
South Carolina. He himself will then have returned
there from Kentucky, and will embark with them for
New Orleans. The rest will embark directly for that
city from New York."

Yrujo could not see the feebleness of the conspiracy. So far as he knew, the story might be true;
and although he had been both forewarned and fore-
armed, he could not but feel uneasy lest Burr should
make a sudden attack on West Florida or Texas. The
Spanish minister was able to protect Spanish interests
if they were attacked; but he would have preferred
to prevent an attack, and this could be done by the
United States government alone. The indifference of
President Jefferson to Burr's movements astounded
many persons besides Yrujo. " It is astonishing,"
wrote Merry in November,[1] " that the Government
here should have remained so long in ignorance of
the intended design as even not to know with certainty at this moment the object of the preparations
which they have learned are now making." Merry
would have been still more astonished had he been
told that the President was by no means ignorant of
Burr's object; and Yrujo might well be perplexed to
see that ignorant or not, the President had taken no
measure for the defence of New Orleans, and that the
time had passed when any measure could be taken.
The city was in Wilkinson's hands. Even of the five
small gunboats which were meant to be stationed at

[1] Merry to C. J. Fox, Nov. 2, 1806; MSS. British Archives.

the mouth of the Mississippi, only one was actually there. That Burr and Wilkinson should meet resistance at New Orleans was not to be imagined. Yrujo saw no chance of checking them except in Ohio and Kentucky.

CHAPTER XII.

HAD Burr succeeded in carrying out his original plan of passing the Falls of the Ohio as early as November 15, he might have reached New Orleans with all his force; but he made too many delays, and tried too far the patience of Ohio. October 1 he returned from Nashville to Lexington, where he was joined by Blennerhassett and Allston. From that moment he was beset by difficulties and growing opposition.

As yet the Government at Washington had not moved, and Burr freely said that his military preparations were made with its knowledge and for the probable event of war with Spain; but he had not foreseen that these tactics might rouse against him the class of men from whom he had least reason to expect opposition. In Kentucky a respectable body of old Federalists still existed, with Humphrey Marshall at their head. The United States District Attorney, Joseph H. Daveiss, was also a Federalist, left in office by Jefferson. Burr's admirers were Republicans, so numerous that the President shrank from alienating them by denouncing Burr, while they in their turn would not desert Burr until the

President denounced him. The Federalists saw here a chance to injure their opponents, and used it.

As early as the year 1787 Governor Miró, the Spanish ruler of Louisiana, tried to organize a party in Kentucky for establishing an independent empire west of the Alleghanies under the protection of Spain. His chief agent for that purpose was James Wilkinson.[1] The movement received no popular support, and failed; but during the next ten years the Spanish governors who succeeded Miró maintained relations with Wilkinson and his friends, always hoping that some change in American politics would bring their project into favor. Godoy's policy of conciliation with America crossed these intrigues. His treaty of 1795 did much to neutralize them, but his delivery of Natchez in 1798 did more. The settlement of boundary came at a moment when Kentucky, under the lead of Jefferson and Breckenridge, seemed about to defy the United States government, and when the celebrated Kentucky Resolutions promised to draw the Western people into the arms of Spain. Talleyrand's indignation at Godoy's conduct[2] was not more acute than the disgust felt by the Spanish officials at New Orleans.

The Spanish intrigues among the Republicans of Kentucky were not wholly unknown to the Federalists in that State; and as time went on, Humphrey Marshall and Daveiss obtained evidence warranting

---

[1] Gayarré's Louisiana; Spanish Domination, pp. 192–199.
[2] See History of First Administration, p. 240.

an assault on the Republicans most deeply implicated.[1] The attempt was a matter of life and death
to the Spanish pensioners; and in a society so
clannish as that of Kentucky, violence was not only
to be feared, but to be counted upon. Daveiss took
the risks of personal revenge, and laid his plans
accordingly.

Burr's appearance on the Ohio and at St. Louis in
Wilkinson's company during the summer of 1805
called attention to the old Spanish conspiracy, and
gave Daveiss the opportunity he wanted. As early
as Jan. 10, 1806, while Burr was still struggling
at Washington to save his plot from collapse for
want of foreign aid, and while John Randolph was
beginning his invectives in Congress, the district-
attorney wrote to the President a private letter
denouncing the old Spanish plot, and declaring that
it was still alive.[2] "A separation of the Union in
favor of Spain is the object *finally*. I know not
what are the means." Assuming that Jefferson was
ignorant of the facts, because he had " appointed
General Wilkinson as Governor of St. Louis, who,
I am convinced, has been for years, and now is,
a pensioner of Spain," Daveiss asserted his own
knowledge, and contented himself with a general
warning; —

---

[1] Marshall's History of Kentucky, ii. 376–384.

[2] Daveiss to Jefferson, Jan. 10, 1806; View of the President's Conduct, by J. H. Daveiss, 1807. Clark's Proofs, pp.
177–179.

" This plot is laid wider than you imagine. Mention the subject to no man from the Western country, however high in office he may be. Some of them are deeply tainted with this treason. I hate duplicity of expression ; but on this subject I am not authorized to be explicit, nor is it necessary. You will despatch some fit person into the Orleans country to inquire."

February 10 Daveiss wrote again calling attention to Burr's movements during the previous summer, and charging both him and Wilkinson with conspiracy.[1] At about the time when these letters arrived, the President received another warning from Eaton. The air was full of denunciations, waiting only for the President's leave to annihilate the conspirators under popular contempt. A word quietly written by Jefferson to one or two persons in the Western country would have stopped Burr short in his path, and would have brought Wilkinson abjectly on his knees. A slight change in the military and naval arrangements at New Orleans would have terrified the creoles into good behavior, and would have made Daniel Clark denounce the conspiracy.

The President showed Daveiss's letter to Gallatin, Madison, and Dearborn ; but he did not take its advice, and did not, in his Cabinet memoranda of October 22,[2] mention it among his many sources of information. February 15 he wrote to

[1] Daveiss to Jefferson, Feb. 10, 1806 ; View, etc.   Cf. Marshall's History of Kentucky, ii. 401.

[2] See p. 278.

Daveiss [1] a request to communicate all he knew on
the subject.   No other acts followed, nor was either
Wilkinson or Burr put under surveillance.

Perhaps this was what Daveiss wished; for if
Jefferson pursued his course much further, he was
certain to compromise himself in appearing to protect
Burr and Wilkinson.   Daveiss not only continued to
write letter after letter denouncing Wilkinson to the
President, without receiving answer or acknowledgment; he not only made a journey to St. Louis in
order to collect evidence, and on his return to Kentucky wrote in July to the President that Burr's object was " to cause a revolt of the Spanish provinces,
and a severance of all the Western States and Territories from the Union, to coalesce and form one government," — but he also took a new step, of which
he did not think himself obliged to inform the President in advance.   He established at Frankfort a weekly
newspaper, edited by a man so poor in character and
means that for some slight gain in notoriety he
could afford to risk a worthless life.   John Wood
was a newspaper hack, not quite so successful as
Cheetham and Duane, or so vile as Callender.   Having in 1801 written a " History of the last Administration," after getting from Colonel Burr, by working
upon his vanity, an offer to buy and suppress the book,
it was probably Wood who furnished Cheetham with
the details of the transaction, and connived at Cheet-

---

[1] Jefferson to Daveiss, Feb. 15, 1806; View, etc.   Clark's
Proofs, p. 179.

ham's "Narrative of the Suppression," in order to give notoriety to himself. Cheetham's "Narrative" called for a reply, and Wood in 1802 printed a "Correct Statement." Both pamphlets were contemptible; but Cheetham was supported by the Clintons, while Wood could find no one to pay for his literary wares. He drifted to Richmond, and thence across the mountains; until, in the winter of 1805–1806, he dropped quietly, unnoticed, into the village of Frankfort, in Kentucky. Humphrey Marshall and District Attorney Daveiss needed such a man.

July 4, 1806, appeared at Frankfort the first number of the "Western World," — a weekly newspaper edited by John Wood. The society of Kentucky was alarmed and irritated to find that the "Western World" seemed to have no other object for its existence than to drag the old Spanish conspiracy to light. Passions were soon deeply stirred by the persistency and vehemence with which this pretended Republican newspaper clung to the subject and cried for an investigation. Wood had no fancy for being made the object of assassination, but he was given a fighting colleague named Street; and while Wood hid himself, Street defended the office. In spite of several attempts to drive Street away or to kill him, the "Western World" persevered in its work, until October 15 it published an appeal to the people, founded on Blennerhassett's "Querist" and on the existence of a Spanish Association. Meanwhile two men in high position dreaded exposure, — Judge

Sebastian, of the Court of Appeals of Kentucky, and Judge Innis, of the United States District Court.

Daveiss was right in thinking the Spanish conspiracy of 1787–1798 closely allied with Burr's conspiracy of 1805. In striking at Sebastian and Innis, he threw consternation into the ranks of Burr's friends, all of whom were more or less familiar with the Spanish intrigue. Senator Adair, bolder than the rest, stood by Wilkinson and defied exposure; but the greater number of Wilkinson's accomplices were paralyzed. Daveiss gave them no respite. In October Burr's appearance in Kentucky offered a chance to press his advantage. Jefferson's persistent silence and inaction left the energetic district-attorney free to do what he liked; and nothing short of compromising the Administration satisfied his ambition.

Burr passed the month of October in Kentucky; but his preparations were far from complete. The delay was probably due to the time consumed in getting Blennerhassett's money. At last Burr paid to Lynch the purchase-money of four or five thousand dollars for Bastrop's grant. He had already ordered the construction of boats and enlistment of men at various points on the Ohio, and especially at Marietta, near Blennerhassett's island; but he waited too long before beginning operations on the Cumberland, for not till November 3 did Andrew Jackson at Nashville receive a letter from Burr, inclosing three thousand dollars in Kentucky bank-notes, with orders for the building of five large boats, the purchase of supplies, and the enlistment of recruits, — all of which was promptly undertaken by Jackson, but required more time than could be spared by Burr.

Meanwhile Burr's affairs were going ill in the State of Ohio. Blennerhassett's foolish " Querist," and the more foolish conversation of both Blennerhassett and Burr, combined with the assaults of the " Western World," drew so much attention to the armaments at the island that Mrs. Blennerhassett, left alone while her husband was with Allston and Burr in Kentucky, became alarmed, and thought it necessary to send them a warning. October 20 she wrote to Burr that he could not return with safety. Thinking the note too important to be trusted to the post, and ignorant of Burr's address, she sent her gardener, Peter Taylor, on horseback, through Chillicothe, to Cincinnati, with orders to ask Senator Smith for the address. Taylor reached Cincinnati October 23, after three days of travel, and went, according to his mistress's orders, directly to Senator Smith's house, which was in the same building with his store, — for Smith was a storekeeper and army contractor. The senator was already too deeply compromised with Burr, and his courage had begun to fail. At first he denied knowledge of Burr or Blennerhassett. In Taylor's words, " He allowed he knew nothing of either of them ; that I must be mistaken ; this was not the place. I said, ' No ; this was the right place, — Mr. John Smith, storekeeper, Cincinnati.' " In the end, Smith took him upstairs, and gave him, with every injunc-

tion of secrecy, a letter to be delivered to Burr at
Lexington. Taylor reached Lexington October 25,
found Burr, delivered his letters, and candidly added:
"If you come up our way the people will shoot you."
The following Monday, October 27, the gardener
started on his return, taking Blennerhassett with him,
and leaving Burr at Lexington to face the storms that
threatened from many quarters at once.

The impossibility of returning to the island was but
one warning; another came from Senator Smith, who
dreaded exposure. The letter he sent by Peter Taylor, dated October 23, affected ignorance of Burr's
schemes, and demanded an explanation of them.
October 26 Burr sent the required disavowal: —

"I was greatly surprised and really hurt," said Burr,[1]
"by the unusual tenor of your letter of the 23d, and I
hasten to reply to it, as well for your satisfaction as
my own. If there exists any design to separate the
Western from the Eastern States, I am totally ignorant
of it. I never harbored or expressed any such intention
to any one, nor did any person ever intimate such design
to me."

From that moment to the last day of his life Burr
persisted in this assertion, coupling it always in his
own mind with a peculiar reservation. What he so
solemnly denied was the intention to separate the
Western States "by force" from the Eastern; what
he never denied was the plan of establishing a Western empire by consent.

[1] Burr to John Smith, Oct. 26, 1806; Senate Report, p. 33.

Of disunion Burr never again dared to speak. On that subject he was conscious of having already said so much as to make his stay in Kentucky a matter of some risk. The leading Republicans would have rejoiced at his departure; but to desert him was more than their tempers would allow. Daveiss saw another opportunity to compromise his enemies, and used it. A week after Blennerhassett and Peter Taylor left Lexington, carrying with them Burr's letter in reply to Senator Smith, on the same day when Andrew Jackson at Nashville received Burr's order, with Kentucky bank-notes for the sum of three thousand dollars, the United States District Court opened its session at Frankfort. Within eight and forty hours, November 5, District-Attorney Daveiss rose in court and made complaint against Burr for violating the laws of the United States by setting on foot a military expedition against Mexico. Besides an affidavit to this effect, the district-attorney asserted in court that Burr's scheme extended to a revolution of all the Western States and Territories.

In the nervous condition of Kentucky society, this attack on Burr roused great attention and hot criticism. The judge who presided over the court was the same Harry Innis who had been privy to the Spanish conspiracy, and was harassed by the charges of the "Western World." Daveiss could count with certainty upon the course which a man so placed would follow. The judge took three days to reflect, and then denied the motion; but Burr could not afford to

rest silent.   November 8, when Judge Innis overruled
the motion and denied the process, Burr appeared in
court and challenged inquiry. The following Wednes-
day, November 12, was fixed for the investigation.
A grand-jury was summoned. Burr appeared, surrounded by friends, with Henry Clay for counsel, and
with strong popular sympathy in his favor.   Daveiss
too appeared, with a list of witnesses summoned ;
but the chief witness was absent in Indiana, and
Daveiss asked a postponement. The jury was discharged ; and after a dignified and grave harangue
from the accused, Burr left the court in triumph.[1]
On the strength of this acquittal he ventured again
to appear in Cincinnati, November 23, in confidential
relations with Senator Smith ; but the term of his
long impunity was soon to end.

October 22, while Burr was at Lexington, President Jefferson held a Cabinet council at Washington.   The Spaniards were then threatening an
attack upon Louisiana, while Wilkinson's force in
the Mississippi and Orleans Territories amounted
only to ten hundred and eighty-one men, with two
gunboats.   Memoranda, written at the time by Jefferson, detailed the situation as it was understood
by the Government : [2] —

" During the last session of Congress, Colonel Burr
who was here, finding no hope of being employed in any
department of the government, opened himself confiden-

[1] Marshall's History of Kentucky, ii. 396.
[2] Cabinet Memoranda, Oct. 22, 1806 ; Jefferson MSS.

tially to some persons on whom he thought he could
rely, on a scheme of separating the Western from the
Atlantic States, and erecting the former into an independent confederacy. He had before made a tour of those
States, which had excited suspicions, as every motion
does of such a Catilinarian character. Of his having
made this proposition here we have information from
General Eaton through Mr. Ely and Mr. Granger. He
went off this spring to the Western country. Of his
movements on his way, information has come to the
Secretary of State and myself from John Nicholson and
Mr. Williams of the State of New York, respecting a
Mr. Tyler; Colonel Morgan, Nevill, and Roberts, near
Pittsburg; and to other citizens through other channels
and the newspapers. We are of opinion unanimously
that confidential letters be written to the Governors
of Ohio, Indiana, Mississippi, and New Orleans; to the
district-attorney of Kentucky, of Tennessee, of Louisiana, to have him strictly watched, and on his committing any overt act, to have him arrested and tried
for treason, misdemeanor, or whatever other offence
the act may amount to; and in like manner to arrest
and try any of his followers committing acts against
the laws. We think it proper also to order some of the
gunboats up to Fort Adams to stop by force any passage
of suspicious persons going down in force. General
Wilkinson being expressly declared by Burr to Eaton to
be engaged with him in this design as his lieutenant,
or first in command, and suspicions of infidelity in Wilkinson being now become very general, a question is
proposed what is proper to be done as to him on
this account, as well as for his disobedience of orders
received by him June 11 at St. Louis to descend with

all practical despatch to New Orleans to mark out the
site of certain defensive works there, and then repair
to take command at Natchitoches, on which business he
did not leave St. Louis till September.   Consideration
adjourned.

    " October 24.   It is agreed unanimously to call for
Captain Preble and Decatur to repair to New Orleans,
by land or by sea as they please, there to take command
of the force on the water, and that the ' Argus ' and
two gunboats from New York, three from Norfolk, and
two from Charleston shall be ordered there, if on a
consultation between Mr. Gallatin and Mr. Smith the
appropriations shall be found to enable us ; that Preble
shall, on consultation with Governor Claiborne, have
great discretionary powers ; that Graham shall be sent
through Kentucky on Burr's trail, with discretionary
powers to consult confidentially with the Governors to
arrest Burr if he has made himself liable.   He is to have
a commission of Governor of [Upper] Louisiana, and
Dr. Browne is to be removed.   Letters are to be written
by post to Governor Claiborne, the Governor of Mississippi, and Colonel Freeman to be on their guard against
any surprise of our posts or vessels by him.   The question as to General Wilkinson postponed till Preble's
departure, for future information."

    Although these measures provided no protection
against the chance of Wilkinson's misconduct, they
could not fail to put an instant stop to Burr's
activity.   All that remained was to carry them out.
Unfortunately Gallatin found that his hands and
those of Robert Smith were tied by Acts of Congress.
The next day the Cabinet met again.

" October 25. A mail arrived yesterday from the westward, and not one word is heard from that quarter of any movements by Colonel Burr. This total silence of the officers of the government, of the members of Congress, of the newspapers, proves he is committing no overt act against law. We therefore rescind the determination to send Preble, Decatur, the ' Argus,' or the gunboats, and instead of them to send off the marines which are here to reinforce, or take place of, the garrison at New Orleans, with a view to Spanish operations; and instead of writing to the Governors, etc., we send Graham on that route, with confidential authority to inquire into Burr's movements, put the Governors, etc., on their guard, to provide for his arrest if necessary, and to take on himself the government of [Upper] Louisiana. Letters are still to be written to Claiborne, Freeman, and the Governor of Mississippi to be on their guard."

The result of this Cabinet discussion, extending from October 22 to October 25, was merely an order to John Graham, Secretary of the Orleans Territory, to stop in Ohio and Kentucky on his way westward and inquire into Burr's movements.

Graham, following orders received from Madison, reached Marietta about the middle of November, when Burr should have already begun his movement, according to the original plan. Blennerhassett, who had been told by Burr that Graham was concerned in the plot, welcomed him with great cordiality, and talked much more freely than wisely. The information which crowded on Graham at Marietta led him to go at the end of November to Chillicothe, where the Legislature was in session, and where he caused a law to be passed, December 2, empowering the governor to use the militia against the conspirators. Had this measure, or one equally energetic, been taken by the President three months earlier, it would have put an end to Burr's projects before they were under way, would have saved many deluded men from ruin, and would have prevented much trouble at New Orleans; but Graham's progress was not quite so rapid, even though late, as it should have been.

Burr had ample warning. November 25 District-Attorney Daveiss renewed his motion in court at Frankfort, and the court appointed December 2 as the day for hearing evidence. Henry Clay became uneasy, and exacted from Burr a written denial of the projects imputed to him. Fortified with this evidence to his own credulity, Clay again went into court with Burr, "for whose honor and innocence," he said, "he could pledge his own," and assailed the district-attorney. A second time the scene of outraged virtue was acted. Once more the witnesses vanished. Senator Smith saddled his horse and fled; Adair would not appear; and the judge lent his weight to the criminal. To crown all, December 5 the grand-jury of twenty-two persons signed a paper declaring that they could discover nothing improper or injurious to the interests of the United States government in the conduct of Burr and Adair. Burr was discharged, with enthusiastic applause, without a stain on his character; and to prove its devotion, the society of Frankfort gave a ball in his honor.[1]

Nov. 25, 1806, was a date to be remembered in the story of Burr's adventures. On that day Daveiss made his second motion in court at Frankfort, while at Washington the Government at length woke to action. An officer, bringing despatches from General Wilkinson at Natchitoches, presented himself at the White House with news so startling that Jefferson immediately called his Cabinet together. Another memorandum in the President's handwriting recorded the action taken : —

" November 25. Present at first the four heads of department; but after a while General Dearborn withdrew, unwell. Despatches from General Wilkinson to myself of October 21, by a confidential officer (Lieutenant Smith), show that overtures have been made to him which decide that the present object of the combination is an expedition by sea against Vera Cruz ; and by comparing the contents of a letter from Cowles Meade to the Secretary of State, with the information from Lieutenant Smith that a Mr. Swartwout from New York, brother of the late marshal, had been at General Wilkinson's camp, we are satisfied that Swartwout has been the agent through whom overtures have been made to Wilkinson. We came to the following determinations, — that a proclamation be issued (see it), and that orders go as follows: To Pittsburg, if we have a military officer there ; . . . Marietta, Mr. Gallatin is to write to the col-

lector ; . . . General Dearborn to write to Governor
Tiffin, . . . and to write to General Jackson, supposed
to be the general of the brigade on the Virginia side of
the river ; . . . Louisville, General Dearborn to write to
the Governor of Kentucky ; . . . Massac, General Dearborn to give orders to Captain Bissell of the same tenor,
and particularly to stop armed vessels suspected on good
grounds to be proceeding on this enterprise, and for this
purpose to have in readiness any boats he can procure
fitted for enabling him to arrest their passage ; Chickasaw Bluffs, give same orders as to Bissell ; New Orleans, General Wilkinson to direct the station of the
armed vessels ; and if the arrangements with the Spaniards will permit him to withdraw, let him dispose of his
force as he thinks best to prevent any such expedition or
any attempt on New Orleans, or any of the posts or military stores of the United States.   (He is also to arrest
persons coming to his camp and proposing a concur-
rence in any such enterprise, and suspected of being
in camp with a view to propagate such propositions.
This addition is made by General Dearborn with my
approbation.) "

The orders to Wilkinson were instantly sent.
" You will use every exertion in your power," Dearborn said,[1] " to frustrate and effectually prevent any
enterprise which has for its object, directly or indi-
rectly, any hostile act on any part of the territories
of the United States, or on any of the territories of
the King of Spain."   Persons found in or about the
military camps or posts, with evident intention of

[1] Dearborn to Wilkinson, Nov. 27, 1806; Report of Committee, Feb. 26, 1811; 3 Sess. 11 Cong. p. 408.

sounding officers or soldiers, were to be arrested, and
if not amenable to martial law, were to be delivered
over to the civil authorities.

The orders were remarkable chiefly for the power
they trusted in the hands of Wilkinson, and the confidence they showed in his good faith.   Yet nothing
could on its face be more suspicious than his report.
The idea that Burr's expedition could be directed
against Vera Cruz was unreasonable, and contrary to
the tenor of the President's information from all
other sources.[1]   A moment's thought should have
satisfied the President that Wilkinson was deceiving
him, and that the city of New Orleans must be the
real point of danger.   In truth, Wilkinson's letters
suppressed more than they told, and were more alarming than the warnings of Eaton or of Daveiss; for
they proved that Wilkinson was playing a double part.
No measure that promised safety could be taken
which would not require an instant removal of Wilkinson and a vigorous support of Claiborne at New
Orleans.

Nov. 27, 1806, the same day with Dearborn's letter, the proclamation was issued.[2]   Without mentioning Burr's name, it announced that sundry
persons were conspiring against Spain, contrary to
the laws ; it warned all persons whatsoever to withdraw from such conspiracy ; and it directed all offi-

[1] See Cabinet Memoranda of October 22, p. 278.

[2] Proclamation of Nov. 27, 1806; Wilkinson's Memoirs, ii.
Appendix, xcvii.

cers, civil and military, of the United States to seize
and detain all persons and property concerned in the
enterprise.

The last chance of stopping the conspirators before
they could enter the Mississippi was at Fort Massac.
Beyond that point they could not easily be molested
until they should reach a country more friendly than
Ohio or Kentucky to their purposes; but the Presi
dent had reason to suppose that his proclamation
came in ample time to stop the conspirators while
they were still on the Ohio River.

The Governor of Ohio, without waiting for the
proclamation, acted promptly. On Graham's re
quest, the necessary law was passed, and measures
were taken to seize Burr's boats at Marietta. The
boats and supplies were brought by Burr's men to
Blennerhassett's island; but finding that militia were
about to take possession of the island itself, the
conspirators, with Blennerhassett in their company,
at midnight of December 10–11, fled down the
river, — a half-dozen ill-fitted boats, with thirty or
forty men, — and passed the Falls of the Ohio
at about the time when Burr and Adair entered
Nashville.

Graham, leaving Ohio, reached Kentucky Decem
ber 22, and induced the Governor and Legislature
December 24, to follow the example of Ohio; but he
lost much time between Chillicothe and Frankfort,
so that even after driving Burr from Ohio to Ken
tucky, and from Kentucky to Tennessee, the quickest

pursuit could not prevent the conspirators from taking their path down the Cumberland. Graham in Ohio heard nothing of Burr's doings in Tennessee, although since November 3 Jackson's close friend Patton Anderson was scouring the country round Nashville for recruits, and had raised a company of seventy-five men. As Burr went farther South, the secrecy of his intimates became more closely guarded, and their movements more obscure.

Burr and Adair reached Nashville December 14, and went directly to the river, where their boats were building. By that time Burr was well trained in the comedy he had within the last month so often played. Senator Smith of Ohio began it October 23, by writing the request that Burr's design should be "candidly disclosed," because Smith had fears that it might interrupt the tranquillity of the country. A month later Henry Clay made the same request. No sooner did Burr reach Clover Bottom, where his boats were building under Andrew Jackson's charge, than he found himself required to repeat the familiar formula. Jackson, in company with General Overton as his witness, soon appeared at Clover Bottom, and intimated as plainly as had been done by John Smith and Henry Clay that his own credit required a disavowal of designs against the Union. Burr, with his usual dignified courtesy, instantly complied; and his denials were accepted as satisfactory by Jackson.

On Jackson's part this conduct was peculiarly sur-

prising, because more than a month before he ha
written to Governor Claiborne [1] at New Orleans
secret denunciation of Burr and Wilkinson, couche
in language which showed such intimate knowledg
of Burr's plans as could have come only from Bu:
himself or Adair. In accepting Burr's disavowal
December 14, Jackson did not mention to Burr h
denunciatory letter written to Claiborne, Novemb
12, in which he had said, "I fear treachery has b
come the order of the day." Like Senator Smit
he was satisfied to secure his own safety; and upo
Burr's denial of treasonable schemes, Jackson, a
though he did not write to Claiborne to withdra
the secret charges, went on building boats, providin
supplies, and enlisting men for Colonel Burr's e:
pedition. His motives for this conduct remained h
own secret. Many of the best-informed persons i
Tennessee and Kentucky, including Burr's avowe
partisans, held but a low opinion of Jackson's cha:
acter or veracity. Eight years afterward Jackso
and John Adair once more appeared on the stage (
New Orleans history, and quarrelled, with charg(
and countercharges of falsehood and insinuations (
treason.

"Whatever were the intentions of Colonel Burr,
wrote Adair in a published letter,[2] "I neither organize
troops at that time, nor did I superintend the building (

---

[1] Jackson to Claiborne, Nov. 12, 1806; Burr's Trial. Anna
of Congress, 1807–1808, p. 571.

[2] Letters of General Adair and General Jackson, 1817.

boats for him ; nor did I write confidential letters recommending him to my friends ; nor did I think it necessary, after his failure was universally known, to save myself by turning informer or State witness."

By that time the people of Nashville had heard what was doing in Ohio and Kentucky. The public impeachment of the conspirators checked enlistments and retarded purchases ; but Burr seemed to fear no such personal danger as had prevented his return to Blennerhassett's island. The Governor and Legislature of Ohio had taken public measures to seize boats and supplies as early as December 2 ; Burr had been driven from Kentucky, and Blennerhassett had fled from his island, by December 11 ; but ten days later Burr was still fitting out his boats at Nashville, undisturbed by the people of Tennessee. December 19 the President's proclamation reached Nashville,[1] but still nothing was done.

At last some unmentioned friend brought to Burr a secret warning that the State authorities must soon take notice of his armaments. The authorities at Nashville could no longer delay interference, and Burr was made to understand that his boats would be seized, and that he was himself in danger unless he should immediately escape ; but between December 19 and 22 he was undisturbed. The announcement that Graham was expected to arrive December 23 probably decided his movements ; for on the 22d he hastily abandoned all except two of his boats, receiv-

[1] Parton's Burr, ii. 87.

ing back from Jackson seventeen hundred and twenty
five dollars and taking the two boats and other arti
cles for his voyage.[1]   Jackson afterward declare
that he suffered in the end a loss of five hundre
dollars by a note which Burr had induced him t
indorse, and which was returned from New Yor
protested.   Without further hindrance Burr the
floated down the Cumberland River, taking wit
him a nephew of Mrs. Jackson, furnished by hi
uncle with a letter of introduction to Governor Cla
borne, — a confidence the more singular because Go
ernor Claiborne could hardly fail, under the warning
of General Jackson's previous secret letter, to seiz
and imprison Burr and every one who should b
found in his company.

Thus, by connivance, Burr escaped from Nashvill
three days after news of the President's proclamatio
had arrived.   The Government had two more chance
to stop him before reaching Natchez.   He must joi
Blennerhassett and Comfort Tyler at the mouth
the Cumberland, and then move down the Ohio Rive
past Fort Massac, garrisoned by a company of th
First Infantry, commanded by a Captain Bissel
Having passed Massac, he must still run the gauntle
at Chickasaw Bluff, afterward called Memphis, wher
another military post was stationed.   The War De
partment sent orders, November 27, to the officer
commanding at Massac and Chickasaw Bluff to b
on their guard.

[1] Parton's Jackson, i. 322.

December 22 Burr left Nashville, while Adair at about the same time started for New Orleans on horseback through the Indian country. At the mouth of the Cumberland, Burr joined Blennerhassett, who had with him the boats which had succeeded in escaping the Ohio militia. The combined flotilla contained thirteen boats, which carried some sixty men and as many stand of arms, the arms being stowed in cases as cargo. December 25 Burr sent a note to Captain Bissell announcing that he should soon reach Fort Massac on his way South, and should stop to pay his respects. Bissell had received neither the President's proclamation nor the orders from the Secretary of War. As an old friend of Burr, he sent a cordial welcome to the party. In the night of December 29 the boats passed the fort, and landed about a mile below. The next morning Captain Bissell went in his own boat to pay his respects to Colonel Burr, who declined invitations to breakfast and dinner, but asked a furlough of twenty days for a Sergeant Dunbaugh, who had been persuaded to join the expedition. Bissell gave the furlough December 31, and Burr's party at once started for the Mississippi. Five days afterward, January 5, Bissell received a letter, dated January 2, from Andrew Jackson, as Major-General of Tennessee militia, warning him to stop any body of men who might attempt to pass, if they should appear to have illegal enterprises in view. The President's proclamation had not yet reached Fort Massac, nor had Captain Bissell received any instructions from Washington.[1]

The proclamation, dated November 27, and sent immediately to the West, reached Pittsburg December 2,[2] and should, with ordinary haste, have reached Fort Massac — the most important point between Pittsburg and Natchez — before December 15. The orders which accompanied it ought to have prevented any failure of understanding on the part of Captain Bissell. Bissell's reply to Jackson, dated January 5, reached Nashville January 8, and was forwarded by Jackson to Jefferson, who sent it to Congress with a message dated January 28. Twenty-three days were sufficient for the unimportant reply; forty days or more had been taken for the orders to reach Massac, although they had only to float down the river. That some gross negligence or connivance could alone explain this shortcoming was evident; but the subject was never thought to need investigation by President or Congress. The responsibility for Burr's escape was so equally distributed between the President himself, the War Department, and the many accomplices or dupes of Burr in Kentucky and Tennessee, that any investigation must have led to unpleasant results.

Burr for the moment escaped, and everything depended on the action of Wilkinson. Dayton and

[1] Bissell to Andrew Jackson, Jan. 5, 1807; Annals of Congress, 1806–1807, p. 1017.

[2] Jefferson to Wilkinson, Jan. 3, 1807; Burr's Trial. Annals of Congress, 1807–1808, p. 580.

the other conspirators who remained in the Eastern
States thought it a matter of small consequence
whether Burr carried with him a party of sixty men
or of six hundred. Doubtless the unexpected energy
shown by the people and the legislatures of Ohio and
Kentucky proved the futility of attempting to revolutionize those States; but if Wilkinson were true to
Burr, and if the city of New Orleans should welcome
him, it remained to be seen whether the Government
at Washington could crush the rebellion. A blockade
of the Mississippi was no easy affair, and slow in its
results; England, France, and Spain might have
much to say.

Meanwhile Humphrey Marshall and his friend
Daveiss enjoyed the triumph they had won. In
spite of silent opposition from the Republican leaders, Marshall drove the Kentucky Legislature into an
inquiry as to the truth of the charge that Judge
Sebastian was a Spanish pensioner. Sebastian instantly resigned. The committee took no notice of
this admission of guilt, but summoned Judge Innis
to testify. Very reluctantly Innis appeared before
the committee and began his evidence, but broke
down in the attempt, and admitted the truth of what
had been alleged.[1] Before the close of the year
Daveiss and Marshall drove Burr and Adair out of
the State, forced Sebastian from the bench, humil-
iated Innis, and threw ridicule upon young Henry

[1] Report of the Select Committee to the Kentucky Legislature,
Dec. 2, 1806; National Intelligencer, Jan. 7, 1807.

Clay and the other aggressive partisans of Jefferson,
besides placing Jefferson himself and his Secretary of
State in an attitude neither dignified nor creditable.
Of all the persons connected with the story of Burr's
expedition, Daveiss and Marshall alone showed the
capacity to conceive a plan of action and the courage
to execute the plan they conceived; but Jefferson
could not be expected to feel satisfaction with services of such a nature.   A few months later he appointed another person to succeed Daveiss in the
office of district-attorney.

CHAPTER XIII.

SAMUEL SWARTWOUT and Peter V. Ogden, the young men whom Burr and Dayton charged with the duty of carrying despatches to Louisiana, crossed the Alleghanies in August and floated down the Ohio River to Louisville.[1] There they stopped to find Adair, for whom they brought letters from Burr. After some search Swartwout delivered the letters, and continued his journey. Adair never made known the contents of these papers; but they probably contained the same information as was conveyed in the despatches to Wilkinson which came in their company.

Supposing Wilkinson to be at St. Louis, the two young men bought horses and rode across the Indiana Territory to Kaskaskias; but finding that the General had gone down the Mississippi, they took boat and followed. At Natchez they learned that the object of their search had gone up the Red River. Swartwout was obliged to follow him; but Ogden went to New Orleans with despatches from Burr to his friends in that city.

[1] Wilkinson's Evidence, Burr's Trial; Annals of Congress, 1807–1808, p. 515.

Among the mysteries that still surround the conspiracy, the deepest covers Burr's relations in New
Orleans. That he had confederates in the city was
proved not only by Ogden's carrying letters, but also
by Erick Bollman's arrival by sea, as early as September 27, with a duplicate of Burr's letter of July
29 to Wilkinson; and above all, by the significant
disappearance of Burr's letters carried by Ogden and
Bollman to persons in New Orleans. The persons
implicated proved their complicity by keeping Burr's
letters and his secret.

One of these correspondents was almost certainly
Judge Prevost, Burr's stepson, whom Jefferson had
appointed District Judge for the Territory of Orleans.
That Daniel Clark was another hardly admits of
doubt. Swartwout assured Wilkinson of the fact;[1]
but apart from this evidence, the same reasons which
obliged Burr to confide in Wilkinson required him to
confide in Clark. The receivers of the letters, who-
ever they were, hastened to make their contents
known to every one whom they could trust. Immediately after the arrival of Bollman and Dayton
about October 1, before any serious alarm had risen
in Ohio, the town of New Orleans rang with rumors
of Burr's projects. The news excited more consternation than hope; for although the creoles had been
bitter in complaints of Claiborne's administration and
of the despotism imposed upon them by Congress,

[1] Wilkinson to Daniel Clark, Oct. 5, 1807; Clark's Proofs,
p. 154.

they remembered their attempt to revolt in 1768, and were far from eager to risk their safety again. Nevertheless, the temper of the people was bad; and no one felt deeper anxiety as to the number of Burr's adherents than Governor Claiborne himself.

Nearly three years had elapsed since Dec. 20, 1803, when the Spanish governor surrendered Louisiana to the United States, and the history of the Territory during that time presented an uninterrupted succession of bickerings. The government at Washington was largely responsible for its own unpopularity in the new Territory, its foreign and domestic policy seeming calculated to create ill-feeling, and after creating it, to keep it alive. The President began by appointing as Governor of Louisiana a man who had no peculiar fitness for the place. Claiborne, in contrast with men like Wilkinson, Burr, and Daniel Clark, rose to the level of a hero. He was honest, well-meaning, straightforward, and thoroughly patriotic; but these virtues were not enough to make him either feared or respected by the people over whom he was to exercise despotic powers; while Claiborne's military colleague, Wilkinson, possessed fewer virtues and a feebler character. The French Prefect, Laussat, who remained for a time in New Orleans to protect French interests, wrote his Government April 8, 1804, an interesting account of the situation as seen by French eyes:[1]

[1] Laussat to Decrès, 18 Germinal, An xii. (April 8, 1804); Archives de la Marine, MSS. Gayarré's Louisiana, iii. 10.

" It was hardly possible that the government of the
United States should have made a worse beginning, and
that it should have sent two men (Messrs. Claiborne,
governor, and Wilkinson, general) less fit to attract
affection.   The first, with estimable private qualities, has
little capacity and much awkwardness, and is extremely
beneath his place ; the second, already long known here
in a bad way, is a flighty, rattle-headed fellow, often
drunk, who has committed a hundred impertinent follies.
Neither the one nor the other understands a word of
French or Spanish.   They have on all occasions, and
without delicacy, shocked the habits, the prejudices, the
character of the population."

Claiborne began his sway, assuming that the creoles
were a kindly but ignorant and degraded people, who
must be taught the blessings of American society.
The creoles, who considered themselves to be more
refined and civilized than the Americans who descended upon them from Kentucky and Tennessee,
were not pleased that their language, blood, and customs should be systematically degraded, in defiance
of the spirit in which the treaty of cession had been
made.   Their anger was not without an element of
danger.   England and France could safely defy public
opinion and trample on prostrate races.   Their empire
rested on force, but that of Jefferson rested on consent ; and if the people of New Orleans should rebel,
they could not be conquered without trouble and expense, or without violating the free principles which
Jefferson was supposed to represent.

The colonists in Louisiana had been for a century

the spoiled children of France and Spain. Petted, protected, fed, paid, flattered, and given every liberty except the rights of self-government, they liked Spain[1]
and loved France, but they did not love the English
or the Americans; and their irritation was extreme
when they saw Claiborne, who knew nothing of their
society and law, abolish their language, establish
American judges who knew only American law,
while he himself sat as a court of last resort, without
even an attorney to advise him as to the meaning of
the Spanish law he administered. At the same time
that as judge he could hang his subjects, as intendant he could tax them, and as governor he could
shoot the disobedient. Even under the Spanish despotism, appeal might be made to Havana or Madrid;
but no appeal lay from Claiborne's judgment-seat.

Before this temporary system was superseded, the
creoles already yearned for a return to French or
Spanish rule. They had but one hope from the
United States, — that, in the terms of the treaty,
Louisiana might be quickly admitted into the Union.
This hope was rudely dispelled. Not only did Congress treat their claims to self-government with indifference, but the Territory was divided in halves, so
that it must be slower to acquire the necessary population for a State; while as though to delay still
longer this act of justice, the growth of population
was checked by prohibiting the slave-trade. Years
must pass before Louisiana could gain admission into

[1] Gayarré, Spanish Domination, p. 627.

the Union; and even when this should happen, it must be the result of American expansion at creole expense.

Jefferson's Spanish policy, which kept the country always on the verge of a war with Spain, prevented the French and Spanish population from feeling that their submission was final. In case of war between the United States and Spain, nothing would be easier than to drive Claiborne away and replace Casa Calvo in the government. Claiborne soon found himself confronted by an opposition which he could neither control nor understand. Even the leading Americans joined it. Daniel Clark, rich, eccentric, wild in his talk and restless in his movements, distinguished himself by the personal hatred which he showed for Claiborne; Evan Jones, another wealthy resident, rivalled Clark; Edward Livingston, who had come to New Orleans angry with Jefferson for removing him as a defaulter from office, joined the old residents in harassing the Governor; while the former Spanish officials, Casa Calvo and Morales, remained at New Orleans under one or another pretext, keeping the Spanish influence alive, and maintaining communications with Governor Folch of West Florida, who controlled the Mississippi at Baton Rouge, and with General Herrera, who commanded the Spanish force in Texas. So bad was the state of feeling that when Oct. 1, 1804, the new territorial system was organized, Messrs. Boré, Bellechasse, Cantrelle, Jones, and Daniel Clark, whom the President had named as members of the legislative council, refused to accept the office ; while Messrs. Sauvé, Destréhan, and Derbigny were deputed by a popular assembly to present their griev- ances at Washington. Two months elapsed before Governor Claiborne could form any council at all ; not until Dec. 4, 1804, was a quorum obtained.

No pretence of disguising their feelings was made by the Spanish population. In French minds the power of Bonaparte was a stronger reliance than the power of Spain ; no Frenchman willingly admitted that Napoleon meant to sacrifice Louisiana forever.[1]

" The President's Message," wrote Governor Claiborne to Madison, Dec. 11, 1804,[2] " has been translated into the French language, and I will take care to have it cir- culated among the people. It will tend to remove an impression which has heretofore contributed greatly to embarrass the local administration ; to wit, that the coun- try west of the Mississippi would certainly be re-ceded to Spain, and perhaps the whole of Louisiana. So general has been this impression, particularly as relates to the country west of the Mississippi, that many citizens have been fearful of accepting any employment under the American government, or even manifesting a respect therefor, lest at a future time it might lessen them in the esteem of Spanish officers."

Under the remonstrances of Sauvé, Destréhan, and Derbigny, and at the intercession of John Randolph, Congress was induced to yield a single point. The

[1] Laussat to Decrès, 18 Germinal, An xii. (April 8, 1804) ; Archives de la Marine, MSS.

[2] Gayarré's Louisiana, iii. 35.

Act of March 2, 1805, gave Louisiana ordinary Territorial rights, an elected legislature, and a delegate to Congress. After its passage, Claiborne wrote to Madison that the people were disappointed; and in fact the concessions were so trivial as to irritate rather than soothe. Claiborne, whom the people obstinately disliked, was re-appointed governor under the Act, and nothing in reality was changed.

Burr visited New Orleans in June and July, 1805. The new Legislature assembled, Nov. 4, 1805, when Claiborne found himself surrounded by a council partly elected by the Legislature, and a Legislature wholly elected by the people. He was soon at odds with both. The leader of opposition was Daniel Clark; and for a moment in May, 1806, the quarrel went so far that the two legislative bodies were on the point of voluntary disbandment, and a majority of the council actually resigned. The Legislature chose Daniel Clark as their delegate to Congress. Claiborne thought that the choice was made merely out of personal spite; but no sooner did he hear of Burr's disunion scheme than he wrote to Madison,[1] —

" If this be the object of the conspirators, the delegate to Congress from this Territory, Daniel Clark, is·one of the leaders. He has often said that the Union could not last, and that had he children he would impress early on their minds the expediency of a separation between the Atlantic and Western States."

[1] Gayarré's Louisiana, iii. 161.

In the same month of May Lieutenant Murray of the artillery, an intimate friend of Daniel Clark, came with a Lieutenant Taylor from Fort Adams to New Orleans, and heard the ordinary conversation of society.

" Lieutenant Taylor and myself," he afterward testified,[1] " were invited to dine with a gentleman there whose name was on the list before mentioned [of persons engaged in an expedition against Mexico] ; it was Judge Workman. We three dined together. After the cloth was removed, Mr. Lewis Kerr came in. . . . After a number of inquiries about Baton Rouge and the Red River country, they proceeded to lay open their plan of seizing upon the money in the banks at New Orleans, impressing the shipping, taking Baton Rouge, and joining Miranda by way of Mexico. . . . When I told Mr. Clark that I was calculated on as the officer to attack Baton Rouge, he advised me by all means to do it. He urged as an inducement that he was coming on to Congress, and would do all he could in my favor ; that he would represent to the Government that it would require a large force to retake it ; and he further observed that, at any rate, if the Government should be disposed to trouble me, before they could send off a sufficient force I should be in a situation to take care of myself."

This attempt to seduce officers of the United States army into Burr's conspiracy was flagrant ; for although Burr's name was not mentioned, no one could fail to see that the seizure of government money in

[1] Report of the Committee to inquire into the Conduct of General Wilkinson, Feb. 26, 1811 ; 3 Sess. 11 Cong. p. 320.

the banks at New Orleans was an act of treason, and that the attack on West Florida implied a permanent military establishment on the Gulf.

June 7, 1806, the first Louisiana legislature adjourned, and Governor Claiborne felt relief as deep as was felt by Jefferson at escaping the stings of John Randolph ; but although for a time Claiborne flattered himself that his difficulties were lessening, he soon became aware that some mystery surrounded him which he could not penetrate. General Herrera began to press upon the Red River from Nacogdoches in Texas with a force considerably stronger than any which Claiborne could oppose to him. The militia showed indifference. August 28 the Governor wrote to the Secretary of War that the French population would not support the government in case of hostilities.[1] September 9 he wrote to Cowles Meade, then acting-governor of the Mississippi Territory, a letter of uneasiness at the behavior of Wilkinson's troops : " My present impression is that *all is not right.* I know not whom to censure, but it seems to me that there is wrong somewhere." The militia could not be stimulated to action against Herrera, and the feeling of hostility between Americans and creoles was so bitter that Claiborne intervened for fear of violence.[2]

October 6, 1806, the Governor returned to New Orleans after a tour of inspection. Erick Bollman had

[1] Gayarré's Louisiana, iii. 151.

[2] Gayarré's Louisiana, iii. 153.

been then ten days in the city, and young Ogden had arrived about October 1, bringing Burr's despatches. According to Bellechasse and Derbigny the creole society was already much excited; but this excitement showed itself to Claiborne in a display of assumed stolidity.

"There is in this city," wrote Claiborne to the Secretary of War October 8,[1] "a degree of apathy at the present time which mortifies and astonishes me; and some of the native Americans act and discourse as if perfect security everywhere prevailed. . . . I fear the ancient Louisianians of New Orleans are not disposed to support with firmness the American cause. I do not believe they would fight against us; but my present impression is that they are not inclined to rally under the American standard."

Claiborne's spirits fluctuated from day to day as he felt the changes in a situation which he could not fathom. October 17 he was elated because the militia of New Orleans unexpectedly, and contrary to the tenor of all its previous conduct, made a voluntary tender of services. November 7 he was again discouraged; and November 15, and even as late as November 25, he fell back into despondency. During all that time the enemies whom he feared were Spaniards in Texas and West Florida; the thought of conspiracy among the apathetic creoles had not yet entered his mind.

Yet around him the city was trembling with excite-

---

[1] Gayarré's Louisiana, iii. 154.

ment; and of all persons in the city Daniel Clark
was the one whose conduct showed most signs of
guilty knowledge. A few months later, he collected
affidavits from four or five of the most important
gentlemen in New Orleans to show what his conduct
had been. At the moment when Bollman and Ogden
arrived, Clark was preparing for his journey to
Washington, where he meant to take his seat in Congress as the Territorial delegate. The news brought
by Bollman and Ogden that Burr was on his way to
New Orleans placed him in a dilemma. Like Senator
Smith and Andrew Jackson, his chief anxiety regarded his own safety; and he adopted an expedient
which showed his usual intelligence. An affidavit of
Bellechasse,[1] on whose character he mainly depended,
narrated that —

" in the month of October, a very few days before Mr.
Clark left this city to go to Congress, he called together
a number of his friends, and informed them of the views
and intentions imputed to Colonel Burr, which were then
almost the sole topic of conversation, and which, from
the reports daily arriving from Kentucky, had caused a
serious alarm ; and he advised them all to exert their
influence with the inhabitants of the country to support
the Government of the United States and to rally round
the Governor, although he thought him incapable of ren-
dering much service as a military man, — assuring them
that such conduct only would save the country if any
hostile projects were entertained against it, and that this
would be the best method of convincing the Government

[1] Clark's Proofs, p. 145.

of the United States of the attachment of the inhabitants of Louisiana, and of the falsity of all the reports circulated to their prejudice. And Mr. Clark strongly recommended to such members of the Legislature as were then present not to attend any call or meeting of either House in case Colonel Burr should gain possession of the city, stating that such a measure would deservedly expose every individual concerned to punishment, and would occasion the ruin of the country."

According to Bellechasse, the society of New Orleans between Oct. 1 and Oct. 15, 1806, was in serious alarm. Burr's intentions formed " almost the sole topic of conversation ; " daily reports were arriving from Kentucky, although in Kentucky, down to October 1, no alarm existed, and Burr's intentions were not even developed. Each of the four affidavits which Clark obtained, one of them signed by Peter Derbigny, affirmed that about the middle of October, 1806, Burr's projects were the general theme of conversation in the city ; but nothing was more certain than that this knowledge of Burr's projects must have come not from Kentucky, but from Burr's own letters and from the messages brought by Ogden and Bollman.

Clark, having thus secured himself from the charge of abetting Burr, sailed for the Atlantic coast, and in due time made his appearance at Washington ; but neither he nor Bellechasse nor Derbigny nor Bouligny, although officers of the government, giving each other excellent advice, communicated to Governor Claiborne what they knew about Burr's plans.

From October 1 to November 25, the projects of Burr were "the exclusive subject of every conversation" in the city, yet the single official who ought to have been first informed, and who bore all responsibility, had not a suspicion that any conspiracy existed. Claiborne's isolation was complete. This isolation was natural, since all the gentlemen of New Orleans quarrelled with the Governor; but the same silence was preserved where their social relations were friendly. Neither Clark nor any of the persons who talked so much with each other about Burr's projects communicated with General Wilkinson, who was in full sympathy with their hatred of Claiborne. Wilkinson stood in relations of close confidence with Clark; intimate letters passed between them as late as October 2.[1] Clark knew that Wilkinson was Burr's most intimate friend; yet he neither warned Claiborne nor Wilkinson nor President Jefferson, although as early as October 15 he warned a number of other gentlemen who needed no warning, and although October 17 the militia of New Orleans, evidently in consequence of his advice, tendered their services to the Governor.

For two months, between September 27 and November 25, Burr's emissaries were busy in New Orleans, without suspicion or hindrance from the United States authorities; while every prominent Frenchman in the Territory knew the contents of Burr's letter to Wilkinson as soon as Wilkinson could have known

[1] Clark to Wilkinson, Oct. 2, 1806 ; Clark's Proofs, p. 157.

them. That Burr had few active adherents might
be true ; but nothing showed that Bollman regarded
the result of his mission as unfavorable. Toward the
end of October Bollman sent letters by a certain Lieutenant Spence, who reached Lexington in due course,
and November 2 delivered his despatches to Burr ;[1]
but whatever their contents may have been, they were
not so decisive against Burr's hopes as to stop his
movement. The people of New Orleans were careful
not to commit themselves, but they guarded Burr's
secret with jealousy. They warned no United States
official of the danger in which the city stood ; they
wrote no letters to the President ; they sent no message to Burr forbidding his approach.

This was the situation in New Orleans Nov. 25,
1806, the day when District-Attorney Daveiss at
Frankfort made his second attempt to procure an
indictment against Burr, and when President Jefferson at Washington was startled into energy by receiving a letter, almost equivalent to a confession,
from General Wilkinson. From the Ohio River to
the Gulf of Mexico the conspiracy had numerous
friends ; and in New Orleans it had the most alarming of all qualities, — silence.

Meanwhile young Samuel Swartwout, after parting
from his friend Ogden, had slowly ascended the Red
River, pursuing General Wilkinson, as Evangeline

[1] Wilkinson's Evidence, Burr's Trial ; Annals of Congress,
1807–1808, p. 518. Evidence of Lieutenant Spence, Report of
House Committee, Feb. 26, 1811 ; 3 Sess. 11 Cong., p. 312.

pursued Gabriel, even as far as " the little inn of the
Spanish town of Adayes." The military point for
Wilkinson to decide was whether he should make
an effort to drive the Spaniards back to their town
of Adayes, or whether he should allow them to fix
themselves on the Red River. The movements of
the Spanish General Herrera, who had brought a
considerable mounted force to Nacogdoches, were
supposed at the moment by many persons to have
been made in concert with Burr ; but in reality they
were doubtless intended only to derange the plan,
recommended by Armstrong and Monroe to Jefferson,
by which Texas should be seized for the United
States, while West Florida for the moment should
be left aside. The Spanish government saw the
danger, and sent a little army of some fifteen hundred
men to the Red River, where they posted a strong
garrison at Bayou Pierre, and pressed close upon
Natchitoches. The Americans, instead of taking the
offensive and advancing with five thousand men, as
Wilkinson wished, to the Rio Grande, were thrown
upon the defensive, and trembled for New Orleans,
protected only by a French militia which neither
Claiborne nor Wilkinson could trust.

Under orders from Washington, General Wilkinson reached Natchitoches September 22, and found
the Spaniards in force between his own post and
the Sabine. For a few days Wilkinson talked loudly,
after his peculiar manner. War seemed imminent.
September 28 he wrote from Natchitoches a letter

to Senator Smith of Ohio, the contractor for his supplies :[1] —

" I have made the last effort at conciliation in a solemn appeal to Governor Cordero at Nacogdoches, who is chief in command on this frontier. Colonel Cushing bore my letter, and is now with the Don. I expect his return in four days ; and then, — I believe, my friend, I shall be obliged to fight and flog them."

Governor Cordero, whose object was probably no more than to restrict American possession within the narrowest possible limits, withdrew his troops from Bayou Pierre, September 27, to the west bank of the Sabine, and left open to Wilkinson the road to the eastern bank. The Spanish forces recrossed the Sabine before September 30, but a week later, October 8, General Wilkinson had not begun his ostentatious march, of some fifty miles, to retake possession of the east bank of the river.

On the evening of October 8, General Wilkinson was sitting with Colonel Cushing, of the Second Infantry, alone in the Colonel's quarters at Natchitoches, discussing the military problem before them, when a young man was introduced who said that his name was Swartwout, and that he brought a letter of introduction from General Dayton. After some little ordinary talk, Colonel Cushing having for a moment been called out of the room, Swartwout slipped into General Wilkinson's hands a packet

[1] Wilkinson to Smith, Sept. 28, 1806 ; Senate Report, Dec. 31, 1807, p. 41.

which he said contained a letter from Colonel Burr.
Wilkinson received the letter, and soon afterward
retired to his chamber, where he passed the rest of
the evening in the labor of deciphering Burr's long
despatch of July 29.[1]

If the falsehoods contained in the letters of Burr
and Dayton found any credit in Wilkinson's mind,
they should have decided him to follow his old
bent toward revolution. Everything beckoned him
on. His secret relations, nearly twenty years old,
with the Spanish officials guaranteed to him the connivance of the Spanish force. The French militia of
Louisiana, deaf to Governor Claiborne's entreaties,
would have seen with pleasure Claiborne deposed.
About five hundred United States troops were under
Wilkinson's command on the Red River, of whom few
were native Americans, or cared for the Government
except to obtain their pay. In New Orleans a breath
would blow away the national authority ; and what
power would restore it ? If it were true, as Burr
wrote, that a British fleet stood ready to prevent a
blockade of the Mississippi, the success of the Western
empire seemed assured.

Severance of the ties that bound him to Dayton
and Burr was not a simple matter for Wilkinson.
That they were old friends was something ; and that
all three had fought side by side under the walls of
Quebec in the winter of 1776, with the father of
young Peter Ogden for a friend, and with Benedict

[1] See p. 253.

Arnold for their commander, was still more; but the most serious difficulty was that Wilkinson stood in the power of these men, who knew his thoughts and could produce his letters, and who, in case of his deserting them, would certainly do their utmost to destroy what character he possessed.

Whatever may have been his reflections, Wilkinson took at once measures to protect his own interests. Like Senator Smith, Andrew Jackson, and Daniel Clark, his first step was to provide against the danger of being charged with misprision of treason. The morning after Swartwout's arrival, Wilkinson took Colonel Cushing aside, and after telling him the contents of Burr's letter, announced that he meant to notify the President of the plot, and that after making some temporary arrangement with the Spaniards, he should move his whole force to New Orleans. In one sense this avowal was an act of patriotism; in another light it might have been regarded as an attempt to sound Colonel Cushing, whose assistance was necessary to the success of the plot.

In any case the deliberation of his conduct proved no eagerness to act. A week passed. Although time pressed, and Burr was to move down the Ohio River November 15, Wilkinson did not yet warn the President or the authorities in Mississippi and Tennessee, or the commanding officers at Fort Adams or Chickasaw Bluffs. About October 15 a troop of militia reached Natchitoches; and Wilkinson confided his plans to Colonel Burling, who accompanied it. One

might almost have suspected that he was systematically sounding his officers.   Not until October 21
did he send the promised letter to President Jefferson,
and in that letter he did not so much as mention
Burr's name.[1]   He spoke of the expedition as destined for Vera Cruz.   " It is unknown under what
authority this enterprise has been projected, from
whence the means of its support are derived, or what
may be the intentions of its leaders in relation to the
Territory of Orleans."   The communication was so
timed as to reach Washington after Burr should have
passed down the Ohio; and it was so worded as to
protect Wilkinson in case of Burr's failure, but in no
event to injure Burr.

After sending this despatch to Washington by a
special messenger, Wilkinson wrote October 23 a
letter of mysterious warning to Lieutenant-Colonel
Freeman, who commanded at New Orleans.[2]   He
wrote also a letter to Burr, which he afterward
recovered at Natchez and destroyed.[3]   He sent his
force forward to the Sabine, and passed ten days in
making an arrangement with the Spanish officers
for maintaining the relative positions of the outposts.
Not until November 5 did he return to Natchitoches.

[1] Wilkinson to Jefferson, Oct. 20 and 21, 1806; Wilkinson's
Memoirs, ii. Appendix, xcv.

[2] Wilkinson to Freeman, Oct. 23, 1806 ; Wilkinson's Memoirs, ii. Appendix, ci.

[3] Wilkinson's Evidence, Burr's Trial ; Annals of Congress,
1807–1808, p. 541.

Then, at last, his movements became as rapid as they had hitherto been dilatory.

November 7 he wrote to Colonel Cushing from Natchitoches : [1] "On the 15th of this month Burr's declaration is to be made in Tennessee and Kentucky. Hurry, hurry after me; and if necessary, let us be buried together in the ruins of the place we shall defend!" He had at last chosen his part; and having decided to act as the savior of the country, he began to exaggerate the danger. "If I mistake not, we shall have an insurrection of blacks as well as whites to combat." [2] "I shall be with you by the 20th instant," he wrote to Freeman the same day; [3] "in the mean time be you as silent as the grave!" He left Natchitoches November 7, and reached Natchez on the 11th, whence he wrote "from the seat of Major Minor" a letter of alarm to the President, confiding to the messenger an oral account of Burr's letter, for Jefferson's benefit : [4] —

"This is indeed a deep, dark, and widespread conspiracy, embracing the young and the old, the Democrat and the Federalist, the native and the foreigner, the patriot of '76 and the exotic of yesterday, the opulent and the needy, the 'ins' and the 'outs;' and I fear it will receive strong support in New Orleans from a quarter little suspected. . . . I gasconade not when I

[1] Wilkinson to Cushing, Nov. 7, 1806 ; Memoirs, ii. Appendix, xcix.

[2] Ibid.   [3] Ibid.

[4] Wilkinson to Jefferson, Nov. 12, 1806 ; Memoirs, ii. Appendix, c.

tell you that in such a cause I shall glory to give my life in the service of my country; for I verily believe such an event to be probable, because, should seven thousand men descend from the Ohio, — and this is the calculation, — they will bring with them the sympathies and good wishes of that country, and none but friends can be afterward prevailed on to follow them. With my handful of veterans, however gallant, it is improbable I shall be able to withstand such a disparity of numbers."

If this was not gasconade, it sounded much like intoxication; but on the same day the writer indulged in another cry of panic. He should have written to Governor Claiborne a month before; but having made up his mind to speak, he was determined to terrify : [1] —

" You are surrounded by dangers of which you dream not, and the destruction of the American government is seriously menaced. The storm will probably burst in New Orleans, where I shall meet it, and triumph or perish ! "

If the courage of Claiborne did not, on the arrival of this letter, wholly desert him, his heart was stout ; but he had yet another shock to meet, for on the same day that Wilkinson at Natchez was summoning this shadowy terror before his eyes, Andrew Jackson at Nashville was writing to him in language even more bewildering than that of Wilkinson : [2] —

[1] Wilkinson to Claiborne, Nov. 12, 1806 ; Memoirs, ii. 328.
[2] Jackson to Claiborne, Nov. 12, 1806 ; Burr's Trial. Annals of Congress, 1807–1808, p. 571.

" I fear treachery has become the order of the day. This induces me to write you. Put your town in a state of defence; organize your militia, and defend your city as well against internal enemies as external. My knowledge does not extend so far as to authorize me to go into details, but I fear you will meet with an attack from quarters you do not at present expect. Be upon the alert! Keep a watchful eye on our General [Wilkinson], and beware of an attack as well from your own country as Spain! I fear there is something rotten in the state of Denmark. . . . Beware of the month of December! . . . This I will write for your own eye and for your own safety. Profit by it, and the ides of March remember!"

A storm of denunciations began to hail upon Claiborne's head; but buffeted as he was, he could only bear in silence whatever fate might be in store, for General Wilkinson, who was little more trustworthy or trusted than Burr himself, arrived in New Orleans November 25, and took the reins of power.

CHAPTER XIV.

For several days after Wilkinson's arrival at New Orleans he left the conspirators in doubt of his intentions. No public alarm had yet been given; and while Colonel Cushing hurried the little army forward, Wilkinson, November 30, called on Erick Bollman, and had with him a confidential interview. Not until December 5 did he tell Bollman that he meant to oppose Burr's scheme; and even then Bollman felt some uncertainty. December 6 the General at length confided to the Governor his plan of defence, which was nothing less than that Claiborne should consent to abdicate his office and invest Wilkinson with absolute power by proclaiming martial law.

Considering that this extraordinary man knew himself to be an object of extreme and just suspicion on Claiborne's part, such a demand carried effrontery to the verge of insolence; and the tone in which it was made sounded rather like an order than like advice.

" The dangers," said he,[1] " which impend over this city and menace the laws and government of the United States from an unauthorized and formidable association

[1] Gayarré's Louisiana, iii. 163.

must be successfully opposed at this point, or the fair fabric of our independence, purchased by the best blood of our country, will be prostrated, and the Goddess of Liberty will take her flight from this globe forever. Under circumstances so imperious, extraordinary measures must be resorted to, and the ordinary forms of our civil institutions must for a short period yield to the strong arm of military law."

Claiborne mildly resisted the pressure, with much good temper refusing to sanction either the impressment of seamen, the suspension of the writ of habeas corpus, the declaration of martial law, or the illegal arrest of suspected persons, while he insisted on meeting the emergency with the ordinary legal means at his disposal. Wilkinson was obliged to act in defiance of his advice.

Sunday, December 14, arrests at New Orleans began. Bollman was first to be seized. Swartwout and Ogden had been arrested at Fort Adams. These seizures, together with that of Bollman's companion, Alexander, and Wilkinson's wild talk, spread panic through the city. The courts tried to interpose, and applied for support to Governor Claiborne. The Governor advised Wilkinson to yield to the civil authorities; but Wilkinson refused, thus establishing in the city something equivalent to martial law. He knew, or believed, that both Judge Workman and Judge Prevost were engaged in the conspiracy with Burr, and he was obliged to defy them, or to risk his own success. The only effect of the attempt to

enforce the writ of habeas corpus in favor of the
prisoners was to draw out what had been hitherto
concealed, — Burr's letter of July 29.   Not until
December 18 did Wilkinson send a written version of
that letter to the President.[1]   In order to warrant
the arrests of Swartwout and Ogden, Wilkinson, December 26, swore to an affidavit which embodied
Burr's letter.

This step brought the panic in New Orleans to a
climax.   Wilkinson's military measures were evidently
directed rather against the city than against Burr.
His previous complicity in the projects of Burr was
evident.   His power of life and death was undisputed.
Every important man in New Orleans was a silent
accomplice of Burr, afraid of denunciation, and at
Wilkinson's mercy.   He avowed publicly that he
would act with the same energy, without regard to
standing or station, against all individuals who might
be participants in Burr's combination; and it would
have been difficult for the best people in New Orleans
to prove that they had no knowledge of the plot, or
had given it no encouragement.   The creole gentlemen began to regret the mild sway of Claiborne when
they saw that their own factiousness had brought
them face to face with the chances of a drumhead
court-martial.

Wilkinson's violence might have provoked an outbreak from the mere terror it caused, had he not

[1] President's Message of Jan. 22, 1807.   Annals of Congress,
1806–1807, p. 43.

taken care to show that he meant in reality to protect and not to punish the chief men of the city.
After the first shock, his arrests were in truth reas-
suring. The people could afford to look on while he
seized only strangers, like Bollman and Alexander;
even in Swartwout and Ogden few citizens of New
Orleans took much personal interest. Only in case
the General had arrested men like Derbigny or
Edward Livingston or Bellechasse would the people
be likely to resist; and Wilkinson showed that he
meant to make no arrests among the residents, and
to close his eyes against evidence that could compromise any citizen of the place. "Thank God!" he
wrote to Daniel Clark, December 10,[1] "your advice to
Bellechasse, if your character was not a sufficient
guaranty, would vindicate you against any foul imputation." In another letter, written early in January,
he added,[2] —

"It is a fact that our fool [Claiborne] has written to
his contemptible fabricator [Jefferson], that you had declared if you had children you would teach them to curse
the United States as soon as they were able to lisp."

Claiborne had brought such a charge only a few
weeks before, and Wilkinson must have heard it
from Claiborne himself, who had already written
to withdraw it on learning Clark's advice to Bellechasse. Nevertheless Wilkinson continued, —

[1] Wilkinson to Daniel Clark, Dec. 10, 1806; Clark's Proofs,
p. 150.
[2] Clark's Proofs, p. 151.

" *Cet bête* [Claiborne] is at present up to the chin in folly and vanity. He cannot be supported much longer, for Burr or no Burr we shall have a revolt if he is not removed speedily. The moment Bonaparte compromises with Great Britain will be the signal for a general rising of French and Spaniards ; and if the Americans do not join, they will not oppose. Take care ! Suspicion is abroad ; but you have a friend worth having."

Clark's business correspondents in New Orleans delivered to Wilkinson a letter which came to them from Burr without address, but which was intended for Bollman.[1] "For your own sake," said the General, " take that letter away ! Destroy, and say nothing of it ! " A year later, when the frightened crew of conspirators recovered from their panic and began to turn upon him with ferocity on account of his treason to them and to Burr, Wilkinson wrote to Daniel Clark a last letter, mentioning in semi-threatening language the written evidence in his possession against Clark himself, and adding,[2] —

" Much pains were taken by Bollman to induce me to believe you were concerned. Swartwout assured me Ogden had gone to New Orleans with despatches for you from Burr, and that you were to furnish provisions, etc. Many other names were mentioned to me which I have not exposed, nor will I ever expose them unless compelled by self-defence. . . ."

[1] Wilkinson to Daniel Clark, March 20, 1807; Clark's Proofs, p. 151.

[2] Wilkinson to Daniel Clark, Oct. 5, 1807; Clark's Proofs, p. 154.

Wilkinson never did expose them, nor did he molest in any serious degree the society of New Orleans.

Had Wilkinson been satisfied to secure the city without magnifying himself, he might perhaps have won its regard and gratitude; but he could do nothing without noise and display. Before many days had passed he put an embargo on the shipping and set the whole city at work on defences. He spread panic-stricken stories of Burr's force and of negro insurrection. He exasperated the judges and the bar, alienated Claiborne, and disgusted the creoles. Nothing but a bloody convulsion or an assault upon the city from Burr's armed thousands could save Wilkinson from becoming ridiculous.

Jan. 12, 1807, the Legislature met. Probably at no time had Burr's project received much avowed support, even among those persons to whom it had been confided. Men of wealth and character had no fancy for so wild a scheme. The conduct of Daniel Clark was an example of what Burr had to expect from every man of property and standing. The Legislature was under the influence of conservative and somewhat timid men, from whom no serious danger was to be expected, and whose fears were calculated to strengthen rather than to weaken the government; yet it was true that Burr had counted upon this meeting of the Legislature to declare Louisiana independent, and to offer him the government. He was to have waited at Natchez for a delegation to bring

him the offer; and he was supposed to be already
at Natchez.   The city had been kept for a month
in a state of continual alarm, distracted by rumors,
and expecting some outbreak from day to day, assured
by Wilkinson that Burr with seven thousand men
might appear at any moment, with a negro insurrection behind him and British ships in the river, when
suddenly John Adair rode into town, and descended
at the door of Madame Nourage's boarding-house.
Judge Prevost, Burr's stepson, was so indiscreet as
to announce publicly that General Adair, second in
command to Burr, had arrived in town with news that
Burr would follow in three days, and that it would
soon be seen whether Wilkinson's tyranny would prevail.[1]   The same afternoon Lieutenant-Colonel Kings-
bury of the First Infantry, at the head of a hundred
and twenty men, appeared at the door of the hotel
and marched Burr's second in command to prison.
Adair afterward claimed that if he had been allowed
forty-eight hours no one could have arrested him,
for he had more friends in New Orleans than the
General had; but even he must have seen that the
conspiracy was dead.   For a moment his arrest,
and a few others made at the same time, caused excitement, and Wilkinson ordered detachments of
troops to patrol the city; but thenceforward confidence began to return and soon the crisis passed
away, carrying with it forever most of the discontent

[1] Deposition of John Shaw, Burr's Trial ; Annals of Congress,
1807–1808, p. 573.

and danger which had marked the annexation of Louisiana. If New Orleans never became thoroughly American, at least it was never again thoroughly French.

Unfortunately for Wilkinson's hopes of figuring in the character of savior to his country, Burr's expedition met with an inglorious and somewhat ridiculous end before it came within sight of Wilkinson or his command. After leaving Fort Massac, the little flotilla entered the Mississippi, and in a few days reached Chickasaw Bluffs, where a small military post of nineteen men was stationed, commanded by a second lieutenant of artillery, who had received no more instructions than had been received by Captain Bissell. So far from stopping the flotilla, Lieutenant Jackson was nearly persuaded to join it, and actually accepted money from Burr to raise a company in his service.[1] January 6, leaving Chickasaw Bluffs, the flotilla again descended the river until, January 10, it reached the mouth of Bayou Pierre, about thirty miles above Natchez. There Burr went ashore, and at the house of a certain Judge Bruin he saw a newspaper containing the letter which he had himself written in cipher to Wilkinson July 29, and which Wilkinson had published December 26.

From the moment Burr saw himself denounced by Wilkinson, his only hope was to escape. The President's proclamation had reached the Mississippi Ter-

[1] Evidence of Lieutenant Jacob Jackson, Burr's Trial; Annals of Congress, 1807–1808, p. 683.

ritory ; Cowles Meade, the acting-governor, had called out the militia. If Burr went on he would fall into the hands of Wilkinson, who had every motive to order him to be court-martialled and shot; if he stayed where he was, Cowles Meade would arrest and send him to Washington. Moving his flotilla across the river, Burr gave way to despair. Some ideas of resistance were entertained by Blennerhassett and the other leaders of the party ; but they were surprised to find their " emperor " glad to abdicate and submit. January 17 Burr met Acting-Governor Cowles Meade and surrendered at discretion. His conversation at that moment was such that Meade thought him insane.[1] January 21 he caused his cases of muskets, which had been at first secreted in the brush, to be sunk in the river. After his surrender he was taken to Washington, the capital of the Territory, about seven miles from Natchez. A grand-jury was summoned, and the attorney-general, Poindexter, attempted to obtain an indictment. The grand-jury not only threw out the bill, but presented the seizure of Burr and his accomplices as a grievance. The very militia who stopped him were half inclined to join his expedition. Except for a score of United States officials, civil and military, he might have reached New Orleans without a check.

Fortunately neither the civil nor the military authorities of the national government were disposed to be made a jest. The grand-jury could grant but

[1] Blennerhassett Papers, p. 426.

a respite, and Burr had still to decide between evils. If he fell into Wilkinson's hands he risked a fate of which he openly expressed fear. During the delay his men on the flotilla had become disorganized and insubordinate ; his drafts on New York had been returned protested ; he knew that the military authorities at Fort Adams were determined to do what the civil authorities had failed in doing ; and his courage failed him when he realized that he must either be delivered to President Jefferson, whom he had defied, or to General Wilkinson, whom he had tried to deceive.

Feb. 1, 1807, after sending to his friends on the flotilla a note to assure them of his immediate return,[1] Burr turned his back on them, and left them to the ruin for which he alone was responsible. Disguised in the coarse suit of a Mississippi boatman, with a soiled white-felt hat, he disappeared into the woods, and for nearly a month was lost from sight. Toward the end of February he was recognized in a cabin near the Spanish frontier, about fifty miles above Mobile ; and his presence was announced to Lieutenant Gaines, commanding at Fort Stoddert, near by. Gaines arrested him. After about three weeks of confinement at Fort Stoddert he was sent to Richmond in Virginia. In passing through the town of Chester, in South Carolina, he flung himself from his horse and cried for a rescue ; but the officer commanding the escort seized him, threw him back like a

[1] Blennerhassett Papers, p. 206.

child into the saddle, and marched on. Like many
another man in American history, Burr felt at last
the physical strength of the patient and long-suffering
government which he had so persistently insulted,
outraged, and betrayed.

Not until the end of March, 1807, did Burr reach
Richmond; and in the mean while a whole session of
Congress had passed, revolution after revolution had
taken place in Europe, and a new series of political
trials had begun for President Jefferson's troubled
Administration. The conspiracy of Burr was a
mere episode, which had little direct connection with
foreign or domestic politics, and no active popular support in any quarter. The affairs of the country at
large felt hardly a perceptible tremor in the midst
of the excitement which convulsed New Orleans;
and the general public obstinately refused to care
what Burr was doing, or to believe that he was so
insane as to expect a dissolution of the Union. In
spite of the President's proclamation of Nov. 27, 1806,
no special interest was roused, and even the Congress
which met a few days later, Dec. 1, 1806, at first
showed indifference to Burr and his affairs.

If this was a matter for blame, the fault certainly
lay with the President, who had hitherto refused to
whisper a suspicion either of Burr's loyalty or of the
patriotism which Jefferson believed to characterize
Louisiana, the Mississippi Territory, and Tennessee.
Even the proclamation had treated Burr's enterprise
as one directed wholly against Spain. The Annual

Message, read December 2, showed still more strongly
a wish to ignore Burr's true objects. Not only did it
allude to the proclamation with an air of apology, as
rendered necessary by "the criminal attempts of private individuals to decide for their country the question of peace or war," but it praised in defiance of
evidence the conduct of the militia of Louisiana and
Mississippi in supporting Claiborne and Wilkinson
against the Spaniards : —

" I inform you with great pleasure of the promptitude
with which the inhabitants of those Territories have tendered their services in defence of their country. It has
done honor to themselves, entitled them to the confidence
of their fellow-citizens in every part of the Union, and
must strengthen the general determination to protect
them efficaciously under all circumstances which may
occur."

On some subjects Jefferson was determined to shut
his eyes. He officially asserted that the Orleans
militia had done honor to themselves and won the confidence of their fellow-citizens at a moment when he
was receiving from Governor Claiborne almost daily
warnings that the Orleans militia could not be trusted,
and would certainly not fight against Spain.

By this course of conduct Jefferson entangled himself in a new labyrinth of contradictions and incon-
sistencies. Until that moment, his apparent interests
and wishes led him to ignore or to belittle Burr's conspiracy ; but after the moment had passed, his interests and convictions obliged him to take the views

and share the responsibilities of General Wilkinson. Thus John Randolph found fresh opportunities to annoy the President, while the President lost his temper, and challenged another contest with Luther Martin and Chief-Justice Marshall.

After shutting his ears to the reiterated warnings of Eaton, Truxton, Morgan, Daveiss, and even to the hints of Wilkinson himself; after neglecting to take precautions against Burr, Wilkinson, or the city of New Orleans, and after throwing upon the Western people the responsibility for doing what the government had been instituted to do; after issuing a proclamation which treated Burr's armament as a filibustering venture like that of Miranda; and after sending to Congress an Annual Message which excused the proclamation on the ground that it was an act of good faith toward Spain, although Spain took no such view of it, — Jefferson could not reasonably expect the opposition in Congress to accept without a protest sudden legislation resting on the theory that the Constitution and the Union were in danger.

The month of December, 1806, passed at Washington without producing a public display of uneasiness on the President's part ; the Government was waiting to hear from Kentucky and Ohio. Outwardly Jefferson continued to rely on the patriotism of the people of Louisiana, but inwardly he was troubled with fears. December 22 Robert Smith, anxious to save himself from possible calamity, wrote to him a letter of remonstrance.

" In the course of our various communications," said
Smith,[1] " in relation to the movements of Colonel Burr in
the Western country, I have from time to time expressed
the opinions which, as they were not at all countenanced
by any of the other gentlemen, I did not deem it expedient to press upon your attention. . . . If, as was proposed on the 24th of October, the sloops-of-war and the
gunboats stationed at Washington, New York, Norfolk,
and Charleston had been sent to New Orleans under the
command of Commodore Preble, with Captain Decatur
second in command, we would at this time have nothing
to apprehend from the military expedition of Colonel
Burr.   Such a naval force joined to the ketches and gunboats now on the Mississippi, would beyond a doubt have
been sufficient to suppress such an enterprise.   But this
step, momentous as it was, the Executive could not take
consistently with the limitations of existing statutes and
with the spirit manifested by the House of Representatives at their last session.   The approaching crisis
will, I fear, be a melancholy proof of the want of forecast in so circumscribing the Executive within such
narrow limits."

Robert Smith, conscious of being the person whom
Congress most distrusted, grasped at the idea of freeing himself from restraint, and did not stop to ask
whether Burr's impunity were due to want of forecast
in Congress or in the Executive.   He was alarmed ;
and the President's reply to his letter showed that
Jefferson was equally uncomfortable.[2]

[1] Robert Smith to Jefferson, Dec. 22, 1806 ; Jefferson MSS.
[2] Jefferson to Robert Smith, Dec. 23, 1806 ; Jefferson MSS.

" What I had myself in contemplation," the President
answered, " was to wait till we get news from Louisville
of December 15, the day of Burr's proposed general rendezvous.   The post comes from thence in twelve days.
The mail next expected will be of that date.   If we then
find that his force has had no effectual opposition at
either Marietta or Cincinnati, and will not be stopped
at Louisville, then, without depending on the opposition
at Fort Adams (though I have more dependence on that
than any other), I should propose to lay the whole matter before Congress, ask an immediate appropriation for
a naval equipment, and at the same time order twenty
thousand militia, or volunteers, from the Western States
to proceed down the river to retake New Orleans, pre-
suming our naval equipment would be there before them.
In the mean time I would recommend to you to be getting ready and giving orders of preparation to the officers
and vessels which we can get speedily ready."

Not a trace of confidence in the people of Louisiana
was to be detected in this plan of operations.   The
duty of the government not only to act, but to act
with extreme quickness and vigor, before Burr should
come within a long distance of New Orleans, was
avowed.   The idea of calling out twenty thousand
men to retake New Orleans showed a degree of alarm
contrasting strongly with the equanimity that pre-
ceded it, and with the inertness which had allowed
such an emergency to arise.   The difference of tone
between this letter and the President's public language was extreme.   Nevertheless, the Western mail
arrived, bringing news that the State of Ohio had

seized the greater part of Burr's boats, that six or eight had escaped, and that Burr had gone to Nashville ; and in this partly satisfactory report the President saw reason for further silence. Next came, Jan. 2, 1807, Wilkinson's letter of November 12 from Natchez, with its pledge to perish in New Orleans, and with messages, not trusted to writing, but orally imparted to the messenger, about Burr's cipher letters and their contents. Still the President made no sign. For want of some clew his followers were greatly perplexed ; and men like John Randolph, who hated the President, and Samuel Smith, who did not love him, began to suspect that at last the Administration was fairly at a standstill. Randolph, with his usual instability, swayed between extremes of scepticism. At one moment he believed that the situation was most serious ; at another, that the conspiracy was only a Spanish intrigue. January 2 he wrote to Monroe, in London, a letter full of the conviction that Spain was behind Burr : [1] " I am informed also, through a very direct and respectable channel, that there is a considerable party about Lexington and Frankfort highly propitious to his views, and with strong Spanish prepossessions. Some names which have been mentioned as of the number would astonish you." Jefferson's conduct irritated him more than that of Burr or Yrujo : —

" The state of things here is indeed unexampled. Although the newspapers teem with rumors dangerous to

[1] Randolph to Monroe, Jan. 2, 1807 ; Monroe MSS.

the peace and safety of the Union, and notwithstanding Government give full faith and credit to the existence of a formidable conspiracy, and have given information and instructions to the several State authorities how to act (under which Ohio has done herself much honor), yet not one syllable has been communicated to Congress on the subject. There are some other curious circumstances which I must reserve for oral communication, not caring to trust them by letter. One fact, however, ought not to be omitted. The army (as it is called) is in the most contemptible state, unprovided with everything, and men and officers unacquainted with their duties."

In what state Randolph expected the army to be, after six years of such legislation as his, could not be guessed. Officers and soldiers, distributed by companies, in forts hundreds of miles distant from each other, could hardly become acquainted with any other duties than those of a frontier garrison. General Smith did not, like Randolph, complain of others for the consequences of his own acts. He too wrote at that moment a confidential letter, describing the situation, to his brother-in-law, Wilson Cary Nicholas : [1] —

" I fear that Burr will go down the river and give us trouble. The proclamation, it seems, in the Western country is very little attended to. They, no doubt, seeing no exertion making, consider that it has originated from false information. The President has not yet given any kind of information to Congress, and gentlemen

[1] Samuel Smith to W. C. Nicholas, Jan. 9, 1807 ; Nicholas MSS.

(Giles among the number) will not believe that there is any kind of danger. . . . Burr's letter to Wilkinson is explicit. (This is secret.) He had passed the Alleghany *never, never* to return; his object, New Orleans, — open and avowed. And yet not one step taken, except the proclamation! Duane calls on Congress to act. How can Congress act? Would you force from the Executive the information they are unwilling to give? This would be imprudent. I have (with consent of the President) introduced a Resolution proposing an addition to our military establishment. Will it pass? That I can't tell. . . . It is curious that the nation should depend on the unauthorized exertions of a man whose honor and fidelity were doubted by all except a very, very few, not five in the United States, for its preservation and character. Had he not disclosed the conspiracy, the President would have folded his arms and let the storm collect its whole strength. Even now, not an energetic measure has been taken except by him [Wilkinson] and Tiffin."

Another week passed. Then at last, January 16, John Randolph rose in the House and moved a Resolution asking the President what he knew about Burr's affairs, and what he had done or meant to do in the matter. "The United States are not only threatened with external war," Randolph said, " but with conspiracies and treasons, the more alarming from their not being defined; and yet we sit and adjourn, adjourn and sit, take things as schoolboys, do as we are bid, and ask no questions!" His Resolution annoyed the democrats; but his sneers were more convincing than his arguments, and after some contradictory and unorganized resistance, a majority supported him. The Resolution was adopted and sent to the President.

Two days afterward, January 18, Wilkinson's despatches from New Orleans to December 18, embracing his first written version of Burr's cipher despatch reached Washington. The country learned that Wilkinson had arrested Bollman and other accomplices of Burr, and in defiance of their legal rights had shipped them to Washington for trial. Jefferson was obliged to decide whether he should sustain or repudiate Wilkinson; and in the light of Burr's revelations and Wilkinson's *quasi* confession, he could not deny that a serious conspiracy existed, or affirm that the General had gone beyond the line of duty, even though he had violated the laws. Dearborn's instructions, indeed, had to some extent authorized the arrests. At that moment if the President had repudiated Wilkinson, he would have only diverted public indignation from Burr, and would have condemned the Executive itself, which after so many warnings had left such power in the hands of a man universally distrusted.

Thus at last Jefferson was obliged to raise his voice against Burr's crimes. Thenceforward a sense of having been made almost a party to the conspiracy gave a sting of personal bitterness to the zeal with which he strove to defend Wilkinson and to punish Burr. Anxiety to excuse himself was evident in the Message which he sent to Congress

January 22, in response to Randolph's Resolution
of January 16.

" Some time in the latter part of September," he said,
" I received intimations that designs were in agitation
in the Western country, unlawful and unfriendly to the
peace of the Union, and that the prime mover in these
was Aaron Burr."

He had received such intimations many times, and
long before the month of September.

" It was not till the latter part of October that the
objects of the conspiracy began to be perceived."

Absolute truth would have required the President
to say rather that it was not till the latter part of October that inquiry on his part began to be made.

" In Kentucky a premature attempt to bring Burr to
justice, without a sufficient evidence for his conviction,
had produced a popular impression in his favor and a
general disbelief of his guilt. This gave him an unfortunate opportunity of hastening his equipments."

Complaint of District-Attorney Daveiss was natural; but the reproof was inexact in every particular.
The attempt to indict Burr, if any attempt were to
be made, was not premature. The impression in his
favor did not give Burr an opportunity to hasten his
equipments, since Graham appeared at Marietta the
same day with the news of Burr's first discharge at
Frankfort. Finally, if Daveiss's attempt failed, the
fault was chiefly with the Government at Washington, which had taken no measures to direct or to

support it, and which was represented on the bench
by a judge himself implicated in the charge.

"On the whole," said the Message, "the fugitives
from the Ohio, with their associates from Cumberland,
or any other place in that quarter, cannot threaten serious
danger to the city of New Orleans."

Yet a conspiracy against the Union existed; the
President communicated Burr's cipher letters; he
proclaimed Burr's expectation of seizing upon New
Orleans, as well as the panic prevailing there; and
he approved Wilkinson's arrest of Bollman and
Swartwout.   Finally, the Message spoke of the people
in New Orleans in a tone of confidence quite different
from that of Wilkinson's despatches, communicated
with the Message itself.[1]

The Senate interpreted the Message in the sense it
was doubtless meant to bear, — as a request from the
President for support.   Bollman and Swartwout, who
would arrive in Washington within a few days or
hours, had been illegally arrested, and they, as well
as the other conspirators, could not without special
legislation be held longer in custody.   Giles at once
introduced a Bill suspending for three months the
writ of habeas corpus with respect to such persons ;
and the necessity of this measure seemed so obvious
to the Senate that the Rules were suspended by
unanimous consent, and the Bill was passed on the

[1] Wilkinson to Jefferson, Dec. 14, 1806 ; Annals of Congress,
1806–1807, p. 1009.

same day through all its stages. Bayard alone voted against it.[1]

Monday, January 26, the Bill was brought before the House, and Eppes of Virginia, the President's son-in-law, immediately moved its rejection. The debate that followed was curious, not only on account of the constitutional points discussed, but also on account of the division of sentiment among the President's friends, who quoted the Message to prove that there was no danger to public safety such as called for a suspension of habeas corpus, and appealed to the same Message to prove the existence of a more wanton and malignant insurrection than any that had ever before been raised against the Government. John Randolph intimated that the President was again attempting to evade responsibility.

"It appears to my mind," said he, "like an oblique attempt to cover a certain departure from an established law of the land, and a certain violation of the Constitution of the United States, which we are told have been committed in this country. Sir, recollect that Congress met on the first of December; that the President had information of the incipient stage of this conspiracy about the last of September; that the proclamation issued before Congress met; and yet that no suggestion, either from the Executive or from either branch of the Legislature, has transpired touching the propriety of suspending the writ of habeas corpus until this violation has taken place. I will never agree in this side way to cover up such a violation by a proceeding highly dan-

[1] Diary of J. Q. Adams (Jan. 23, 1807), i. 445.

gerous to the liberty of the country, or to agree that this invaluable privilege shall be suspended because it has been already violated, — and suspended, too, after the cause, if any there was for it, has ceased to exist. . . . With whatever epithets gentlemen may dignify this conspiracy, . . . I think it nothing more nor less than an intrigue ! "

The Bill was accordingly rejected by the great majority of one hundred and thirteen to nineteen. On the same day the attorney-general applied to Judge Cranch of the District Court for a warrant against Bollman and Swartwout on the charge of treason, filing Wilkinson's affidavit and a statement given under oath by William Eaton in support of the charge. The warrant was issued ; Bollman and Swartwout at once applied to the Supreme Court, then in session, for a writ of habeas corpus. February 13 Chief-Justice Marshall granted the writ ; February 16 their counsel moved for their discharge ; and February 21 the chief-justice decided that sufficient evidence of levying war against the United States had not been produced to justify the commitment of Swartwout, and still less that of Bollman, and therefore that they must be discharged. Adair and Ogden, who had been sent to Baltimore, were liberated by Judge Nicholson.

The friends of the Administration, exasperated at this failure of justice, again talked of impeaching the judges.[1] Giles threatened to move an amendment of

[1] Diary of J. Q. Adams (Feb. 21, 1807), i. 459.

the Constitution taking all criminal jurisdiction from the Supreme Court. Meanwhile Randolph and the Federalists assailed Wilkinson, and by implication the President. They brought forward a Resolution declaring the expediency of making further provision by law for securing the privilege of habeas corpus; and in the warm debate raised by this manœuvre John Randolph made himself conspicuous by slurs upon Wilkinson, whom he did not scruple to charge with double treason, — to the Constitution and to Burr. By a close vote of sixty to fifty-eight this Resolution was indefinitely postponed; but the debate showed the settled drift of Randolph's tactics. He meant to attack the President by attacking Wilkinson; and the President could no longer evade responsibility for Wilkinson's acts. To be thwarted by Chief-Justice Marshall and baited by John Randolph; to be made at once the scapegoat of Burr's crimes and of Wilkinson's extravagances, — was a fate peculiarly hard to bear, but was one which Jefferson could not escape.

Thenceforward the situation changed. What seemed to be the indictment and trial of Burr became, in a political point of view, the trial of Wilkinson, with John Randolph acting as accuser and President Jefferson as counsel for the defence, while Chief-Justice Marshall presided in judgment. No more unpleasant attitude could be readily imagined for a man of Jefferson's high position and pure character than to plead before his two most formidable and unforgiving enemies as

the patron and protector of a client so far beneath
respect.   Driven by forces which allowed no choice of
paths, he stood by the man who had saved him;
but in order to understand precisely what he effected in sustaining Wilkinson, Americans must look
in the archives of the King of Spain for knowledge
of facts disbelieved by the President of the United
States.

"According to appearances," wrote Yrujo Jan. 28,
1807,[1] "Spain has saved the United States from the
separation of the Union which menaced them.   This
would have taken place if Wilkinson had entered cor-
dially into the views of Burr, — which was to be expected,
because Wilkinson detests this government, and the separation of the Western States has been his favorite plan.
The evil has come from the foolish and pertinacious perseverance with which Burr has persisted in carrying out
a wild project against Mexico.   Wilkinson is entirely
devoted to us.   He enjoys a considerable pension from
the King.   With his natural capacity and his local and
military knowledge, he anticipated with moral certainty
the failure of an expedition of this nature.   Doubtless he
foresaw from the first that the improbability of success in
case of making the attempt would leave him like the dog
in the fable with the piece of meat in his mouth; that is,
that he would lose the honorable employment he holds
and the generous pension he enjoys from the King.
These considerations, secret in their nature, he could
not explain to Burr; and when the latter persisted in an
idea so fatal to Wilkinson's interests, nothing remained

[1] Yrujo to Cevallos, Jan. 28, 1807 : MSS. Spanish Archives.

but to take the course adopted. By this means he as-
sures his pension; and will allege his conduct on this
occasion as an extraordinary service, either for getting
it increased, or for some generous compensation. On
the other hand this proceeding secures his distinguished
rank in the military service of the United States, and
covers him with a popularity which may perhaps result
in pecuniary advantages, and in any case will flatter his
vanity. In such an alternative he has acted as was to
be expected; that is, he has sacrificed Burr in order to
obtain, on the ruins of Burr's reputation, the advantages
I have pointed out."

Whether Yrujo was right in his theory of Wilkinson's motives might be doubted, but on one point he
could not be mistaken. The general-in-chief of the
United States Army was in the employment of Don
Carlos IV.; he enjoyed a pension of two thousand dollars a year in consideration of secret services, and
for twenty years the services had been rendered and
the pension had been paid.[1]

[1] Clark's Proofs against Wilkinson, 1809.

CHAPTER XV.

JEFFERSON'S effort to suppress the scandal of Burr's disunion scheme had its source in motives both pure and generous. Distressed by the factiousness of the last session, he could feel no wish more ardent than to restore harmony to his party. The struggle for the succession threatened to tear from his brows the hard-won laurels which were his only pleasure, and the reward for infinite labors and mortifications. So far as he could, he stifled discussion in regard to the coming change.

" The question," he wrote to Leiper of Pennsylvania,[1] " cannot be touched without endangering the harmony of the present session of Congress, and disturbing the tranquillity of the nation itself prematurely and injuriously. . . . The present session is important as having new and great questions to decide, in the decision of which no schismatic views should take any part."

In this spirit the President shaped his acts. Reunion in a common policy, a controlling impulse, was the motive of his gentleness toward Randolph and the Virginia schismatics, as it was that of his blindness to the doings of Burr.

[1] Jefferson to Leiper, Dec. 22, 1806; Jefferson MSS.

The Annual Message of December, 1806, was intended to unite the party on a new plane of action,
and to prepare the way for Madison's gentle rule.
Foreign affairs were to be allowed to drop from sight;
France, England, and Spain were to be forgotten ;
Florida was to be ignored ; political energy was to be
concentrated upon the harvesting of fruits already
ripe. For six years, carrying out the policy of discharging public debt, Gallatin had pursued his economies, in the opinion of many good men pressing
them so far as to paralyze Government. The time
had come when he could do no more. Twenty-four
millions of debt had been paid. Of the remainder
about ten millions only could be dealt with ; and arrangements were made for discharging these ten millions before Jefferson's term should end. Meanwhile
the revenue was growing ; the surplus must be disposed of, and the period of pinching economies might
cease. Henceforward Republicans, Democrats, and
Federalists might agree on some common system of
expenditure.

" The question now comes forward," said the Annual
Message, " to what other objects shall these surpluses
be appropriated, and the whole surplus of impost, after
the entire discharge of the public debt, and during those
intervals when the purposes of war shall not call for
them ? Shall we suppress the impost, and give that advantage to foreign over domestic manufactures ? On a
few articles of more general and necessary use the suppression in due season will doubtless be right ; but the

great mass of the articles on which impost is paid are foreign luxuries, purchased by those only who are rich enough to afford themselves the use of them. Their patriotism would certainly prefer its continuance and application to the great purposes of the public education, roads, rivers, canals, and such other objects of public improvement as it may be thought proper to add to the constitutional enumeration of federal powers. By these operations new channels of communication will be opened between the States, the lines of separation will disappear, their interests will be identified, and their union cemented by new and indissoluble ties. Education is here placed among the articles of public care, not that it would be proposed to take its ordinary branches out of the hands of private enterprise, which manages so much better all the concerns to which it is equal; but a public institution can alone supply those sciences which, though rarely called for, are yet necessary to complete the circle, all the parts of which contribute to the improvement of the country, and some of them to its preservation."

With an air of apology, as though his old opinions were no longer of practical interest, the President added that an amendment to the Constitution would be necessary in order to bring these new functions within the enumerated objects of government; but to such an amendment he saw no objection, nor did he apprehend difficulty in obtaining it. A broad system of internal improvements; a national university; "a steady, perhaps a quickened, pace in preparations for the defence of our seaport towns and waters; an early settlement of the most exposed and vulnerable parts of our country; a militia so organized that its effective portions can be called to any point in the Union, or volunteers instead of them, to serve a sufficient time," — these were the objects to which Congress should devote its energies, in order that when the two remaining years of Jefferson's power should come to an end, the fabric of Republican government might be complete.

That Federalist and Democrat could join in accepting such a scheme of action, and could lay aside forever their old, unprofitable disputes, seemed no wild dream. The hope was strengthened by a paragraph of the Message which held out the prospect of removing another serious barrier to perfect harmony : —

" I congratulate you, fellow-citizens, on the approach of the period at which you may interpose your authority constitutionally to withdraw the citizens of the United States from all further participation in those violations of human rights which have been so long continued on the unoffending inhabitants of Africa, and which the morality, the reputation, and the best interests of our country have long been eager to proscribe."

Almost ignoring foreign politics, Jefferson recommended Congress to abolish the slave-trade, begin a system of national roads and canals, found a national university, fortify the coasts, and organize the national militia; and had Congress been able or willing to follow promptly his advice, many difficulties would have been overcome before the year 1810 which seemed even twenty years later to bar the path of national progress. Congress, indeed, never succeeded in rising to the level of Jefferson's hopes and wishes; it realized but a small part of the plan which he traced, and what it did was done with little system. The slowness with which political movement lagged behind industrial and social progress could be measured by the fate of President Jefferson's scheme of 1806 for crowning the fabric of Republican government. Not by means of the government, or by virtue of wisdom in the persons trusted with the government, were Jefferson's objects destined at last to be partially attained.

Notwithstanding the favor shown to internal improvements, John Randolph exulted in the President's Message, which he regarded as expressing his own views. He scoffed at the Smiths, Crowninshields, and other orators who in the last session had talked loudly of war.[1]

"The Message," he wrote to Nicholson, "was, as you supposed, wormwood to certain gentry. They made wry faces, but in fear of the rod and in hopes of sugar-plums swallowed it with less apparent repugnance than I had predicted."

General Smith and the politicians who wanted armaments were annoyed.

"We have established theories," wrote Smith,[2] "that would stare down any possible measures of offence or

[1] Adams's Randolph, p. 206.
[2] Adams's Randolph, p. 208.

defence. Should a man take a patriotic stand against
those destructive and seductive fine-spun follies, he will
be written down very soon.   Look at the last Message!
It is such that the President cannot recommend (although he now sees the necessity) any augmentation of
the army.   Nay I, even *I*, did not dare to bring forward
the measure until I had first obtained his approbation.
Never was there a time when Executive influence so completely governed the nation ! "

No man of ordinary sense could fail to feel some
shame at the recollection of what had taken place in
regard to Florida, or to wish that it might be forgotten ; and the friends of Madison had every reason for
ignoring it and for welcoming Randolph's followers
back into the party, if they would consent to come.
The session took character from this spirit of reconciliation.   The first Bill adopted by Congress suspended, at the President's judgment, the operation of
the Non-importation Act passed in April ; and Randolph did not fail to suggest that his sarcasms against
those who had urged this law were justified by its
instant suspension.   The next important measure,
brought forward under the President's patronage,
was the abolition of the duty on salt ; and Randolph
reminded the House that this relief from taxation
followed close upon his own strenuous efforts of the
year before.   Throughout the session Randolph took
the tone of a dictator ; and on most questions a
majority of the House tried only to vie with him in
the race for popularity.   Old subjects of dispute were

laid aside ; the Yazoo claims were forgotten. In
regard to the army and navy, Randolph was allowed
to have his way ; in the case of Bollman and Swartwout, he stopped the attempt to suspend the writ of
habeas corpus ; in sympathy with his opinions the
House cut down appropriations, refused to fortify New
York, declined to increase the army, and reverted to
the first principles of the Republican party. The session of 1806–1807 was a perpetual effort to win back
the confidence and support of Virginia for Madison,
and leave no excuse for defection to Monroe.

General Smith thought Executive influence more
powerful than ever, but the President seemed to influence only by disguising his weakness.   Little or no
attention was paid to his wishes.   He would gladly
have built ships of the line, he would willingly have
fortified New York, he would have liked two more
regiments to garrison the military posts ; but he could
do nothing in face of the reaction which, at Randolph's bidding, swept the Southern Republicans back
to their practices of 1801 and their professions of
1798.   The force of reactionary feeling was shown
in speeches which revealed a dangerous chasm between North and South.   On the question of fortifying New York, Southern Republicans took ground
which caused New York Democrats to feel toward
Virginia a disgust as deep as ever had been felt by
Burr. Nelson of Maryland favored abandoning the
cities altogether in case of attack : [1] " When the

[1] Annals of Congress, 1806–1807, p. 389.

enemy comes, let them take our towns, and let us retire into the country." Holland of North Carolina regarded the seaboard cities as so many enemies : [1]

" If New York and our other cities were only tolerably fortified, Mr. Holland was confident that we should go to war. He lamented the consequences of that disposition that is for novelty in this country, — a disposition that cannot be quelled. Our commercial towns are defence-less, and that is our only safety at present. I want to see not a single ship, or any preparation for war."

Eppes of Virginia, the President's son-in-law, spoke hotly against the doctrine of defence : —

" If there is any principle which ought to be hooted at in a Republican government, it is the very principle laid down by the gentleman from New York as the basis of his reasoning, — that to preserve peace we ought to be prepared for war. Sir, it is this very principle which is the source of all the miseries of Europe."

John Randolph also favored abandoning New York in case of attack : [2] —

" Suppose New York ever so well fortified, an army may land above the city and cut off its intercourse with the country. A fortification there would be made for the enemy. Not a man of our army would have escaped in the last war from Long Island, if the enemy's general had not been treacherous to his duty ; and all the calami-ties of that campaign might have been avoided if our army had retreated into the country."

[1] Annals of Congress, 1806–1807, p. 598.
[2] Annals of Congress, 1806–1807, p. 610.

Answer to arguments like these was of course impossible. The only final answer was to take the Southern people at their word, and to assert as a principle the rule that seaboard cities, being entitled to no protection from government in case of attack, should have the right to protect themselves by inviting the enemy to occupy them. Boston and New York had no reason to fear the operation of such a rule, if it suited the interests of Virginia; but as an argument even this logic would have availed nothing, because so deep was Virginian antipathy to cities that Randolph and all his friends would have answered with one voice, " We expect no better!"

The unwillingness of the Southern Republicans to fortify extended only to forts and ships, not to gunboats. Randolph had not much faith in gunboats; but his friends were willing to spend comparatively large sums on these cheap defences. Their theory was reasonable. A coast like that of America could not be protected by fixed fortifications alone, — only some system of movable batteries could answer the whole purpose; but in such a system everything depended on the effectiveness of the battery to be selected, and no one could say that the gunboat would prove to be effective. Most sea-going people pronounced it a failure; and in the navy, gunboat service was never popular. The real argument for gunboats was their assumed cheapness; but Gallatin and the Northern Democrats, as well as the Federalists, foresaw that the supposed economy was a delusion. A gunboat cost some ten thousand dollars or less, and a whole flotilla of gunboats could be built for the price of a frigate; but no one could say how much this flotilla would cost in annual repairs or in actual service. The life of a gunboat was short.

These doubts had no effect on the majority of the House. " Fortifications will be of no possible service unless they are manned," argued Nelson,[1] " and to man them we must have a large standing army." He wanted to know whether the House was prepared to adopt a system that would require the raising of above one hundred thousand men. If forts were of no possible service unless they were always manned, — new as the assertion was, — surely gunboats were open to the same objection; yet Nelson wanted to spend three hundred thousand dollars in building gunboats, and he was willing to build any number of gunboats the navy might ask for.[2]

The Northern seaboard representatives rejected the offer of gunboats, and allowed the Southern States to dispose of them. No appropriation for fortifying New York could be obtained. The theory that seaboard cities could not be defended received general assent; but many of the members went further, and declared that no danger to those cities existed. A policy of neglecting defence might be safe in peace, when foreign nations had every interest to avoid a war; but nothing could warrant the common asser-

[1] Annals of Congress, 1806-1807, p. 398.
[2] Annals of Congress, 1806-1807, p. 400.

tion that danger of war existed only from America herself, at a moment when France was attacking American commerce by measures of actual warfare, when England was hesitating whether to permit America to trade at all except with the British Islands, and when diplomatic relations with Spain had ceased, the ministers at Madrid and Washington had been withdrawn, and a Spanish army was threatening New Orleans.

Willis Alston of North Carolina, chiefly known as an object of Randolph's peculiar contempt and personal violence, took as strong ground as Randolph himself on these questions. On the other hand Josiah Quincy showed in a high degree the art of irritating opponents by his manner of expressing a low opinion of their sense and motives; and the Southern members resented this treatment the more because Quincy was a man well born and well educated, whose social standing could not be questioned. In reply to his taunts Alston resorted to the well-worn commonplaces of the Republican party. "The present Administration," said he, "has taken up a new system of defence, — it is that of saving the public money. This system is new, and not known in Federal times. We have not gone on increasing taxes, like our predecessors." The assertion could not be denied; but Quincy's retort was not the less pungent. "The Federal Administration," he replied, "saved the country from danger and disgrace: I wish I could say as much of their successors."

The whole issue lay in these short charges and counter-charges. To some extent the President, his Cabinet, and the Senate had become converted to Federalist views ; but the influence of Randolph and of popular prejudices peculiar to Southern society held the House stiffly to an impracticable creed. Whatever the North and East wanted the South and West refused. Jefferson's wishes fared no better than the requests of the State and city of New York ; the House showed no alacrity in taking up the subject of roads, canals, or universities. The only innovation which made its way through Congress was the Act of Feb. 10, 1807, appropriating fifty thousand dollars for the establishment of a coast survey, for this was an object in which the Southern States were interested as deeply as the Northern. Even the Senate's appropriation for beginning the Cumberland Road was indefinitely postponed by the House.

This jealousy of government could not without illtemper be so severely enforced. Randolph's manners were unconsciously imitated by the men who imitated his statesmanship, and the Southern Republicans treated their Northern allies with autocratic harshness as offensive as that of Randolph. The Federalist members, for the most part able to hold their own and even to return such treatment with manners still more arrogant, enjoyed the irritation of Democrats like Sloan and Smilie, Bidwell and Varnum. If the Southern planters refused to aid in fortifying New York, the Federalists were the stronger for the

refusal; and if Virginia was anxious not to risk her
tobacco and corn for the sake of Boston, New York,
and Philadelphia, the Federalists for the most part
hoped that the Northern cities might be induced to
take care of themselves.   Yet although the Federalists were not sorry to see the Pennsylvania Democrats ground under the heel of Virginia, they were
surprised to find how rapidly the sectional spirit increased in the Southern States when slavery was in
question.   The debate on the abolition of the slave-
trade startled Democrats and Federalists alike.

The paragraph in the President's Message which
related to the slave-trade was regularly referred to
a special committee.   Peter Early of Georgia was
chairman, while Thomas Mann Randolph of Virginia, John Campbell of Maryland, Thomas Keenan
of North Carolina, and three Northern representatives completed the number.   Early took the subject
promptly in hand, and Dec. 15, 1806, reported a Bill,
which was referred to the House in committee, and
came up two days afterward for debate.   The Bill
declared the importation of negroes as slaves unlawful; imposed a fine on the importer, with forfeiture
of ship and cargo; and authorized the President to
employ the armed vessels of the United States in
enforcing the law.

Under the Act which prescribed rules for forfeiture, the cargo of a forfeited vessel was to be sold on
behalf of the United States government.   The cargo
of a slave-ship consisted in negroes.   Under Early's

Bill, every negro imported thenceforth into the country became forfeit to the United States, and must be sold by the United States government to the highest bidder.

The Pennsylvania Democrats, imbued with Quaker principles in regard to slavery, could scarcely be expected to approve of a policy which made the government an owner and trader in slaves. The New Englanders, though the slave-trade had been to a great extent a Rhode Island interest, were little inclined to adopt a law under which any cargo of negroes that might be driven on their coast must be sold at public auction in the streets of Newport or Boston; and perhaps even some of the Southern members might have admitted that the chance of collusion between importers and buyers was a serious objection to the Bill. No one could suppose that such a measure would pass without strenuous opposition, and no one could have felt surprise at seeing Sloan of New Jersey immediately rise to offer an amendment providing that every forfeited negro should be entitled to freedom.[1]

Upon this amendment a debate began which soon became hot. Early took the ground that without his provision for forfeiture and sale, the law would be ineffectual; that no man in the South would inform against the slave-dealer if his act were to turn loose a quantity of savage negroes on the public at large.

[1] Annals of Congress, 1806–1807, p. 168.

" We must either get rid of them or they of us ; there is no alternative ; and I leave it to gentlemen to be determined which course would be pursued. There can be no doubt on this head. I will speak out ; it is not my practice to be mealy-mouthed on a subject of importance. Not one of them would be left alive in a year."

The Southern members supported Early, and the Northern members knew not what to propose. The negroes could not be returned to Africa, because they were all brought from the interior, and the coast tribes would re-enslave or massacre them. Pennsylvania and Ohio were little more anxious than Virginia to receive such citizens. Binding them to masters for a term of years was suggested, but objections were made on both sides.

The debate was adjourned, resumed, adjourned again ; and although the Northern speakers were forbearing, the Southern members more and more lost their temper.

" You have got into a great difficulty," said David R. Williams of South Carolina ; [1] " you are completely hobbled. It is so bad that you cannot go on, and you must stick where you are. Let me ask what is the usual conduct of legislatures on local subjects. Do they not inquire of those who are informed? Are they not guided by those who are competent to judge? The gentlemen from the South, who understand this subject, tell you how this business must be done ; but the gentlemen over the way seem anxious now, as on a former occasion, to draw a revenue from the blood and sweat of the mis-

[1] Annals of Congress, 1806-1807, p. 183.

erable Africans. I will not say that this is their motive, but their conduct certainly justifies a suspicion
that their object is to pass such a law as will connive
at the continuance of the trade for the emoluments of
their constituents."

The discussion was further embittered by a motion
made by Smilie of Pennsylvania to make the importation of negroes a felony to be punished by death.
This proposition called out another display of Early's
frankness.

" We have been asked," said he,[1] " what punishment
can be considered too severe for so atrocious a crime.
Without answering the question in the abstract, it will
be sufficient to answer it by a practical view of the
subject. How do people consider the transaction? Do
they consider it such an atrocious crime? They do not."

The Pennsylvania philanthropists had assumed that
they could at least follow Jefferson in holding slavery
to be an evil and the slave-trade to be a violation of
human rights; but even these points were no longer
conceded.

" All the people in the Southern States," continued
Early, " are concerned in slavery. It is not, then, considered as criminal. . . . I will tell the truth, — a large
majority of people in the Southern States do not consider
slavery as even an evil."

The death-penalty was rejected by a vote of sixty-
three to fifty-three, almost the whole Pennsylvania
delegation voting in its favor. Bidwell of Massachu-

[1] Annals of Congress, 1806-1807, p. 238.

setts then moved an amendment, "that no person shall be sold as a slave by virtue of this Act;" and the House divided, sixty against sixty,[1] nearly all the Pennsylvanians supporting Bidwell, while ten of the seventeen New York members showed the influence of slavery in their State by voting with the Southern slave-owners. Six Southern men, including the member for Delaware, joined the Pennsylvanians and New Englanders in this protest against turning the government into a slave-trading agency; while but two Northern men besides the members from New York voted with the South. Macon, the Speaker, by his casting vote threw out the amendment.

Even after this point was carried, notwithstanding the time wasted in going over and over again the same arguments on either side, the Bill made no progress. Men like Sloan and Smilie were not gifted with great genius, but found infinite resources in their patient obstinacy; and no one could fail to see that the true sympathies of the House were with them. Their first object was to prevent the forfeiture of the negroes, because forfeiture implied title, and the United States government could have no title in these human beings, mere captives in war of barbarous tribes; but on that point the House was decidedly against them, and even Josiah Quincy insisted that they were wrong. Forced to yield on the issue of forfeiture, they resisted with the greater obstinacy the sale of the forfeited negroes; and their objections were so obviously sound

[1] Annals of Congress, 1806–1807, p. 267.

that in spite of adverse votes they held the Bill in suspense, and even secured its recommittal to a select committee of their own choice.

The Southerners, who insisted that their knowledge and experience should guide the House on a matter which they then preferred to consider local, chafed under the patient stolidity of Quaker conscientiousness, but submitted, rather in defiance than in conciliation, to throw the Bill into Northern hands. The recommittal was ordered Jan. 8, 1807, by a vote of 76 to 46; January 20 the new Bill was reported, and the struggle began again as at first. January 28 the Senate sent down a Bill of its own for the same purpose. The Senate debates during the session were not reported, and those of the House were reported only in part, and briefly; but by some means the Senate was persuaded to introduce one rigorous provision into its Bill, prohibiting the coastwise domestic slave-trade in vessels of less burden than forty tons, so that small craft found at sea with cargoes of slaves could not escape under pretence of being engaged in the domestic slave-trade. At best, the Bill could not be effective. The Southern members frankly said that they could frame no Bill likely to be executed, which would prevent slave-traders from smuggling negroes across the Florida boundary or from the West Indian Islands; but the prohibition of the coastwise transport of negroes in small vessels seemed necessary in order to maintain even a pretence of stopping the trade, and the Senate saw no objection to it.

The House hesitated painfully between Pennsylvanian and Virginian influence. Very rarely did the Pennsylvanians assert themselves, and they did so with great moderation; but they were conscientious men, and they had behind them not only the moral support of Jefferson, but also the steady influence of Secretary Gallatin, whose determined hostility to slavery and the slave-trade was proved at every moment of his public life. When, Feb. 9, 1807, the debate was resumed in Committee of the Whole, a majority began by voting in favor of the death-penalty. The next question rose on a new section in regard to forfeitures. The Pennsylvania Bill provided that the forfeited negroes should be indentured for a term of years in some free State or Territory. The proposition seemed reasonable in itself, and calculated to give no offence to the South; but Early declared that the inhabitants of the Southern States would resist this provision with their lives.[1] " We want no civil wars, no rebellions, no insurrections, no resistance to the authority of the government. Give effect, then, to this wish, and do not pass this Bill as it now stands."

Even Pennsylvania patience was disturbed by an outbreak so extravagant. Smilie, who was Irish by birth, obliged Early to take back and explain away his words; but the flash of temper answered its purpose, — Early carried his point. Throughout the struggle the Southern representatives took the ground

[1] Annals of Congress, 1806–1807, p. 477.

that the subject belonged to them; that they were
well aware of the defects in the Bill; that they did
not expect wholly to stop the trade, although they
wished to do so; but that any stronger measure
would revolt public opinion in the South, and would
leave the trade open, because no one would venture
to enforce the Act. Under such circumstances, seeing that in any case the trade would continue, the
Pennsylvanians naturally argued that if only in order
to assert a principle, the law should be made severe;
but they were abandoned by the New Englanders, and
beaten. Eleven of the Pennsylvanians clung to the
death-penalty in spite of Quaker principles; while
not only Barnabas Bidwell, but even Josiah Quincy
deserted them. The House ended by leaving to each
State the decision as to the fate of the forfeited
negroes; and at length, February 13, weary of the
interminable dispute, the House adopted the Senate
Bill with some amendments.

Hitherto John Randolph had taken little part in
the debate; he voted steadily with the Southern representatives, but his well-known antislavery theories
kept him quiet. His silence did not last. The
Senate disagreed to one of the amendments which
had passed the House; a committee of conference
reported, and the Bill came up again on their report.
In a final debate the Southern members attacked the
prohibition of the coastwise trade, the whole measure being thus in their eyes vitiated. Early declared
that the Act would not prevent the introduction of

a single slave; Randolph asserted that the coastwise prohibition touched the right of private property:[1] " He feared lest, at a future period, it might be made the pretext of universal emancipation; he had rather lose the Bill, he had rather lose all the Bills of the session, he had rather lose every Bill passed since the establishment of the government, than agree to the provision contained in this slave-bill. It went to blow up the Constitution in ruins." He prophesied that if ever the time of disunion between the States should arrive, the line of severance would not be between Eastern and Western, but between slave-holding and non-slaveholding States. He said that if ever the time should come when the South should have to depend on the North for assistance against the slaves, he should despair. " All he asked was that the North should remain neutral; that it should not erect itself into an abolition society." The vehemence of the Southern orators was in this instance natural, for the coastwise prohibition cut far more deeply into the constitutional rights of slave-owners than all the other provisions of the Bill which they had so obstinately and successfully resisted; yet on the division they were beaten by the large majority of sixty-three to forty-nine. New York, which cared little for the slaves, cared less for the Constitution, and reversed its former vote. The Senate Bill, Feb. 26, 1807, was sent to the President.[2]

[1] Annals of Congress, 1806–1807, p. 626.
[2] Annals of Congress, 1806–1807, p. 635.

That Randolph and other State-rights Republicans should be deeply irritated was a matter of course. In their effort to tone the Bill to make it suit the opinions of slaveholding communities, they exhausted their strength and the public patience ; and they found a precedent slipped upon them, which would warrant almost any legislative interference with slavery. Randolph, alive to the bearings of all legislation which touched his class interests, at once introduced a Bill to explain and amend the Act. Josiah Quincy promptly moved its reference. The day was February 27, and in another week the Ninth Congress would expire. Randolph opposed the reference, and urged the immediate passage of his Bill, but was defeated by a vote of sixty to forty-nine. His Bill was referred to the House in committee ; it was even made an order for the next day, but it was never taken up.

Randolph declared the hope that should his Bill fail, the Virginia delegation would wait on the President and remonstrate against his signing the Act for Prohibiting the Slave Trade ; but no such step was taken, and March 2, 1807, President Jefferson approved this alarming measure. He at least had no constitutional scruples, and paid no attention to the scruples of others. The only result of the long sectional struggle was to disgust the Southern Republicans and their Pennsylvanian allies alike ; while, so far from obtaining a law which should suit Southern views of the slave-trade, their Act shocked the pride and threatened the property of every slave-owner in the South.

The disasters of the Southern, or what was afterward known as the State-rights, party were largely due to temper. The habit of command, giving self-confidence and vigor of will, opened a boundless field for extravagances. The strength of men like Randolph and Early was their chief weakness; they had every sense except the sense of proportion. The mole-hill which tripped them seemed as serious an obstacle as the distant mountain range, where a false step would dash them to fragments; and when at last they reached the mountain range, with its impassable chasms, where temper was helpless, they saw in it only a mole-hill. That men like Sloan, the butt of the house, and like Smilie and Findley, the ordinary representatives of an intellectual mediocrity somewhat beneath the Pennsylvanian average, should habitually end in carrying their points, in singular and unexpected ways, against the ablest leaders of New England Federalism and the most gifted masters of Virginian oratory; that they should root up everything in their path, and end by giving to the whole country the characteristics of their own common-place existence, — was partly due, not to their energy or their talents, but to the contempt which their want of genius inspired. Not their own wisdom, but their antagonists' errors decided the result, and overthrew successively Church and State in New England and a slave-owning oligarchy throughout half the continent. The Southern gentry could not learn patience. John Randolph, in many respects the most gifted man produced by the South in his generation, and certainly the one who most exaggerated the peculiar qualities and faults of his class, flung away the advantages of every success by attempting to punish his opponents, — as though the hare had stopped in his race to beat the tortoise with a whip. Punishment of Pennsylvania Democrats was waste of time and strength; sarcasm did not affect them; social contempt did not annihilate them; defeats made no impression upon them. They had no leaders and no well-defined policy, but they gravitated like inert weights to an equilibrium. What they wanted they were sure in the end to get.

Randolph's disappointment in regard to the slave-bill was but a single example of a law. After domineering over the House during the whole session, and impressing his own character upon its acts, he attempted at the end to coerce it into a quarrel with the Senate. A Bill for repealing the salt-tax and continuing the Mediterranean Fund was sent to the Senate, and the Senate sent it back with an amendment which reduced the duty on salt from twenty cents a bushel to twelve cents, without wholly abolishing it. Usage and courtesy required that a committee of conference should be appointed; but Randolph insisted that the House should abruptly adhere to its original Bill, and he carried his point by the large majority of ninety-three to twenty.[1] The Senate accepted the challenge, and in its turn voted to adhere. The Bill was lost; and while the salt-tax continued in force, producing some five hundred thousand dollars, the Mediterranean Fund, producing one million two hundred thousand dollars, must expire by limitation. Congress reached this point February 26, the same day when the slave-bill was passed against Randolph's protest.

The Pennsylvania members allowed themselves to be drawn into this step; but they had hardly given their votes before waking to their mistake. The next day a committee was moved to reconsider the subject; and in spite of Randolph's remonstrances, the motion was carried by sixty to forty, every Pennsylvanian changing his vote. Randolph, exasperated to the last degree, attempted to block the measure by obstinacy. When the new Bill was taken up in committee of the whole House February 28, he consumed the day in dilatory motions, calling the yeas and nays until he could no longer induce one fifth of the members to support him in asking for them. The House sat until half-past one in the morning; and when at last the Bill came to a vote, Randolph and his friends left the House without a quorum.[2] After several counts, a quorum was reported, and the Bill was passed ; but the yeas and nays were not taken, and many suspicions were ex-

[1] Annals of Congress, 1806–1807, p. 635.

[2] Diary of J. Q. Adams, i. 464.

pressed that a quorum was not actually present. Nevertheless the Pennsylvanians won their victory; the Bill became law at the last moment of the session. Randolph's conduct ended in destroying his own influence; and the Pennsylvanians felt that the time had come when an alliance with the Democrats of New England against the oligarchy of Virginia could no longer be postponed.

This was the situation at Washington when, on the last day of the Ninth Congress, a messenger arrived from England bringing from Monroe and Pinkney a treaty of commerce. The President's attempt to unite his party on a liberal domestic policy had not succeeded; and many years were to pass before Congress should see another session devoted to domestic affairs.

CHAPTER XVI.

WHILE the summer of 1806 was passing in America, carrying Burr and his insane projects to failure, General Armstrong in Paris was watching the progress of another adventurer, whose plans were as dark as those of Burr, but whose genius was of a very different order. Talleyrand's mysterious instructions regarding Florida were given to Armstrong early in September, 1805. Ulm capitulated October 17; the battle of Trafalgar was fought October 21. Napoleon was thenceforward master of the Continent, and England of the ocean. December 2 Napoleon won the decisive battle of Austerlitz, and December 26 he signed the treaty of Pressburg which humbled Austria.

The wit of man often lagged behind the active movement of the world; but never had diplomatists a harder task than to keep abreast of Napoleon. Other men had moments of repose; but Napoleon's mind seemed never to rest. His schemes were developed, and swept over Europe like so many storm-centres. His plans sometimes succeeded and sometimes failed, but the success or the failure equally implied a greater effort behind; and while Armstrong and his brother diplomatists speculated about the Emperor's motives in pursuing one object, the Emperor was already devising and using new machinery for gaining another. At the close of the war with Austria, Armstrong needed to learn whether Napoleon still wanted money, whether Talleyrand favored the sale of Florida, whether the treaty of Pressburg had or had not left American affairs where they were ; and none of these questions could be answered except by Napoleon himself, who was already far advanced in schemes which no one could fathom, and which largely depended for their success on the skill with which he could conceal them from Jefferson.

Armstrong could only wait. Through the winter of 1805–1806, while John Randolph's opposition delayed Madison's instructions to the minister at Paris, Armstrong had nothing to do. The Emperor and Talleyrand returned to Paris at midnight Jan. 26, 1806. More powerful than ever and more absolute, Napoleon came back from Vienna rich with the contributions he had levied in Germany, but angry at the condition into which Marbois had brought the Treasury of France. Within twelve hours after arriving at the Tuileries he called a council of his ministers, disgraced Marbois, and appointed Mollien in his place.

That this revolution in the Cabinet had some bearing upon American interests was more than likely ; for not only was Marbois an honest man and a warm friend of the United States, but the weight that dragged him down was nothing less than the weight of Spanish finances. The story may be shortly told.[1] Napoleon's wars and repudiation of every inconvenient debt threw the French mercantile class into general bankruptcy. In the want of coin to supply the demands of the Emperor and of the merchants, the Bank of France issued dangerous amounts of paper money. To support these issues specie had to be obtained ; and the empire which produced specie was Spain. Spain might be forced to give up her treasures ; her arrears of subsidy alone would if paid add greatly to Marbois's resources. Yet the treasures of Spain were shut in Mexico and Peru ; they could be brought to Europe only under danger of capture ; and a means by which ten or twenty million Mexican dollars could run the gauntlet of British cruisers and reach in safety the Bank of France was a matter of necessity to Marbois.

The ordinary business of the Treasury in discounts and contracts was conducted through a firm called the " Négociants réunis," consisting of three capitalists, — Messrs. Ouvrard, Desprez, and Vanlerberghe. Ouvrard, the most active of the three, went to Madrid ; and by lending assistance to the sorely pressed Treasury and trade of Spain induced the Spanish government to give him the privilege of importing bullion from Mexico at the rate of seventy-five cents on the dollar. The risk of importation was worth twenty-five per cent on any cargo ; but Ouvrard meant to

[1] Thiers, Consulat et Empire, vi. 30.

escape all risk.   He had plans of his own, involving partnership with the British government itself through the Hopes and Barings of Amsterdam and London; he proposed to draw some five million dollars from Mexico by giving to the United States government drafts on South America in settlement of the Spanish spoliations, besides getting no less than ten million dollars from the United States government for the Floridas.

The unnamed negotiator who came to Armstrong in September, 1805, with Talleyrand's autograph instructions was an agent of Marbois and Ouvrard, whose errand was doubtless known to the Emperor. Meanwhile the Treasury, the Bank, and the "Négociants réunis" supported each other by loans, discounts, and indorsements, largely resting on Spanish bonds, and made face as well as they could against commercial embarrassments and Napoleon's arbitrary calls for great sums of coin; but the Treasury, being in truth the only solvent member of the partnership, must ultimately be responsible for the entire loss whenever matters should come to liquidation.

This was the state of the finances when, Jan. 27, 1806, Napoleon called Marbois and Ouvrard before him.   No one charged criminality on any of the parties to the affair.   In truth one person alone was to blame, and that person was the Emperor himself; but men who served such masters were always in the wrong, — and in fact Marbois, Ouvrard, Desprez, and Vanlerberghe accepted their fate.   Marbois was disgraced; while the three others were obliged to surrender all their property under the alternative of going to Vincennes, with its memories of the Duc d'Enghien.

The dismissal of Marbois and the ruin of Ouvrard had no immediate effect on the Florida negotiation. So far from discouraging Armstrong's hopes, they seemed at first likely to bring about some arbitrary decision, after the Emperor's well-known style of settling questions in which he had an interest. In the middle of February Armstrong wrote in some alarm to Madison: [1] —

"All the points in controversy between his Catholic Majesty and the United States were submitted on the 14th instant to this Government by the Spanish ambassador, with an order from his Court to solicit the immediate interposition of the Emperor and King. That his Majesty will take upon himself the mediation is not to be questioned; but the form he may think proper to give to it is a point equally doubtful and important. Should this movement on the part of Spain have been spontaneous, growing merely out of her own policy and feelings, there is reason to believe that I may be able to prevent any sudden and unfavorable determination from being taken; but if, on the other hand, it should have been either dictated or invited by this Cabinet, the presumption is strong that the decision is already taken, and will present only the alternative, — submission or hostility. Of the two conjectures, the latter is the more probable."

[1] Armstrong to Madison, Feb. 17, 1806; MSS. State Department Archives.

For the moment, while Napoleon was struggling with the confusion of his finances, he held Florida in reserve as a resource for extremity. Armstrong was officially or semi-officially told that the Emperor supposed the whole matter of the Spanish-American dispute to be regularly before him by consent of both parties.[1] He had another long interview with his unnamed negotiator, who pressed him to accept Spanish drafts on South America in payment of the claims for Spanish spoliations, and who argued with much obstinacy that Florida was well worth ten million dollars to the United States.

During all this time Armstrong had heard not a word from his Government. While the minister was listening to these whispers of imperial policy at Paris, Madison had but begun to write the long-delayed instructions which were in effect an acceptance of Talleyrand's proffered terms. The long-delayed "Two-Million Act" received the President's signature Feb. 13, 1806; but not until March 13 did Madison sign the instructions which contained the project of a convention.[2] This despatch was accompanied by another of March 15, which contained an explanation of the Miranda affair and long complaints of Yrujo's conduct. The law prohibiting trade with St. Domingo, "although it must be understood to have proceeded

---

[1] Armstrong to Madison, March 9, 1806; MSS. State Department Archives.

[2] Madison to Armstrong and Bowdoin, March 13, 1806; MSS. State Department Archives.

. . . not from any rightful requisition on the part of France, and still less from a manner of pressing it which might have justly had a contrary tendency," was enclosed in the despatch, with instructions to sound the French government in the hope of inducing Napoleon to lay aside his objections to the traffic.

The packet sailed at once; and after a voyage of the usual length arrived in France in time to bring the despatches, May 1, to Armstrong's hands. No apparent change had then taken place in the Emperor's plans; but during the three months of labor since his return from Austria he had succeeded in restoring order to his finances and was richer than ever before. The Spanish government sent to Paris a certain Señor Izquierdo as special agent to make a financial arrangement with Napoleon; and through him much business was done unknown to the department over which Talleyrand presided. In short the situation had changed, although no one, even among the Emperor's immediate household, knew what had taken place.

In pursuance of the secret memorandum in Talleyrand's handwriting, Armstrong, May 1, sent a note to the Foreign Office in the language of his instructions. Talleyrand acted promptly; May 2 he carried Armstrong's note to Napoleon's closet.[1] Without discussing the matter the Emperor said : " I have some papers in relation to that business which you have not

[1] Armstrong to Madison (private), May 4, 1806; MSS. State Department Archives.

seen." The next day these papers were given to him. They consisted in maps and charts of the Floridas, with many arguments to prove their military and naval importance to Spain, and a formal declaration from Don Carlos IV. that on no account would he consent to alienate them either by sale or otherwise.

Talleyrand immediately sent for the American minister and told him what had occurred. Only a few weeks before, with equal appearance of seriousness, Armstrong had been assured that the whole matter was in the Emperor's hands by the request of the Spanish government. May 3 he was suddenly told that King Charles would on no account consent to alienate Florida. If the first story were true the second must be false. Armstrong hinted as much. "Though I have not seen the overture on paper," said he, "yet I am not the less assured that it had existence; and if I have not been much deceived, it may at this moment be found in the portfolio of M. Ouvrard."

"That may be," replied Talleyrand; "but it is not the less true that circumstances have produced an entire change in the dispositions of Spain." Then, as though to protect himself from the charge of deception by making a counter-charge against Armstrong, he suddenly hinted that Armstrong's own conduct had much to do with alarming the pride of Spain.

"Do you know," said he, "that Mr. Erving has communicated to the Prince of Peace the confidential propositions of which you were made the depository last summer, and that they were derived from Mr. Bowdoin, as it would appear for the express purpose of being so communicated?"

At this unexpected shock, coming instantly after the other, Armstrong was thunderstruck.

"You may readily imagine my confusion and astonishment at this discovery," he continued in his narrative to Madison. "I had confided the propositions to Mr. Bowdoin under the most solemn injunctions of secrecy. . . . Could I believe that a man to whom his country has committed so high an office could so flagrantly violate a trust so sacred?"

His anger was diverted from Talleyrand to his colleague; but in spite of this successful diversion, one might suppose Armstrong capable, even in anger, of seeing that Talleyrand's story was not altogether clear, — that he was trying to distract attention from his own failures.

The more closely Ouvrard's scheme was brought to light, the more clearly it seemed to take the form of an intrigue or a job. The notorious corruption that surrounded Talleyrand explained the favor shown it by the French Foreign Office; but neither the Emperor of France nor the King of Spain was ruled in such matters by subordinates, and Armstrong began to feel the error of making his own Government the instrument of Ouvrard's speculations. Too deeply involved to draw back he took refuge in caution, and said even to the Secretary of State as little as he could. Above all, he avoided reference to possible corruption involved in the bargain. His colleague Bowdoin, whose garrulity had already annoyed him, did not imitate Armstrong's reticence, but wrote to the President the facts which Jefferson least cared to know. The profits on the Louisiana stock, he said,[1] had stimulated jobbery; fifteen per cent discount on one million seven hundred and ten thousand dollars had been divided among the individuals concerned. The two Floridas were offered by Daniel Parker, agent of the Hopes in Amsterdam, who came with a letter of recommendation from Labouchere, Sir Francis Baring's son-in-law, and who held or pretended to hold powers of transfer from the Prince of Peace. The highest point to which the propositions could be traced was to one Cazeneau, Parker's friend, who lived in Talleyrand's house. Some time afterward Bowdoin added[2] that a new negotiator had appeared, — a former private secretary to Talleyrand, — a M. Dautremont, who came to Skipwith, the American consul at Paris, and after explaining that the X. Y. Z. business and the jealousy of the American government had caused much uneasiness in matters of this delicate nature, suggested that other means less exposed than money to observation might be devised. He thought well of land-grants to Talleyrand's brother, in which Skipwith might take a share.

With so many different persons and interests in-

---

[1] Bowdoin to Jefferson, May 20, 1806; Jefferson MSS.

[2] Bowdoin to Jefferson, Oct. 20, 1806; Jefferson MSS.

volved in the Floridas and the claims, Armstrong might feel confident that a single rebuff from the Emperor would not end the matter. After a few weeks Talleyrand quietly instigated the American minister to renew his request, which was done by a note of May 25 ;[1] and May 28 Armstrong received in reply an official assurance of " his Majesty's wishes to see the controversy amicably terminated, and his readiness to lend himself to that object." Talleyrand was not only in earnest but in haste ; for on the same day, May 28, he wrote to M. de Vandeul, who was in charge of the French embassy at Madrid, a cautious letter of instructions. The United States government, he said,[2] seemed disposed to renew negotiations with Spain. He ran over the points in dispute, and sketched the outlines of an arrangement, including the cession of West Florida.

" You will have, sir, to express no official opinion on this point," he said. " I need only tell you, in order that you may make use of it in your conversations, that this part of the Floridas must be warmly desired by the Americans, because it closes the mouths of several rivers which have a great part of their course within the United States. Under another Power Florida, so situated, can intercept American commerce ; and since the Province is thinly populated and very accessible by land, it is to be presumed that the United States would seize the first

[1] Armstrong to Madison, Oct. 10, 1806; MSS. State Department Archives.

[2] Talleyrand to Vandeul, May 21, 1806; Archives. des Aff. Étr., MSS.

pretext for invasion. If Spain is not bent on preserving this colony, she may listen to the American propositions; and all that she would have to remark in making this arrangement is that West Florida, which brings very little revenue to her, would be a much more valuable possession for the United States."

Vandeul was intimate with G. W. Erving, the American *chargé* at Madrid; and with friendly zeal he entered into the negotiation. Taking Talleyrand's despatch and Armstrong's note, a copy of which was inclosed for his guidance, he went to the Prince of Peace, with whom he had a long conversation June 18, 1806.

" To tell your Excellency the truth," he wrote the next day to Talleyrand,[1] " I ought to inform you that the Prince of Peace appears to me to hold pronounced opinions excessively opposed to the conciliatory views which I should have wished to find in him. Nevertheless I did my best to bring him to less passionate ideas, and asked him whether he did not think it a matter of general interest that the old relations should be restored between Spain and the United States, even admitting (for this is one of the Prince's allegations) that they were only suspended for the moment as to official forms. He answered me that this state of things was in no way prejudicial to the interests of the two countries; that commerce continued between them under the safeguard of reciprocal good faith; and that this mode of existence might last a long time without disquieting Spain."

[1] Vandeul to Talleyrand, June 19, 1806; Archives des Aff. Étr., MSS.

Vandeul was obliged to urge the Emperor's wish for a reconciliation and the advance made by Armstrong at Paris. Thereupon Godoy suddenly changed his tone. "At bottom," said he, "we are quite ready to see where they want to come out; you may assure your Court of that." Vandeul thanked him, and added that he hoped the Prince would be pleased to have the matter negotiated at Paris. "Well, granted again!" answered Godoy; "I see no inconvenience in consenting to that." "Your Excellency authorizes me to inform M. de Talleyrand by my first despatch?" "By your first despatch."

Greatly pleased at his success, Vandeul immediately wrote to Talleyrand. A few days afterward he returned to the Prince of Peace, and in a long interview undertook to dispose of the whole subject.[1] Godoy objected chiefly that as yet no official representation had been made on which the Government of Spain could act. Vandeul urged that Armstrong's note and Talleyrand's instructions were sufficient proof that the Americans had changed their tone and system. In his earnestness he insisted upon expressing his opinion on all the points in dispute, including the cession of West Florida.

"Then the Prince gave way entirely to the accession that I asked; and in a manner that I found not only open, but even friendly, told me to renew to you what he had previously authorized me to write to you, and to add

[1] Vandeul to Talleyrand, June 23, 1806; Archives des Aff. Étr., MSS.

that ministerial measures should decidedly be taken for a suitable expression of the intentions of the Spanish Court both to your Highness and to the American ministers, with views of conciliation and definite arrangement, in the dispute with the United States."

Vandeul was convinced that the Prince spoke the truth, and he hurried to tell Erving. The American *chargé*, though far from friendly to Spain, believed that Godoy was honest; and he hastened to notify Armstrong. Armstrong had no doubt that all was well, and lost no time in consulting Talleyrand, who had every motive to feel sure of success. The Spanish imbroglio seemed on the verge of a friendly settlement.

Suddenly occurred one of the scenes of melodrama to which the Emperor's servants were accustomed. When Talleyrand brought Vandeul's despatch to his master, Napoleon broke into a passion. Rebuking Talleyrand sharply for having pressed the matter in its first stages, he threatened to degrade and punish Vandeul; and he ordered Talleyrand not only to reprimand his subordinate in the severest manner, but himself to meddle no more with the subject.[1] His orders were instantly followed with the blind obedience which marked the Emperor's service. Vandeul was still congratulating himself on his success, and waiting for a letter of approval from Paris, when a despatch arrived which shivered his diplo-

[1] Armstrong to Madison, Oct. 10, 1806; MSS. State Department Archives.

matic triumph. Without a word of explanation,
Talleyrand administered the reproof he had been
ordered to give. Vandeul was told that he had gone
altogether beyond his instructions : [1] —

" To cause the negotiations of these two Governments
to be opened under his Majesty's eyes would be to associate him in all their quarrels and to render him more
or less responsible for the results. He will see with
pleasure the return of a good understanding between the
two countries ; but they alone can judge what means of
reconciliation suit their respective interests."

A few days afterward came another and sharper
reprimand : [2] —

" In demanding that the negotiation should take place
at Paris, in making overtures to the United States minister while he has not even received instructions from his
Government, in leading the Prince of Peace to believe
that everything would be done under the mediation of
France, — you exceed the instructions marked out for
you ; and such is the effect of one false step, that it
inevitably draws others after it before the system which
has been forsaken can be resumed. That Spain and the
United States should seek a reconciliation is to be desired ; but leave to them the opening of negotiation, and
take only such steps as are marked out for you, — such
are his Majesty's orders. The United States and Spain
will communicate their intentions to each other. You
cannot charge yourself with the always embarrassing

[1] Talleyrand to Vandeul, July 3, 1806 ; Archives des Aff.
Étr., MSS.

[2] Talleyrand to Vandeul, July 12, 1806; Archives des Aff.
Étr., MSS.

functions of an intermediary without being formally authorized to do it; for the Government alone can know whether this step is consistent with its interests of the moment and with the general plan it has formed for itself."

That the words of this despatch were taken from the Emperor's lips is more than likely. Talleyrand's notes always repeated as nearly as possible the exact expressions of his master; and the expressions of this note were Napoleonic even in their confusion of facts and ideas. Above all, the concluding sentence, which was probably as mysterious to Talleyrand as to the Americans, marked the proceeding with the peculiar stamp of Napoleon's mind. No one but himself should judge whether the cession of Florida was " consistent with his interests of the moment and with the general plan he had formed for himself." Probably for the first time, July 12, 1806, Talleyrand learned that Napoleon had a general plan which was inconsistent with complete reconciliation between Spain and the United States ; yet he could no longer doubt that the same general plan had controlled the Emperor's conduct at least as far back as May 1. From this reticence he might infer that his own fall approached. Another proof that his credit waned came in a form more gracious, but not less convincing. Napoleon conferred on him an Italian principality. The Ex-Bishop of Autun became Prince of Benevento.

Had Armstrong been allowed to know every de-

tail of this transaction, he could not have penetrated
Napoleon's secret; but for weeks he was kept in
dense ignorance. Aware that the Prince of Peace
had consented to negotiate, informed that Izquierdo
had received powers and was authorized to proceed,
Armstrong still found an invisible barrier across his
path, — frivolous difficulties of form and unmeaning
references to Madrid, — which no effort of his could
remove. At a hint from Talleyrand he went to
Marshal Duroc, a man of high character and abilities, who stood as near as the nearest to the Emperor, and who was conducting with Izquierdo the
Spanish negotiations which Napoleon had taken from
Talleyrand. Duroc seemed well disposed toward
America; and through him Armstrong succeeded in
putting into Napoleon's hands the project of a treaty
between the United States and Spain. After reading it attentively, the Emperor quietly returned it,
without a word.

Foiled again by this impenetrable mystery, Armstrong dreamed of forcing the Emperor's hand. He
could at least, by an official note, compel Talleyrand
and Izquierdo either to act or to explain their inaction; but from this step he was dissuaded by Talleyrand and Duroc, who reasoned that precipitancy
might do harm, but could do no good.

Meanwhile Talleyrand wrote a despatch [1] to Turreau at Washington; and if Turreau understood its

[1] Talleyrand to Turreau, July 31, 1806; Archives des Aff.
Étr., MSS.

meaning, his insight was clearer than that of the Prince of Benevento himself. The tone of this instruction varied between a caress and a threat; but the threat came last, and was most significant: —

"His Majesty would be pained to remark that the United States, to whose prosperity France has at all times contributed, — that Spain, in whom she takes a like interest, — should revive in America quarrels that are beginning to slumber in Europe. The United States, which owe their fortune to commerce, are interested in peace; they have reason to wish it with their neighbors; and if, comparing their force with that of a colony, they can promise themselves success at first, they can also bear in mind (*reconnaître*) that the colonies are not alone, and that Europe has always gone to their aid. Take care, sir, to maintain the United States in the views of conciliation with which the news of the events of the last campaign may have inspired them. A sense of their true interests would suffice to make them true to this disposition, even though they had not bound themselves to it by the demand they have made on his Majesty the Emperor to intervene in their discussions with Spain, and to employ his good offices for the re-establishment of a perfect harmony between the two Powers. His Majesty, without putting himself forward as mediator in circumstances where other interests, which directly concern his empire, ought to fix his whole attention, will regard whatever the United States and Spain may do toward a reconciliation as an evidence of friendship toward himself."

Sept. 25, 1806, the Emperor returned to Germany to begin a war with Prussia which was to lead him

far. His departure put an end to whatever hopes
Armstrong still cherished, while it left the United
States in a mortifying attitude. After having been
defied by Spain, Jefferson found himself deluded by
France. No imagination could conceive the purpose
for which Napoleon meant to use the United States
government; but that he had some scheme, to which
President Jefferson must be made subservient, was
clear. Armstrong tried in vain to penetrate the
mystery. Whatever it might be, it was as yet hidden
in the recesses of Napoleon's mind.

No sooner had the Emperor left Paris than the
American minister, September 30, wrote a note of
inquiry to Izquierdo, who replied in substance that
his powers had been suspended or recalled. Nothing
remained but for Armstrong to inform the President
of all the facts connected with the failure of his negotiation, and then to wait at Paris, with what patience
he could command, for the moment when Napoleon
should consent to reveal the meaning of these mysterious manœuvres. Yet in diplomacy as in war,
nations were commonly lost when they allowed Napoleon to take the initiative, and to choose his own time
and place for attack. The United States government
had every reason to be on its guard.

Napoleon reached the battle-field of Jena Oct. 14,
1806, and crushed the Prussian army. October 27
the conquering French battalions made a triumphal
entry into Berlin. November 25, — the day so frequently occurring in the story of Burr's conspiracy,

when Jefferson received General Wilkinson's despatch, and when Wilkinson himself reached New Orleans, — the Emperor Napoleon left Berlin for Poland and Russia. Before leaving Berlin he signed a paper destined to become famous throughout the world under the name of the Berlin Decree. This extraordinary mandate, bearing the date of Nov. 21, 1806, began by charging that England disregarded the law of nations. She made non-combatants prisoners of war; confiscated private property; blockaded unfortified harbors and mouths of rivers, and considered places as blockaded though she had not a single ship before them, — even whole coasts and empires. This monstrous abuse of the right of blockade had no other object than to raise the commerce and industry of England on the ruin of the commerce and industry of the Continent, and gave a natural right to use against her the same weapons and methods of warfare. Therefore, until England should recognize and correct these violations of law, it was decreed — (1) That the British Isles were in a state of blockade; (2) That all intercourse with them was prohibited; (3) That every Englishman found within French authority was a prisoner of war; (4) That all British property, private as well as public, was prize of war; (5) That all merchandise coming from England was prize of war; (6) That half the product of such confiscations should be employed to indemnify merchants whose property had been captured by British cruisers; (7) That no ship coming from

England or her colonies should be admitted into any port; (8) That every vessel trying to elude this rule by means of false papers should be confiscated.

This decree, which cut the roots of neutral rights and of American commerce with Europe, was published at Paris in the "Moniteur" of Dec. 5, 1806. At the same time news arrived that Hamburg, and nearly all the north coast of Germany along the German Ocean and the Baltic, had fallen into Napoleon's hands, or was certain soon to become his prey. When Armstrong, watching with keen interest the rapid progress of French arms, took up the "Moniteur" which contained the Berlin Decree, he might well have started to his feet with the cry that at last he understood what the Emperor would be at. A part of the enigma which had perplexed diplomacy was explained, and what was not yet revealed might vaguely be divined.

December 10 Armstrong wrote to Decrès, the Minister of Marine, to ask of him, in Talleyrand's absence, an explanation of the decree. For some days no answer was received. "Much is said here," he wrote to Madison, "of qualifications which are to be given to the *arrêté* of November 20 [21], and which would indeed make it very harmless; but these are rather to be hoped for than believed in." When Decrès' reply arrived, dated December 24, it went far to confirm Armstrong's fears, by avoiding decisive and official explanation.[1]

[1] Armstrong to Madison, Dec. 24, 1806; State Papers ii. 805.

" I consider the imperial decree of the 21st of November last," wrote Decrès, " as thus far conveying no modification of the regulations at present observed in France with regard to neutral navigators, nor consequently of the convention of Sept. 30, 1800, with the United States of America; . . . but it will be proper that your Excellency should communicate with the Minister of Exterior Relations as to what concerns the correspondence of citizens of the United States with England. . . . It will not escape General Armstrong that my answers cannot have the development which they would receive from the Minister of Exterior Relations, and that it is naturally to him that he ought to address himself for these explanations, which I am very happy to give him, because he wishes them, but upon which I have much less positive information than the Prince of Benevento."

With this explanation, such as it was, Armstrong was obliged to content himself; and the year 1806 closed, leaving President Jefferson at the mercy of battles soon to be fought in the most distant corner of Germany, where the Emperor Alexander of Russia was gathering his forces for a conflict more terrible than Europe had yet seen.

CHAPTER XVII.

WHILE Armstrong coped with Napoleon in Paris, Monroe enjoyed a brief moment of sunshine on the other side of the Channel. After his diplomatic disasters he might think himself happy, though he only threw from his own shoulders upon those of Armstrong and Bowdoin the Florida negotiation which had thus far injured the reputation of every man connected with it; but he had double cause of rejoicing. He not only escaped from Talleyrand and Godoy, but also from William Pitt, whose body he saw carried amidst the pompous mournings of London in funeral state to Westminster Abbey, and left in solemn grandeur by the side of his great father. Pitt died Jan. 23, 1806, exhausted by the anxieties of office.

At last Fortune smiled upon Monroe with caresses more winning than any she had shown since her last sudden appearance before his eyes under the outward semblance of Barbé Marbois in Livingston's garden on the Boulevard Montmartre. Old King George, knowing no Tory competent to succeed Pitt or capable of controlling Parliament, summoned Lord Grenville and submitted to Charles James Fox. Grenville became First Lord of the Treasury; Fox took charge of

the Foreign Office ; Erskine became Lord Chancellor ;
Sidmouth, Lord Privy Seal.   The union of different
party chiefs was so general as to give the Ministry
the nickname of All the Talents.   By February 7 the
revolution was completed.

Monroe was greatly pleased, as well he might be,
for his position in England had been hitherto far
from comfortable.   To soothe the Tories, — who were
prejudiced against him not only as American minister, but also as having when minister to France
actively sympathized with the French Directory in
hostility to England, — Monroe had thought himself
obliged to shun the society of the Whigs, and had
been restricted to such social relations as Pitt's
friends would supply, which under the best of circumstances were neither extensive nor amusing.   Fox
made amends for this self-denial.   His statesmanship
was broad and liberal, his manners charming, and he
had the quality, most rare in politics, of entire frankness and truthfulness.   In a few days Monroe wrote
home that he had enjoyed his first interview with the
new secretary, " who in half an hour put me more
at my ease than I have ever felt with any person in
office since I have been in England." [1]   Fox said
little, but held out hopes ; and Monroe had so long
been left without even hope to nourish him that he
gladly fed upon the unaccustomed diet.   Nevertheless, more than a month passed before he ventured

[1] Monroe to Madison, Feb. 12, 1806; MSS. State Department
Archives.

to make formal application [1] for an order to suspend
the seizure and condemnation of American vessels
under the rule established by Pitt and Sir William
Scott. At length, April 17, at the Queen's drawing-
room Fox took the American minister aside and
announced himself ready to begin negotiation, and to
pursue it without delay till it should be concluded.[2]
He said that no trouble need be feared about the
colonial trade, but that there would be objections to
making payments for property already taken; meanwhile the seizures and condemnations were to be
stopped.

The 1st of May arrived. Three months had passed
since the new Ministry took office, yet nothing had
been publicly done to satisfy the United States. The
reason was well known. Fox was obliged to overcome many kinds of opposition both in and out of
the Cabinet. The West Indian colonies, the royal
navy, the mercantile shipping interest, the Tory country gentlemen, and the Court were all opposed to
concessions, and only the Treasury favored them.
To increase Fox's difficulties, news began to arrive
from the United States of the debate in Congress on
the Non-importation Act, of the loose talk of Congressmen and the vaporings of the press; and to
crown all came the story that the mob of New York
had taken the punishment of Pierce's manslaughter
into its own hands. The English people honestly

[1] Monroe to Madison, April 3, 1806; State Papers, iii. 115.

[2] Monroe to Madison, April 18, 1806; State Papers, iii. 116.

believed the Americans to be cheating them in the matter of the colonial trade; they suspected that their Yankee cousins were shrewd, and they could plainly see that Jefferson and Congress were trying to hide behind the shadow of Napoleon. Nonimportation and commercial restriction had no other object than to give England the alternative of surrendering either to France or to America what she believed to be the price of her existence without the chance of fighting for it. Two thirds of the British people understood the Non-importation Act as a threat, — as though the Americans said, " Surrender to us your commerce and your shipping, or surrender your liberties to France."

Whatever were the faults or sins of England, they were at least such as Americans could understand. Her Government was guided, as a rule, by interests which were public, permanent, and easily measured. The weight of interests which had driven Pitt into his assault on American commerce was not lessened by the death of Pitt or by the return of Lord Grenville to power. On every side Fox found these interests active in opposition and earnest in pressing arguments against concession. Englishmen were used to giving and receiving hard blows. Seldom long at peace, they had won whatever was theirs by creating a national character in which personal courage was as marked a quality as selfishness; for in their situation no other than a somewhat brutal energy could have secured success. They knew what to think of war,

and could measure with some approach to exactness
its probable costs and returns, but they were quite
unused to being conquered by peace; and they listened with as much contempt as anger to the American theory that England must surrender at discretion
if Americans should refuse any longer to buy woollen shirts and tin kettles. Englishmen asked only
whether America would fight, and they took some
pains to make inquiries on that point; but it happened that of all the points in question this, which
to Englishmen was alone decisive, could be answered
in a syllable: No! America would not fight. The
President, Congress, the press of both parties in the
United States agreed only in this particular. John
Randolph's speech on Gregg's Resolution was reprinted in London with a long preface by James Stephen, and proved conclusively that America would
submit. Merry came as near to a laugh as his gravity
would permit in expressing his contempt for the idea
of war, and in urging his Government to resent the
Non-importation Act; and although Fox probably
thought poorly of Merry's judgment, he could not but
show his despatches to the Cabinet if the Cabinet
wished to read them. After the slaughter of Pierce,
when the Federalist newspapers in New York and
the irresponsible mob of seamen clamored for warlike
measures, the only effect of the outcry upon England
was to stimulate the anti-American prejudice and to
embarrass the well-meant efforts of Fox, until his
chief newspaper, the " Morning Chronicle," in a

moment of irritation plainly told the Americans that they were much mistaken if they thought a war would be so very unpopular in England; and if they knew this, they would not hector or bully so much. Even the powerful interests directly engaged in trade with the United States made no attempt to protect themselves; they did not see that the British nation was ready and eager to cut its own throat in its desperate anxiety to save its own life. The contest with France had made all Europe violent and brutal; but England could boast that at the sound of British cannon the chaos had become order, that the ocean had been divided from the land, and as far as the ocean went, that her fleets made law. Two Powers only remained to be considered by Great Britain,— Russia and the United States. Napoleon showed an evident intention to take charge of the one; England thought herself well able to give law to the other.

Against such public inclination toward measures of force Fox struggled as he could, without united support even in the Cabinet. Men like Lord Sidmouth were little inclined to risk the fate of the new Administration by concessions to America; and the Tories, led by Canning and Spencer Perceval, profited by every English prejudice in order to recover their control of the government. Fox could carry his point only by adopting half-measures. Instead of procuring a new judicial decision or issuing an Order in Council, as had been done in previous times, for replacing American commerce in its old privileges, he caused Government to adopt a measure intended to produce the same effect, but resting on a principle quite as objectionable to Americans as the Rule of 1756 itself had ever been. May 16, 1806, the ministers of neutral Powers were notified that the King had ordered a blockade of the whole French and German coast from Brest to the river Elbe, but that this blockade was to be strict and rigorous only between Ostend and the Seine; while elsewhere neutral ships should not be liable to seizure in entering or leaving the blockaded ports except under the usual conditions which made them seizable in any case. Under this blockade an American ship laden in New York with sugar, the product of French or Spanish colonies, might sail in safety for Amsterdam or Hamburg. Monroe wrote : [1] " It seems clearly to put an end to further seizures on the principle which has been heretofore in contestation."

English statutes, like English law, often showed peculiar ingenuity in inventing *a posteriori* methods of reaching their ends; but no such device could be less satisfactory than that of inventing a fictitious blockade in order to get rid of a commercial prohibition. Interminable disputes arose in the course of the next few years in regard to the objects and legality of this measure, which came to be known as Fox's blockade, and as such became a point of honor with England; but its chief interest was its reflection of the English mind. To correct a dangerous principle by

[1] Monroe to Madison, May 17, 1806; State Papers, iii. 124.

setting an equally dangerous precedent; to concede
one point by implication, and in doing so to assert
another not less disputed; to admit a right by appearing to deny it; and to encourage commerce under the
pretence of forbidding it, — was but admitting that
the British government aimed at illegitimate objects.
America had always contested the legality of paper
blockades as emphatically as she had contested the
Rule of 1756, and could no more submit to the one
than to the other, although in this case the paper
blockade was invented in order to conciliate and satisfy
her. The measure was intended for a temporary expedient pending negotiation; yet such was the condition of England that Fox's blockade became six years
afterward one of the chief pretexts under which the
two countries entered upon a war.

Another fortnight elapsed, but Monroe made no
further progress. Whenever he saw Fox the subjects
in dispute were discussed; but news arrived that the
Non-importation Act had passed both Houses of Congress, and the difficulty of obtaining favors was increased by the attempt at compulsion. Fox showed
less and less willingness to concede principles, although
he did not, as Monroe feared, declare that the Act relieved him from any promises he might have made or
from the fulfilment of any hopes he might have held
out. Thus the matter stood, balanced almost equally
between opposite chances, when, May 31, 1806, news
arrived from America that Monroe's powers were superseded by the appointment of a special mission, in

which he was to be associated with William Pinkney
of Maryland.

The blow to Monroe's pride was great, and shook
his faith in the friendship of Jefferson and Madison.
Three years had elapsed since he had himself been
sent abroad to share Livingston's negotiations, and he
had the best reason to know how easily the last comer
could carry away the prizes of popularity. The nomination of a colleague warned him that he had lost
influence at home, and that Jefferson, however well
disposed, no longer depended on him. This was in
substance the truth; but other and graver troubles
were revealed in part to Monroe's eyes when William
Pinkney arrived in London June 24, bringing with
him the new instructions which were to become the
foundation of the treaty.

These instructions [1] began by treating the Non-
importation Act as at once a domestic and a foreign
regulation, a pacific and a hostile act, a measure with
which England had no right to be angry, and one
which was calculated to anger her, — strictly amicable and at the same time sharply coercive. After
this preamble, in which the threat was clearer than
the explanation, followed an order precluding the possibility of successful negotiation. Monroe was to
begin by imposing an ultimatum. The British government must expressly repudiate the right and forbid
the practice of impressment, or not only could no

[1] Madison to Monroe and Pinkney, May 17, 1806; State
Papers, iii. 119.

treaty be made, but the Non-importation Act should be enforced. " So indispensable is some adequate provision for the case that the President makes it a necessary preliminary to any stipulation requiring a repeal of the Act shutting the market of the United States against certain British manufactures."

Besides this condition precedent, the instructions prescribed as another ultimatum the restoration of the trade with enemies' colonies on its old foundation and indemnity for the captures made under Sir William Scott's late decisions. Three ultimata, therefore, were fixed as conditions without which no treaty could receive the President's assent or procure a repeal of the Non-importation Act. The numerous requests to be further made upon Fox concerned many different points in dispute, — contraband, blockade, discriminating duties, immunity of neutral waters, East and West Indian trade, and trade with Nova Scotia ; but these were matters of bargain, and the two negotiators might to some extent use discretion in dealing with them. Yet every demand made by the United States required a corresponding concession from England, for which no equivalent could be offered by the American negotiators except the repeal of the Non-importation Act.

Monroe knew that Jefferson had ever strongly opposed any commercial treaty with Great Britain, and that he never spoke of Jay's treaty except with disgust and something like abhorrence. Again and again Jefferson had said and written that he wished for no

treaty; that he preferred to rely on municipal legislation as his safeguard against attack; and that he
would not part with this weapon in order to obtain
the doubtful protection of an agreement which England could always interpret to suit herself. Pinkney
could add that Jefferson, as every one in Washington
was aware, had been unwillingly driven into the present negotiation by the Senate, and that as the measure
was not his its success would hardly be within his expectation; that it would embarrass his relations with
Napoleon, endanger if not ruin the simultaneous negotiation for Florida, and exalt Monroe, the candidate
of Randolph, at the expense of Madison, who was already staggering under the attacks of his enemies.

Monroe was well informed of the efforts made to
raise or to depress his own fortunes at Washington,
and could see how easily his rival, the Secretary of
State, might play a double part. Nothing could be
simpler than such tactics. Madison had only to impose on Monroe the task of negotiating a treaty under
impossible conditions. If the treaty should fail, the
blame would fall upon Monroe; if it should succeed,
the credit would be divided with Pinkney. No one
could suppose that Madison would make any great
effort to secure the success of a negotiation when
success might make the negotiator the next President
of the United States.

Monroe could not doubt the President's coldness
toward the treaty; he could not fail to see that the
secretary's personal wishes were rather against than

for it; and when he studied the instructions he could not but admit that they were framed, if not with the intention, at all events with the effect, of making a treaty impossible. No harder task could well have been imposed than was laid upon Monroe. Not even when he had been sent to Madrid in defiance of Talleyrand and Godoy, to impose his own terms on two of the greatest Powers in the world, had his chance of success been smaller than when his Government required him to obtain from England, after the battle of Trafalgar, concessions which England had steadily refused when she was supposed to be drawing almost her last gasp. For a British ministry to abandon the Rule of 1756 was to challenge opposition; to throw open the colonial trade was to invite defeat; but to surrender the so-called right of impressment was to rush upon destruction. No minister that had ever ruled over the House of Commons could at such a moment have made such a treaty without losing his place or his head.

If America wanted such concessions she must fight for them, as other nations had done ever since mankind existed. England, France, and Spain had for centuries paid for their power with their blood, and could see no sufficient reason why America should take their hard-won privileges without a challenge. Jefferson thought otherwise. In his opinion, all the three Powers would end by conceding American demands, not as a matter of abstract right but for fear of throwing the United States into the arms of an enemy. The instructions to Monroe rested on this idea ; and that no doubt might remain, Jefferson wrote to Monroe a private letter which expressed the doctrine in set terms.

" No two countries upon earth," said the President,[1] " have so many points of common interest and friendship ; and their rulers must be great bunglers indeed if with such dispositions they break them asunder. The only rivalry that can arise is on the ocean. England may by petty-larceny thwartings check us on that element a little ; but nothing she can do will retard us there one year's growth. We shall be supported there by other nations, and thrown into their scale to make a part of the great counterpoise to her navy. If, on the other hand, she is just to us, conciliatory, and encourages the sentiment of family feelings and conduct, it cannot fail to befriend the security of both. We have the seamen and materials for fifty ships of the line and half that number of frigates ; and were France to give us the money and England the dispositions to equip them, they would give to England serious proofs of the stock from which they are sprung and the school in which they have been taught, and added to the efforts of the immensity of sea-coast lately united under one Power would leave the state of the ocean no longer problematical. Were, on the other hand, England to give the money and France the dispositions to place us on the sea in all our force, the whole world, out of the continent of Europe, might be our joint monopoly. We wish for neither of these scenes. We ask for peace and justice from all nations, and we will remain uprightly neutral in fact."

[1] Jefferson to Monroe, May 4, 1806; Works, v. 12.

This was masterful not to say dictatorial language ; for it came in support of categorical claims which, however just, were vehemently opposed by every conservative interest in England. The claims which Monroe was to make as ultimata could not be conceded by England without opening the door to claims more sweeping still. In the same breath with which the President threatened England with fifty ships of the line in case she would not abjure the right of impressment and the Rule of 1756, he added : —

" We begin to broach the idea that we consider the whole Gulf Stream as of our waters, in which hostilities and cruising are to be frowned on for the present, and prohibited as soon as either consent or force will permit us. We shall never permit another privateer to cruise within it, and shall forbid our harbors to national cruisers. This is essential for our tranquillity and commerce."

These were bold words, but not well suited to Monroe's task or likely to encourage his hopes. President Jefferson was not only bent upon forcing England to abandon by treaty the right of impressment and the control of the colonial trade ; he not only asked for liberal favors in many different directions, which required the whole fabric of British legislation to be reconstructed, without equivalent on the part of the United States, — but he had also " begun to broach the idea " that he should dictate where England's line-of-battle ships might sail upon the ocean. Monroe knew how such language would sound to English

ears strained to hear the distant thunders from Trafalgar, and how such words would look to English
eyes, dim with tears, as they watched their hero borne
through the shrouded streets of London to rest in his
glory beneath the dome of St. Paul's. That England was inflated with her triumphs, mad in her pretensions, intolerable in her arrogance, was true. A
people that had swept the ocean of enemies and held
the winds and waves for subjects could hardly fail to
go mad with the drunkenness of such stormy grandeur. The meanest beggar in England was glorified
with the faith that his march was o'er the mountain waves and his home upon the deep; and his
face would have purpled with rage at the idea that
Jefferson should dare to say that the squadrons of
England must back their topsails and silence their
broadsides when they reached the edge of the Gulf
Stream.

With this picture before his eyes, Monroe could
feel no great confidence either in his own success
or in the good faith of the President's instructions,
which tied him to impossible conditions. Nevertheless he accepted the task; and as he had gone to
Spain with the certainty of defeat and mortification,
he remained in London to challenge a hopeless contest. As though to destroy his only chance of success, on the very day of Pinkney's arrival Fox fell ill.
His complaint was soon known to be dropsical, and
his recovery hopeless. Two months passed, while the
American envoys waited the result. Aug. 20, 1806,

Fox, being still unable to do business, appointed Lord
Holland and Lord Auckland to carry on the negotiation in his place. No better men could have been
selected. Lord Holland especially, Fox's favorite
nephew and the most liberal of all Whig noblemen,
was warmly disposed to make the negotiation a success; but much invaluable time had been lost, and
Napoleon was on the eve of Jena.

The negotiation began in earnest August 27, but
proved to be long and arduous. The two British
commissioners, though courteous and friendly, stood
in constant fear of the charge that they had surrendered vital English interests under American threats.
They were especially hampered by the Admiralty, the
atmosphere of which, as Lord Holland complained,[1]
made those who breathed it shudder at anything like
concessions to the Americans; while the Treasury,
though naturally still less yielding, listened willingly
to every expedient that offered hope for the revenue.
September 1 began the struggle over impressments;
and from the outset Monroe saw that the American
claim had no chance of success, while the case of
the West Indian trade was almost equally desperate.
Only one serious discussion had taken place when the
death of Fox, September 13, produced a new delay
of several weeks; and on resuming the negotiation,
Monroe and Pinkney were required to deal with a new
Foreign Secretary, — Charles Grey, Lord Howick, —
to be better known in English history as Earl Grey.

[1] Memoirs of Lord Holland, ii. 98–103.

Such a change boded no good to the Americans. All Fox's influence could not counteract the Tory instincts of Parliament; and what Fox could not do when the Whigs were strong could much less be done by Lord Howick when the Ministry was every day tottering to its fall.

November 11 the American negotiators wrote home that they had decided to disregard their instructions and to abandon impressments,—accepting, instead of a formal article on the subject, a note in which the British commissioners pledged their government to exercise the strictest care not to impress American citizens, and to afford prompt redress should injury be inflicted while impressing British seamen. Having thus made up his mind to violate instructions on the chief point of negotiation, Monroe found nothing to prevent his doing so in other respects. His progress under William Pinkney's influence was rapid; his good nature, in the face of Lord Holland's difficult position, was extreme; and at the end of a few weeks, Dec. 31, 1806, Jefferson's favorite diplomatic agent set his name to a treaty which, taking its omissions and admissions together, surpassed Jay's treaty in outraging Jefferson's prejudices and express desires.

That a people, like an individual, should for a time choose to accept a wrong, like impressment or robbery, without forcible resistance implied no necessary discredit. Every nation at one time or another had submitted to treatment it disliked and to theories of international law which it rejected. The United States might go on indefinitely protesting against belligerent aggressions while submitting to them, and no permanent evil need result. Yet a treaty was a compromise which made precedent ; it recorded rules of law which could not be again discarded; and above all, it abandoned protest against wrong. This was doubtless the reason why Jefferson wished for no treaties in the actual state of the world ; he was not ready to enforce his rights, and he was not willing to compromise them.

The treaty signed by Monroe and Pinkney Dec. 1, 1806, was remarkable for combining in one instrument every quality to which Jefferson held most strenuous objections. The three ultimata were all abandoned ; impressments were set aside under a diplomatic memorandum which rather recorded the right than restrained its exercise ; no indemnity was obtained for the ravages made on American commerce in 1805 ; and in regard to the colonial trade, a compromise was invented which no self-respecting government could admit. Article XI. of the treaty imposed the condition that West Indian produce, coming from French or Spanish colonies, and *bonâ fide* the property of United States citizens, might be exported from American ports to Europe on condition that it should have paid to the United States custom-house a duty of not less than two per cent *ad valorem*, which could not be returned in drawback ; while European merchandise might in the same way be re-exported from the United States to the West Indies, provided it paid not less than one per cent *ad valorem* in duties to the American Treasury. This provision was only to be compared with Article XII. of Jay's treaty, in which Lord Grenville insisted and Jay agreed that the United States should export no cotton. Even Pitt had never proposed anything so offensive as the new restriction. He had indeed required that the American merchant whose ship arrived at Baltimore or Boston with a cargo of sugar or coffee from Cuba should unload her, carry the hogsheads and cases into a warehouse, and pass them through all the forms of the American custom-house; after which he must turn about and stow them again on shipboard, — an operation which was usually reckoned as equivalent, in breakage, pilfering, and wages, to a charge of about ten per cent on the value of the cargo; but he had not ventured to levy a duty upon them to be paid to the United States government. One step more, and — as a clever London pamphleteer suggested — the British government would require the American stevedores to wear the King's livery.[1] Had it been stipulated that the custom-house payments should be taken as full proof of neutrality and complete protection from seizure, the American merchant might have found a motive for submitting to the tax; but the treaty further insisted that both goods and vessel must be in good faith American property, — a condition which left the door open as widely as ever to the arbitrary seiz-

[1] Oil without Vinegar, Medford, London, 1807.

ures of British cruisers and to the equally arbitrary decisions of admiralty courts.

" We flatter ourselves," wrote Monroe and Pinkney to Madison,[1] " that the sum agreed to be paid will not be felt as a heavy one by our merchants, whose patriotism will be gratified by the recollection that the duty which they pay will redound to the advantage of their country."

Mercantile patriotism was proverbially elastic ; yet in the present instance not so much the merchants' gratification as that of the President was to be considered, — and Jefferson's patriotism could hardly approve this tax for the protection of British shipping and produce, which would on the one hand excite the anger of Napoleon, while on the other it conferred advantages merely during the period of war. Another objection existed which in Jefferson's eyes was fatal. He believed implicitly in the efficacy of commercial restrictions ; he thought the Non-importation Act a better guaranty of good treatment than the best treaty ever made, and was quite ready to try the experiment of such a measure against England. Yet Article V. of Monroe's treaty pledged him for ten years to abstain from every attempt to discriminate against British commerce.

The smaller points conceded by Monroe and Pinkney were not less likely than the greater ones to disturb Jefferson's temper. The British commission-

[1] Monroe and Pinkney to Madison, Jan. 3, 1807; State Papers, iii. 145.

ers refused to remove the export duty of two and a half per cent on British manufactures which Americans paid in excess of what was paid by European consumers. Trade with the British East Indies was restricted to ships which should sail directly from America and return directly thither, — a provision less favorable than Jay had secured. The trade with the British West Indies was a subject so delicate in Parliament that the two Englishmen refused to touch it, saying that any sanction of this trade, coupled with their sanction of the neutral trade with French and Spanish colonies, would endanger the treaty. They would enter into no arrangement of the trade with Nova Scotia, New Brunswick, and Canada. They also refused to accept Madison's ideas in regard to blockades.

Bad as all this was, and contrary to Madison's instructions and Jefferson's private letters, it was not yet the worst. After Monroe had violated his orders, — had abandoned the ultimata and accepted the commercial restrictions which the President disliked, — when the four commissioners were about to sign the treaty, Monroe and Pinkney were startled to hear that the two Englishmen meant to append an explanatory note to their signatures. News of the Berlin Decree had reached England, and its gravity was at once recognized. The British negotiators formally notified Monroe and Pinkney that unless the American government, before ratification, should give security that it would not recognize the decree, his Majesty George

III. would not consider himself bound by the signatures of his commissioners.[1]   Signature under such a condition seemed rather the act of a suppliant people than of one which had not yet so much as bought the sword it should have used.   Nevertheless Monroe signed.

Monroe was often called a very dull man.   He was said to follow the influence of those who stood near him, and was charged by different and opposed politicians with having a genius for blunders; but either Jefferson or Madison might be excused for suspecting that no man on whom they implicitly relied could violate instructions, sacrifice the principles of a lifetime, and throw infinite embarrassments on his Government without some ulterior motive.   They could not be blamed for suspecting that Monroe, in signing his treaty, thought more of the Federalist vote than he did of Madison's political promotion.

Monroe afterward defended his treaty in writings more or less elaborate, but his most candid account of his diplomacy in these years was given in a letter to Colonel Taylor of Caroline, written in the year 1810. Of the British treaty, he said: [2] —

"The failure of our business with Spain and the knowledge of the renewal of the negotiation and the manner of it, which were known to every one, were sensibly felt in our concerns with England.   She was not willing to yield

[1] American State Papers, iii. 151.
[2] Monroe to Colonel Taylor, 10 Sept., 1810; Monroe MSS., State Department Archives.

any portion of what she called her maritime rights, under the light pressure of the non-importation law, to a Power which had no maritime force, not even sufficient to protect any one of its ports against a small squadron, and which had so recently submitted to great injuries and indignities from Powers that had not a single ship at sea. Under such circumstances, it seemed to me to be highly for the interest of our country and to the credit of our government to get out of the general scrape on the best terms we could, and with that view to accommodate our differences with the great maritime Power on what might be called fair and reasonable conditions, if such could be obtained.   I had been slighted, as I thought, by the Administration in getting no answers to my letters for an unusual term, and in being subjected to a special mission, nothwithstanding my remonstrance against it on a thorough conviction of its inutility, and by other acts which I could not but feel ; yet believing that my service in England would be useful there, and by means thereof give aid to the Administration and to the Republican cause at home, I resolved to stay, and did stay for those purposes.   The treaty was an honorable and advantageous adjustment with England.   I adopted it in the firm belief that it was so, and nothing has since occurred to change that opinion."

CHAPTER XVIII.

MONROE was singularly unfortunate in diplomacy. His disasters came not in any ordinary form of occasional defeat or disappointment, but in waves and torrents of ill-luck. No diplomatist in American history, except Monroe and Pinkney, ever signed a treaty in flagrant contradiction to orders, and at the same time submitted to be told that the opposite party to the contract reserved a right to break it; but if any other man had taken such a step it would have answered for a lifetime, and his mortifications would have ended there. No one could assume that the British ministry would care to do more, pending the ratification of its own treaty. Fox's successor, one of the most liberal Whig noblemen, having imposed on the United States terms which would have been hard as the result of war, with the addition that even these terms were conditional on a declaration of hostilities between the United States and France, the liberal Whigs might be supposed willing to wait for some new pretext before publicly tearing their own treaty to pieces.

If Monroe flattered himself that he had for the moment checked British aggression, he quickly

learned his error.   The treaty had been signed barely
a week when a new Order in Council appeared, which
surpassed any belligerent measure of the Tories.[1]
Beginning with the premise that Napoleon's Berlin Decree " would give to his Majesty an unquestionable right of retaliation, and would warrant his
Majesty in enforcing the same prohibition of all
commerce with France which that Power vainly
hopes to effect against the commerce of his Majesty's subjects," the order added that King George
felt himself bound " to retort upon them the evils
of their own injustice," and therefore " ordered that
no vessel shall be permitted to trade from one port
to another, both which ports shall belong to, or
be in the possession of, France or her allies."
In other words the Whig ministers, ignoring their
fresh treaty with the United States and even the
note appended to it, declared that they would not
wait for America to resent the Berlin Decree, but
that United States vessels must in future, as a
retort for that decree, be deprived of the right to
sail from one European port to another.   The custom had hitherto prevailed among American shippers
of seeking a market according to ruling prices, partly
perhaps at Bilbao or Bordeaux, partly at some
other French or Mediterranean port.   Lord Howick's
order of Jan. 7, 1807, which cut short this coasting
privilege, was a blow to American commerce sharper

[1] Order in Council, of Jan. 7, 1807; American State Papers,
iii. 267.

than the famous decision of Sir William Scott in the case of the " Essex." Its apparent effect was to double the cost and risk of neutral commerce, while incidentally it asserted a right to prohibit such trade altogether.

Unfortunately more remained behind. The new order was not only an act of violence ; it was, according to the Tories, also one of meanness. On its face it purported to be a measure of retaliation, taken in order to retort upon France the evils of Napoleon's injustice. In the Parliamentary debate four weeks afterward, when the order was attacked, all parties argued it as a matter of retaliation. The King's advocate, Sir John Nicholls, who defended it, took the ground that for the moment no severer retaliation was needed ; while Spencer Perceval and Lord Castlereagh held that Napoleon's decree should have been retaliated in full.

" You might turn the provisions of the French decree against themselves," said Perceval ; [1] " and as they have said that no British goods should sail freely on the seas, you might say that no goods should be carried to France except they first touched at an English port. They might be forced to be entered at the custom-house, and a certain entry imposed, which would contribute to advance the price and give a better sale in the foreign market to your own commodities."

Sir John Nicholls replied : [2] —

[1] Cobbett's Debates, viii. 632.
[2] Cobbett's Debates, viii. 635.

" It was not denied that some steps in retaliation were necessary ; and the question was how far the steps that had been taken were adequate. . . . It was necessary to allow a fair trial to what ministers had adopted."

All this seemed clear and frank ; it was equivalent to saying that the rules of international law were henceforth to be laid aside, and that the doctrine of retaliation was to be the measure of England's rights. Yet this was not the form in which Lord Howick addressed President Jefferson.

" His Majesty," wrote Lord Howick to Erskine,[1] "with that forbearance and moderation which have at all times distinguished his conduct, has determined for the present to confine himself to the exercise of the power given him by his decided naval superiority in such a manner only as is authorized by the acknowledged principles of the law of nations."

In Parliament the measure was represented as an extra-legal act, justified by the illegality of the Berlin Decree. In diplomacy it was represented as an act " authorized by the acknowledged principles of the law of nations." The reason of the self-contradiction was evident. Only a week before this letter was written, the ministers had concluded a treaty with the United States involving the rights of neutrals, and had attached to it a note to the effect that if the United States failed to resist the Berlin Decree England would acquire the right to retaliate, but had not

[1] Howick to Erskine, Jan. 8, 1807; Cobbett's Debates, x. 558. Erskine to Madison, March 12, 1807; American State Papers, iii. 158.

hinted that retaliation was intended until the case of acquiescence should happen. As the matter stood, the British government had no right to retaliate, but was bound to wait for America to act; and Lord Howick's order, from that point of view, could not be defended.

From every other point of view the Order was equally indefensible; and within a year the Whigs were obliged to take the ground that it was not an act of retaliation at all, but an application of the Rule of 1756. Strange to say, this assertion was probably true. Unlikely as it seemed that Earl Grey, Lord Holland, and Lord Grenville could be parties to a transaction so evasive, their own admissions left no doubt that Napoleon's Berlin Decree was the pretext, not the cause, of Lord Howick's order; that Lord Howick's true intention was to go one step further than Pitt in applying the Rule of 1756 against United States commerce; that he aimed only at cutting off the neutral trade at one end of the voyage, as Pitt had cut it off at the other.

This criticism of the Whig ministry was made not so much in America as in England. The Whigs never offered an intelligible defence. Lord Grenville and Lord Howick argued at much length in Parliament, but convinced no one that their argument was sound; even the " Edinburgh Review " was ashamed of the task, and became unintelligible when it touched upon this party measure.[1]   Whether the conduct of

[1] Edinburgh Review, xxii. 485.

Lord Grenville's administration was, as a vigorous
Tory pamphleteer said,[1] a piece of chicanery of which
an attorney's clerk would have been ashamed, was
a matter for English historians to decide.   In England at that day none but a few merchants or Republicans believed in the honor or honesty of the United
States government or people; but in this instance it
was not the honor or honesty of Americans that
the English critics denied : it was, on the contrary,
the good faith of their own most distinguished and
most trusted noblemen, — Lord Grenville and Lord
Sidmouth, Earl Grey and Lord Holland, Lord Erskine
and Lord Lansdowne, Lord Ellenborough and Earl
Fitzwilliam ; and in the light of such conduct and
criticism, Americans could not be greatly blamed if
they refused to admit the ground on which these English gentlemen claimed a better reputation for truth
or honesty than they were willing to allow Napoleon.
Robbery against robbery, the English mode of pil-
lage seemed on the whole less respectable than the
French.

The Whigs were liberal by tradition and instinct ;
well disposed toward peace and commerce with all
nations, they knew that neutral ships alone could
carry British manufactures to a European market.
Every impediment put in the way of neutral commerce was an additional burden on British produce ;
every market closed to neutrals was a market closed

[1] T. P. Courtney's Additional Observations on the American
Treaty, London, 1808, p. 89.

to England. From a Whig point of view Lord Howick's order violated the rules of political economy and
common-sense; not to be defended or excused, it
equalled in violence the aggressions of Pitt, and in
bad faith rivalled the deceptions of Napoleon. Yet
this measure was the last act of a Ministry more
liberal than England was destined to see again for
twenty years. Hardly had Lord Grenville made this
concession to Tory prejudice when the old King,
nearly blind and on the verge of insanity, clinging
to his prejudices with the persistence of age, seized
the pretext of some small concession to the Roman
Catholics and turned the Whigs out of his councils.
March 26, 1807, Lord Grenville and Lord Howick announced to the two Houses of Parliament their dismissal from office.

If the friendly Whigs, after imposing on the
United States such a treaty, had thought themselves still obliged to lop off another main limb of
American commerce, which Pitt had spared, the
Tories were not likely to rest until they had put an
end to American neutral commerce altogether. This
result was foreshadowed by Spencer Perceval and
Lord Castlereagh in their speeches on Lord Howick's
order, and was the end to which the legislation and
public opinion of England had pointed for years.
The time for negotiation had gone by, and nothing
remained for the United States but a trial of
strength.

For this final test Jefferson was ready. Congress

had placed in his hands powers which in his opinion
were ample to protect American interests abroad and
at home. On sufficient provocation he could exclude
British ships-of-war from American waters, and if
they should refuse to depart he might enforce the
Non-importation Act against British commerce. His
conduct proved that he felt neither fear nor hesitation. He had never expected a satisfactory treaty
from England, and he had good reason to know that
Monroe's treaty, if Monroe should succeed in making
one, must be worse than none. Early in February,
1807, arrived the despatch from Monroe and Pinkney announcing that the two envoys had decided to
depart from their instructions and to abandon the
impressment ultimatum. Madison replied,[1] February
3, that no such treaty would be ratified, and that it
would be better to let the negotiation quietly terminate, leaving each party to follow an informal understanding; but that if such a treaty should have been
signed, the British commissioners should be candidly
apprised of the reasons for not expecting its ratification. That Monroe's treaty, if he made one, would
be rejected and returned without ratification to the
British government was certain long before it reached
America.

On that point, as on the inflexibility of England, no
doubt could exist. President Jefferson and Secretary
Madison were as determined, in case of necessity, to

[1] Madison to Monroe and Pinkney, Feb. 3, 1807; State
Papers, iii. 153.

attack British manufactures as Spencer Perceval and George Rose were bent upon cutting off American trade; but although the Americans fully meant to use commercial weapons against British aggression, they earnestly wished for a good working arrangement under which, without a treaty, peace and commerce could be secure. So far from challenging a rupture, they were anxious only to encourage cordial relations. Throughout the winter of 1806–1807 Jefferson made of his attachment to England a foundation for all his policy at home and abroad. Congress, under the security of Fox's friendship, left foreign affairs alone, and quarrelled only about domestic matters; while General Turreau's temper was made more irritable by the attentions lavished upon David Montague Erskine, the new British minister, who, Nov. 4, 1806, put an end to the adventures of Merry at Washington, and began the easy task of winning popularity.

The winter of 1805–1806 had been favorable to Turreau, who saw France control American policy toward Spain and St. Domingo; while a stringent Act of Congress prohibiting the importation of British manufactures brought within his sight the chief object of French diplomacy in America, — a war between the United States and England. The winter of 1806–1807 promised to undo this good work, and even to bring the United States to the verge of war with France. The first measure recommended by the President and adopted by Congress — the suspension of the Non-importation Act — annoyed Turreau.

Monroe's treaty was signed in London December 1 ;
at Washington Turreau wrote, December 12,[1] soon
after Congress met, —

" If I am to judge by the talk and countenances of the
great people, this Congress will be more favorable to
England than the last was ; and already its leader, under
the President's own invitation, shows a benevolent disposition toward the British government. I had the honor
to see Mr. Jefferson the evening before Congress met,
and to say to him, on the subject of Spanish differences,
that probably all the negotiations entered into by the
Government with that Power, as well as with England,
would succeed. ' Really,' replied the President, ' I have
reason to think that the English are going to make an
arrangement with us, and that it would be already done
if Mr. Fox's death had not interrupted negotiation. Perhaps we shall even obtain,' he added, ' the right to extend our maritime jurisdiction, and to carry it as far
as the effect of the Gulf Stream makes itself felt, —
which would be very advantageous both to belligerents
and to neutrals.' "

To persons who knew that Jefferson was then
angry with Napoleon for his faithless conduct in
preventing the new Florida negotiation, this assurance of English friendship gave a measure of the
President's diplomacy. He was willing to irritate
and alarm the French minister, and he succeeded.
Turreau took refuge in speculations and sharp
criticisms : —

[1] Turreau to Talleyrand, Dec. 12, 1806 ; Archives des Aff.
Étr., MSS.

"I know not whether to attribute this first effect of pronounced favor in regard to England to the last despatches of the two envoys negotiating at London, or to the first overtures of Mr. Erskine, who arrived here a few days ago, and with whom they seem already infatuated (*très engoué*) ; . . . or, finally, whether it may not be the result of some hints from Alexander, — for whom the Federal government, and particularly Mr. Jefferson, have an admiration which borders on delirium. And your Excellency may recall that last spring the President talked of making overtures to the Russian sovereign relative to a plan of unarmed maritime confederation, which was then his great object, and which, as he assured me in our last interview, he has not given up, — making, as his custom is, a grand eulogium of Alexander and his savages."

Madison, even in prosperous times never a favorite with General Turreau, managed as usual to draw upon himself the chief weight of diplomatic suspicion and wrath.

"The unexpected change in the views of the Federal government," continued Turreau, "is such that the secretary's bearing toward me is deranged by it. Not that he has renounced his system of attentions (*prévenances*) toward the minister of France, whom he does not love, and whom, as I have unfortunately good reason to know, he distrusts ; not that he has weakened his protestations, reiterated to satiety, of personal attachment to the interests of France, and of the Government's constant wish to maintain and strengthen the friendly relations which unite it with that Power, — but the Secretary of State has forgotten that at the beginning of this year

[1806], and particularly after the event of Austerlitz, the only subject of our private conversations was complaint of England, and the fixed resolution of the Federal government to stop the course of her wrongs either by repression or reprisals. He has forgotten that the steps taken by the Executive to obtain from Congress the famous Non-importation Bill, now suspended, were so marked and ill-concealed that John Randolph called attention to them, and flung severe, or rather humiliating, taunts at the agents of ministerial influence. Now Mr. Madison no longer talks to me about England; he tries to keep out of our conversations whatever relates to that Power, and far from making complaints of her, the Federal government ' has to congratulate itself that the ministry of Mr. Fox, though unfortunately too short, has nevertheless sufficed to bring the Cabinet of St. James to moderate sentiments.' "

Neither Jefferson nor Madison took direct notice of Napoleon's conduct in regard to Florida, but they led Turreau to think that England was their favorite; and Turreau's dislike of America and Americans became in consequence more decided. He hoped for Burr's success in order to relieve the pressure upon him : [1] —

" It seems to me that Burr's success cannot be contrary to the interests of France, although I am convinced that England will favor him, — doubtless with other hopes; but if we had to-day the Floridas, the importance of which I have felt it my duty to recall to you, I think I

[1] Turreau to Talleyrand, Jan. 12, 1807; Archives des Aff. Étr., MSS.

can guarantee that New Orleans would be ours if we only
showed a wish for it. All reports, and I have had such,
both official and positive, agree as to the regrets expressed by the great majority of inhabitants at not living
under French rule."

In the middle of February, at a moment when
Americans expected daily the arrival of a British
treaty marked by generous concessions, Napoleon's
Berlin Decree reached the United States. Commerce
was instantly paralyzed, and merchants, Congressmen, Cabinet, and President turned to Turreau anxiously inquiring what was meant by this blockade of
the British Islands by a Power which could not keep
so much as a frigate at sea. Turreau could give them
no answer. " Your Excellency will readily believe,"
he wrote home,[1] " that this circumstance does not
put us in a better position here." The influence
of France in the United States was never lower than
at the moment when England turned Lord Grenville
and Lord Erskine out of power, in order to install
Spencer Perceval and Lord Eldon at the head of
a Tory reaction. Jefferson's objections to a British
treaty would have had no weight with the Senate
if the treaty had been tolerable ; the Berlin Decree
and the Emperor's conduct in regard to Florida would
have reconciled Madison to almost any British alliance.
Turreau was so well aware of the danger that he
exerted himself in remonstrances and semi-threats,

[1] Turreau to Talleyrand, Feb. 23, 1807 ; Archives des Aff.
Étr., MSS.

and told [1] one member of the Cabinet after another
that "at a moment when Europe, leagued together
against the maritime tyranny of England, was laboring to throw off the yoke of that Power and to secure
for all navigating nations freedom of commerce and
the seas," it was particularly improper for the United
States to accept any treaty which did not expressly
secure all disputed points, and that no treaty would
be observed by England unless made under the auspices and by the guaranty of Napoleon.

In view of the recent fate that had overtaken
Powers like Switzerland and Venice, which had put
themselves under the auspices of Napoleon, this
argument produced no conviction. Turreau might
better have left to the English the task of repairing
Napoleon's mistakes; but these mistakes had accumu-
lated until it depended upon England alone whether
the United States should join her in the war. Not
only had the Emperor offended Jefferson and Madison
by his peremptory stoppage of the Florida purchase,
— he had also declared war upon American commerce
in a decree which Jefferson and Madison could not
but suspect to be in some mysterious way connected
with his sudden change of front toward Spain and
Florida; while in the face of these difficulties he left
his own minister at Washington in such discredit that
Turreau was reduced to beg sixty thousand dollars
from the American Treasury to meet consular expen-

[1] Turreau to Talleyrand, April 1, 1807; Archives des Aff.
Étr., MSS.

ditures at a moment when he should have been pressing complaints about the frigate " Impétueux," destroyed by the English within American jurisdiction, and when he should have been threatening the most fatal consequences if President Jefferson should sign any treaty whatever with England.[1]

In this temper all parties waited for the news from England, which could not long be delayed; until March 3, 1807, the last day of the session, a rumor reached the Capitol that a messenger had arrived at the British legation with a copy of the treaty negotiated by Pinkney and Monroe. The news was true. No sooner did Erskine receive the treaty than he hurried with it to Madison, " in hopes that he would be induced to persuade the President either to detain the Senate, which he has the power by the Constitution to do, or to give them notice that he should convene them again." Unlike Merry, Erskine was anxious for a reconciliation between England and America; he tried honestly and over-zealously to bring the two governments into accord, but he found Madison not nearly so earnest as himself :

" The first question he asked was, what had been determined on the point of impressment of seamen, claimed as British, out of American ships ; and when I informed him that I had not perceived anything that directly referred to that question in any of the Articles of the copy of the treaty which I had received, he expressed the

[1] Turreau to Talleyrand, May 15, 1807 ; Archives des Aff. Étr., MSS.

greatest astonishment and disappointment. . . . The note which was delivered in to the American commissioners, previous to the signature of the treaty, by Lords Holland and Auckland, relative to Bonaparte's decree of November 21, particularly attracted his attention; and he observed that the note itself would have prevented, he was convinced, the ratification of the treaty, even if all the Articles of it had been satisfactory, and all the points settled upon the terms that had been required by their commissioners."[1]

At ten o'clock the same night the two Houses of Congress, when ready to adjourn, sent a joint committee to wait upon the President, who was unwell, and unable to go as usual to the Capitol. Dr. Mitchill, the senator from New York, a member of this committee, asked the President whether there would be a call of the Senate to consider the treaty.[2] "Certainly not," replied Jefferson; and he added that " the only way he could account for our ministers having signed such a treaty under such circumstances was by supposing that in the first panic of the French imperial decree they had supposed a war to be inevitable, and that America must make common cause with England. He should, however, continue amicable relations with England, and continue the suspension of the Non-importation Act."

The senators received this rebuff with ill-concealed annoyance. Jefferson's act in refusing to consult

---

[1] Erskine to Howick, March 6, 1807; MSS. British Archives.
[2] Diary of J. Q. Adams, i. 495.

them about a matter so important as a British treaty
— and one which from the first had been their own
rather than the President's scheme — was another
instance of the boldness which sometimes contradicted
the theory that Jefferson was a timid man. To ordinary minds it seemed clear that the President needed
support; that he could not afford single-handed to
defy England and France; that the circle of foreign
enemies was narrowing about him; and that to suppress of his own will a treaty on which peace and
war might depend, exposed him to responsibilities
under which he might be crushed. Although the
treaty was not yet published, enough had been
said to make senators extremely curious about its
contents; and they were not pleased to learn that
the President meant to tell them nothing, and cared
too little for their opinion to ask it. Of all the senators the most formidable intriguer was Samuel Smith
of Maryland, who wrote the next day confidentially to
Wilson Cary Nicholas a letter full of the fresh impressions which gave life to Smith's private language:[1]

" A copy of the treaty arrived last evening. The
President is angry with it, and to Dr. Mitchill and Mr.
Adams (who carried the last message) expressed his
anger in strong, very strong terms, telling in broad language the cause of his wrath. He requested the doctor
to tell the senators his objections. If the doctor repeated
correctly, then I must be permitted to think there was

[1] S. Smith to W. C. Nicholas, March 4, 1807; Nicholas
MSS,

not a little of the heightening. He said the President
was at present determined to send the original back the
moment it shall be received, without submitting it to the
Senate. He was sick, it is true, — vexed and worried;
he may think better of it, for Madison (expecting less
than he had) differs with him as to calling the Senate,
and R[obert] S[mith] concurs in opinion with M[adi-
son]. . . . I stopped here, and I have seen the President
and Mr. M[adison].   It seems the impressment of seamen was a *sine qua non* in the instructions. The P[resi-
dent] speaks positively that, without full and formal
satisfaction shall be made thereupon, he will return the
treaty without consulting the Senate; and yet he admits
the treaty, so far as to all the other points, might be
acceptable, — nay, that there are but few exceptions to it
in his mind. I fancy the merchants would be perfectly
pleased therewith.   If then in all other points it would
please, will the responsibility not be very great on him
should he send it back without consulting the Senate?
M[adison] in answer to this query said, 'But if he
is determined not to accept, even should the Senate advise, why call the Senate together?' I could give no
answer to this question. If by his unusual conduct the
British continue or increase their depredations (which he
cannot prevent), what will be the outcry? *You* may
advise him.   He stumped us by his positive manner.
. . . Will not M[onroe] and P[inkney] both conceive
themselves insulted, and return to make war on the
Administration? The whole subject ought, I conceive,
to have been treated as one of great delicacy."

In another letter, written the same day, General
Smith rehearsed the story in a few words, which

proved that Smith had a full share of the shrewdness that was lacking in Jefferson. He saw the future as clearly as politicians often saw what philosophers overlooked; but his jealousy of Jefferson appeared in every word:[1] —

"The Senate, agreeably to the first construction (given by General Washington and his Administration, of which Jefferson was one, — given, too, immediately after the knowledge of what was the intention of the convention that framed it), did *unanimously* advise the President to negotiate a treaty with Great Britain. The Senate agreed to his nomination of the negotiators. A treaty was effected. It arrives. It is well known that he was *coerced* by the Senate to the measure; and he refuses to submit it to their approbation. What a responsibility he takes! By sending it back he disgraces his ministers, *and Monroe is one.* Monroe and Pinkney come home, and in justification publish the treaty. It may appear good to the eyes of all unprejudiced men, — I suspect it will. By a refusal to accede to it the British continue their depredations, to the amount perhaps of their whole system of 'You shall not trade in time of war where you are refused in time of peace;' the impressment is carried to an excess bounded only by their power; immense losses are sustained; a general outcry will ensue; all will say, 'If Monroe's treaty had succeeded, those losses would not have happened; why was it refused?' Jealousy of Monroe, and unreasonable antipathy by Jefferson and Madison to Great Britain! — this will be said, this will be believed. And Monroe will be brought forward; new parties will arise, and those

[1] S. Smith to W. C. Nicholas, March 4, 1807; Nicholas MSS.

adverse politically will be brought together by interest.
. . . Shall we put all to jeopardy because we have not
got all we ask? Will we go to war? No! What will
we do to coerce? More non-importation. Will Congress
under such circumstances consent to continue their non-
importation? I suspect not; I cannot believe they will.
Then where shall we be? J. Randolph will take his
stand and ask, ' Shall we hazard everything for a set
of men who, etc.? What, put the landed interest to
such inconvenience! The fair merchant is satisfied;
the country is flourishing,' etc. But I have not time to
make a speech. Monroe will be called a martyr, and
the martyr will be the President. And why? Because
he has done right, and his opponent has advised wrong.
The people care little or nothing about the seamen."

The more closely the subject was studied the more
clearly it appeared that Monroe had to all appearance
knowingly embarrassed the Administration by signing a treaty in contravention of the President's orders; but Jefferson added unnecessarily to his embarrassment by refusing the treaty before he read it.
Tacit abandonment of impressments was the utmost
concession that the President could hope from England, and even this he must probably fight for; yet
he refused to consult the Senate on the merits of
Monroe's treaty for a reason which would have caused
the withholding of every treaty ever made with England. That the public should be satisfied with this
imperious treatment was an extravagant demand.
No act of Jefferson's administration exposed him to
more misinterpretation, or more stimulated a belief in

his hatred of England and of commerce, than his refusal to lay Monroe's treaty before the Senate.

Perhaps the President would have been less decided
had he known at first how faulty the treaty was.
Not until it had been studied for weeks did all its
faults become evident; and not until it was read
in the light of Lord Howick's Order in Council
did its character admit of no more doubt.   When
news of this order reached Washington, about ten
days after the treaty, Madison wrote to Erskine a
letter[1] which showed an effort to treat the new restriction of neutral trade as though it might have
some shadow of legality in the background, and as
though it were not directed solely against America;
but the truth soon became too evident for such mild
treatment, and Madison was obliged ten days afterward to interrupt his study of Monroe's treaty in
order to tell Erskine that the operation of the new
order " would be a proceeding as ruinous to our commerce as contrary to our essential rights." [2]

To Monroe the President wrote with the utmost
forbearance and kindness.[3]   Instead of reproaching,
Jefferson soothed the irritation of his old friend,
contradicted newspaper reports which were calculated to wound Monroe's feelings, and pressed upon
him the government of New Orleans Territory : " It is
the second office in the United States in importance,

[1] Madison to Erskine, March 20, 1807 ; State Papers, iii. 158.

[2] Same to same, March 29, 1807 ; Ibid., 159.

[3] Jefferson to Monroe, March 21, 1807; Works, v. 52.

and I am still in hopes you will accept it; it is impossible to let you stay at home while the public has so much need of talents." In regard to the treaty he said little; but what he did say was more severe than any criticism yet made to others. "Depend on it, my dear Sir, that it will be considered as a hard treaty when it is known. The British commissioners appear to have screwed every Article as far as it would bear, — to have taken everything and yielded nothing." He urged Monroe, if nothing better could be got, "to back out of the negotiation" as well as he could, letting it die insensibly, and substituting some informal agreement until a more yielding temper should rise. Next the President wrote privately to Bowdoin, his wandering minister to Spain, to whom Armstrong had shut the doors of the legation at Paris for betraying its secrets, and who in return was abusing Armstrong with recriminations. If a quarrel should arise with England, it might at least be made to bring Florida again within reach.

"I have but little expectation," wrote the President to Bowdoin,[1] "that the British government will retire from their habitual wrongs in the impressment of our seamen, and am certain that without that we will never tie up our hands by treaty from the right of passing a non-importation or non-intercourse Act to make it her interest to become just. This may bring on a war of commercial restrictions. To show, however, the sincerity of our desire for conciliation, I have suspended

[1] Jefferson to Bowdoin, April 2, 1807 ; **Works, v. 63.**

the Non-importation Act. This state of things should be understood at Paris, and every effort used on your part to accommodate our differences with Spain under the auspices of France, with whom it is all important that we should stand in terms of the strictest cordiality. In fact we are to depend on her and Russia for the establishment of neutral rights by the treaty of peace, among which should be that of taking no persons by a belligerent out of a neutral ship, unless they be the soldiers of an enemy. Never did a nation act toward another with more perfidy and injustice than Spain has constantly practised against us; and if we have kept our hands off of her till now, it has been purely out of respect to France, and from the value we set on the friendship of France. We expect, therefore, from the friendship of the Emperor that he will either compel Spain to do us justice or abandon her to us. We ask but one month to be in possession of the city of Mexico."

In reality Jefferson needed somewhat more than a month to be in possession of Mexico, although the Spaniards might without much difficulty have reached New Orleans in less time. Had the Federalist press been able to print the letter to Bowdoin, with its semi-admissions of intent to wage a commercial war against England in dependence upon Napoleon in order to gain the Floridas, the scandal would have been as great as that caused by the famous letters to Mazzei and Paine; but in truth this flighty talk had no influence or importance, and the time was close at hand when Jefferson was to become helpless.

Between the will of England and France on one side
and the fixed theories of Virginia and Pennsylvania on
the other, Jefferson's freedom of action disappeared.

Madison, who rarely accepted either horn of a dilemma with much rapidity, labored over new instructions to Monroe which were to make the treaty tolerable, and called Gallatin and General Smith to his
aid, with no other result than to uncover new and
insuperable difficulties.   April 20 he wrote to Jefferson at Monticello : [1] —

" The shape to be given to the instructions to our commissioners becomes more and more perplexing.   I begin
to suspect that it may eventually be necessary to limit
the treaty to the subject of impressments, leaving the
colonial trade, with other objects, to their own course
and to the influence which our reserved power over our
imports may have on that course.   In practice the colonial trade and everything else would probably be more
favored than they are by the Articles forwarded, or
would be by any remodifications to be expected.   The
case of impressments is more urgent.   Something seems
essential to be done, nor is anything likely to be done
without carrying fresh matter in the negotiation.   I am
preparing an overture to disuse British seamen, in the
form of an ultimatum, graduated from an exception
of those who have been two years in our navigation
to no exception at all other than such as have been
naturalized."

A few days later news arrived that the Whigs had
been driven from office, and a high Tory ministry had

[1] Madison to Jefferson, April 20, 1807 ; Jefferson MSS.

come into power.   Madison was more than ever perplexed, but did not throw aside his treaty.

" A late arrival from London," he wrote again,[1] April
24, " presents a very unexpected scene at St. James's.
Should the revolution stated actually take place in the
Cabinet, it will subject our affairs there to new calculations.   On one hand the principles and dispositions of
the new Ministry portend the most unfriendly course.
On the other hand, their feeble and tottering situation
and the force of their ousted rivals, who will probably
be more explicit in maintaining the value of a good
understanding with this country, cannot fail to inspire
caution.   It may happen also that the new Cabinet will
be less averse to a *tabula rasa* for a new adjustment than
those who formed the instrument to be superseded."

Jefferson's reply to these suggestions showed no
anxiety except the haunting fear of a treaty, — a fear
which to Monroe's eyes could have no foundation.
" I am more and more convinced," the President
wrote April 21,[2] " that our best course is to let the
negotiation take a friendly nap ; " and May 1 he
added : [3] " I know few of the characters of the new
British Administration.   The few I know are true
Pittites and anti-American.   From them we have
nothing to hope but that they will readily let us back
out."   In view of George Canning's character and
antecedents and of Spencer Perceval's speeches, Jefferson's desire to be allowed to back out of his

[1] Madison to Jefferson, April 24, 1807 ; Jefferson MSS.

[2] Jefferson to Madison, April 21, 1807 ; Works, v. 69.

[3] Jefferson to Madison, April 21, 1807; Works, v. 74.

treaty was superfluous. That Canning and Perceval
would make any effort to hold him to his bargain
was quite unlikely, but that they would let him back
out was still more so. They had in view more expe-
ditious ways of ejecting him.

Nevertheless Madison was allowed to perfect his
new instructions to Monroe and Pinkney. May 20
they were signed and sent. Before they reached
London a British frigate had answered them in
tones which left little chance for discussion.

CHAPTER XIX.

MARCH 30, 1807, in a room at the Eagle Tavern in Richmond, Aaron Burr was brought before Chief-Justice Marshall for examination and commitment. Although Burr had been but a few days in the town, he was already treated by many persons as though he had conferred honor upon his country. Throughout the United States the Federalists, who formed almost the whole of fashionable society, affected to disbelieve in the conspiracy, and ridiculed Jefferson's sudden fears. The Democrats had never been able to persuade themselves that the Union was really in danger, or that Burr's projects, whatever they were, had a chance of success; and in truth Burr's conspiracy, like that of Pickering and Griswold, had no deep roots in society, but was mostly confined to a circle of well-born, well-bred, and well-educated individuals, whose want of moral sense was one more proof that the moral instinct had little to do with social distinctions. In the case of Burr, Jefferson himself had persistently ignored danger; and no one denied that if danger ever existed, it had passed. Burr was fighting for his life against the power of an encroaching government; and human nature was too simply or-

ganized to think of abstract justice or remote principles when watching the weak fight for life against
the strong. Even the Democrats were more curious
to see Burr than to hang him; and had he gone
to the gallows, he would have gone as a hero, like
Captain Macheath amidst the admiring crowds of
London.

Between Captain Macheath and Colonel Burr was
more than one point of resemblance, and the "Beggar's Opera" could have been easily paralleled within
the prison at Richmond; but no part of Burr's career
was more humorous than the gravity with which he
took an injured tone, and maintained with success
that Jefferson, being a trivial person, had been deceived by the stories of Eaton and Wilkinson, until,
under the influence of causeless alarm, he had permitted a wanton violation of right. From the first
step toward commitment, March 30, to the last day
of the tedious trials, October 20, Burr and his counsel never ceased their effort to convict Jefferson;
until the acquittal of Burr began to seem a matter of
secondary importance compared with the President's
discomfiture.

Over this tournament the chief-justice presided as
arbiter. Blennerhassett's island, where the overt act
of treason was charged to have taken place, lay within
the chief-justice's circuit. According as he might
lean toward the accused or toward the government,
he would decide the result; and therefore his leanings
were a matter of deep interest. That he held Feder-

alist prejudices and nourished a personal dislike to Jefferson was notorious; but apart from political feelings he had given no clew to his probable legal bias except in his recent decision upon the case of Bollman and Swartwout. In discharging these two agents of Burr on the ground that no overt act of levying war was alleged against them, Marshall had taken occasion to define the law of treason as a guide to the attorney-general in the coming indictment of Burr : —

" It is not the intention of the Court to say that no individual can be guilty of this crime who has not appeared in arms against his country. On the contrary, if war be actually levied, — that is, if a body of men be actually assembled for the purpose of effecting by force a treasonable purpose, — all those who perform any part, however minute, or however remote from the scene of action, and who are actually leagued in the general conspiracy, are to be considered as traitors. But there must be an actual assembling of men for the treasonable purpose, to constitute a levying of war."

On the strength of this opinion, the attorney-general undertook to convict Burr of treason for the acts committed under his direction at Blennerhassett's island, although at the time when these acts were committed Burr himself was in Kentucky, two hundred miles away.

The task was difficult, and Burr's experience as a lawyer enabled him to make it more difficult still. He retained the ablest counsel at the bar. First of

these was Edmund Randolph, prominent among the
older Virginia lawyers, who had been attorney-general
and Secretary of State in President Washington's
Cabinet.   Edmund Randolph's style of address was
ponderous, and not always happy ; to balance its defects Burr employed the services of John Wickham,
another Virginian, whose versatility and wit were
remarkable.   A third Virginian, Benjamin Botts, was
brought into the case, and proved a valuable ally.
Finally Luther Martin was summoned from Baltimore ; and Martin's whole heart was with his client.
In defending Justice Chase, Luther Martin had made
a great name ; but hatred for the Democrats and
their President became a secondary passion in his
breast.   His zeal for Burr was doubled by a sudden
idolatry which the sexagenarian conceived for Burr's
daughter Theodosia, who came to her father's side at
Richmond.

The government was represented by no one of
equal force with these opponents.   John Breckinridge, the Attorney-General of the United States, died
in December, 1806.   Jan. 20, 1807, President Jefferson appointed Cæsar A. Rodney to the post.   Although Rodney's abilities were respectable, he could
hardly have wished to be confronted at once by the
most important and difficult State prosecution ever
tried under Executive authority.   Rodney's duties
or his health prevented him from attendance.   He
barely appeared at Richmond in the preliminaries,
and then left the case in the hands of the district-

attorney, George Hay, who took his orders directly from Jefferson, with whom he was in active correspondence. To assist Hay the President engaged the services of William Wirt, then thirty-five years old, and promising to become an ornament to the bar; but in the profession of the law age gave weight, and Wirt, though popular, conscientious, admired, and brilliant in a florid style of oratory, suffered as a lawyer from his youth and his reputation as an orator. He was hardly more capable than Hay of conducting a case which drew upon every resource of personal authority. The third counsel, Alexander McRae, Lieutenant-Governor of Virginia, was inferior both in ability and in tact to either of his associates. His temper irritated Hay and offended the Court, while his arguments added little strength to the prosecution.

The first object of the government was to commit Burr for trial on the charge of treason as well as of misdemeanor; but Marshall promptly checked all hopes of obtaining aid from the court. April 1 the chief-justice delivered an opinion on the question of commitment, and took that opportunity to give the district-attorney a warning. Declining to commit Burr for treason without evidence stronger than the affidavits of Eaton and Wilkinson, Marshall blamed the Executive with asperity for neglect of duty in providing proof of treason: —

"Several months have elapsed since this fact did occur, if it ever occurred. More than five weeks have elapsed since the opinion of the Supreme Court has declared the necessity of proving the fact if it exists. Why is it not proved? To the Executive government is intrusted the important power of prosecuting those whose crimes may disturb the public repose or endanger its safety. It would be easy in much less time than has intervened since Colonel Burr has been alleged to have assembled his troops, to procure affidavits establishing the fact."

Accordingly Burr was committed only for misdemeanor, and five securities immediately offered themselves on his behalf. At three o'clock on the afternoon of April 1 he was again at liberty, under bonds for ten thousand dollars to appear at the next circuit court, May 22, at Richmond.

Marshall's reproof of Executive slowness was not altogether respectful to the co-ordinate branch of government. No doubt treasonable assemblages had taken place in December, and affidavits could have been brought from Marietta or Nashville within six or eight weeks had the government known precisely what would be needed, or where the evidence was to go; but no judge could reasonably require that the Executive should within five weeks obey a hint from the Supreme Court which implied a long correspondence and inquiry at spots so remote as Blennerhassett's island, Lexington, Nashville, Fort Massac, and Chickasaw Bluffs. Jefferson was naturally indignant at being treated with so little courtesy. He wrote with extreme bitterness about Marshall's "tricks to force trials before it is possible to collect the evidence." [1] He returned threat for threat, with something in addition : —

" In what terms of decency can we speak of this? As if an express could go to Natchez or the mouth of the Cumberland and return in five weeks, to do which has never taken less than twelve ! . . . But all the principles of law are to be perverted which would bear on the favorite offenders who endeavor to overturn this odious republic ! . . . All this, however, will work well. The nation will judge both the offender and judges for themselves. If a member of the Executive or Legislature does wrong, the day is never far distant when the people will remove him. They will see then and amend the error in our Constitution which makes any branch independent of the nation. They will see that one of the great co-ordinate branches of the government, setting itself in opposition to the other two and to the common-sense of the nation, proclaims impunity to that class of offenders which endeavors to overturn the Constitution, and are protected in it by the Constitution itself ; for impeachment is a farce which will not be tried again. If their protection of Burr produces this amendment, it will do more good than his condemnation would have done ; . . . and if his punishment can be commuted now for a useful amendment of the Constitution, I shall rejoice in it."

In substance Jefferson said that if Marshall should suffer Burr to escape, Marshall himself should be removed from office. No secret was made of this intention. The letter in which Jefferson announced the threat was written to the Virginia senator William

[1] Jefferson to W. B. Giles, April 20, 1807; Works, v. 65.

B. Giles, who had been foremost in every attack upon the Judiciary, and would certainly lead the new one; but Giles was not the confidant of a secret, — the idea was common, as Marshall knew. The little society that swarmed in the court-room and in the streets of Richmond could see without an effort that the President courted a challenge from Marshall, and that the chief-justice on his side, for a second or third time, welcomed a trial of skill and address with the President. If Marshall was in truth the gloomy and malignant conspirator that Jefferson imagined him to be, he might easily excuse or justify the President's intended course.

Punctually, May 22, the next act began. The question of commitment had been a matter of no great consequence; that of indictment was vital. Burr must be indicted, not merely for misdemeanor, but for treason; and to leave no doubt of success, the government summoned a cloud of witnesses to appear before the grand jury. The town swarmed with conspirators and government agents. The grand jury — containing some of the most respected citizens of Virginia — was sworn, and the court instructed the clerk to place John Randolph as foreman. A long delay ensued. General Wilkinson, the most important witness for government, was on his way from New Orleans; and while waiting his arrival from day to day, the grand jury took evidence and the court listened to the disputes of counsel. The district-attorney moved to commit Burr on the charge of treason, while Burr on his side moved for a subpœna *duces tecum* to be directed to the President, requiring him to produce certain papers in evidence. This motion was evidently part of a system adopted by the defence for annoying and throwing odium on the Executive, — a system which Burr's counsel rather avowed than concealed, by declaiming against the despotism of government and the persecution of which Burr was a victim. Luther Martin, at the first moment of his appearance in court, launched into an invective against Jefferson : —

" The President has undertaken to prejudge my client by declaring that ' of his guilt there can be no doubt. He has assumed the knowledge of the Supreme Being himself, and pretended to search the heart of my highly respected friend. He has proclaimed him a traitor in the face of that country which has rewarded him. He has let slip the dogs of war, the hell-hounds of persecution, to hunt down my friend. And would this President of the United States, who has raised all this absurd clamor, pretend to keep back the papers which are wanted for this trial, where life itself is at stake ? "

A long argument followed. Hay, while admitting that the President might be generally subpœnaed as a witness, held that no need of a subpœna had been shown, and that in any case a subpœna *duces tecum* ought not to be issued. The chief-justice, after hearing counsel on both sides, read June 13 an elaborate decision, which settled the point in Burr's favor.

"If upon any principle," said he, "the President could be construed to stand exempt from the general provisions of the Constitution, it would be because his duties as chief magistrate demand his whole time for national objects. But it is apparent that this demand is not unremitting ; and if it should exist at the time when his attendance on a court is required, it would be sworn on the return of the subpœna, and would rather constitute a reason for not obeying the process of the court than a reason against its being issued. . . . It cannot be denied that to issue a subpœna to a person filling the exalted station of the chief magistrate is a duty which would be dispensed with much more cheer-fully than it would be performed ; but if it be a duty, the court can have no choice in the case."

Nothing could irritate Jefferson more sensibly than this decision. Only a few months before, in the trial of Smith and Ogden for complicity with Miranda, he had ordered his Cabinet to disregard the summons of the court. Luther Martin did not fail to fling reproach on him for this act. "In New York, on the farcical trial of Ogden and Smith, the officers of the government screened themselves from attending, under the sanction of the President's name. Per-haps the same farce may be repeated here." To be insulted by Martin and to be ordered about the country by Marshall, exasperated Jefferson beyond reason. He wrote letter after letter to Hay, filled with resentment : —

"The leading feature of our Constitution is the inde-pendence of the Legislature, Executive, and Judiciary of each other; and none are more jealous of this than the Judiciary. But would the Executive be independent of the Judiciary if he were subject to the *commands* of the latter, and to imprisonment for disobedience; if the smaller courts could bandy him from pillar to post, keep him constantly trudging from north to south and east to west, and withdraw him entirely from his executive duties?" [1]

The Judiciary never admitted the propriety of this reasoning,[2] which was indeed no answer to Marshall's argument. Unless the President of the United States were raised above the rank of a citizen, and endowed with more than royal prerogatives, no duty could be more imperative upon him than that of lending every aid in his power to the Judiciary in a case which involved the foundations of civil society and government. No Judiciary could assume at the outset that Executive duties would necessarily be interrupted by breaking Jefferson's long visits to Monticello in order to bring him for a day to Richmond. Consciousness of this possible rejoinder disturbed the President's mind so much that he undertook to meet it in advance: —

"The Judge says '*it is apparent* that the President's duties as chief magistrate do not demand his whole time, and are not unremitting.' If he alludes to our annual retirement from the seat of government during the sickly season, he should be told that such arrangements are made for carrying on the public business, at and between

[1] Jefferson to Hay, June 20, 1807; Works, v. 102.

[2] U. S. *vs.* Kendall, Cranch's Circuit Court Reports, v. 385.

the several stations we take, that it goes on as unremittingly there as if we were at the seat of government."

The district-attorney would hardly have dared tell this to the chief-justice, for he must have felt that Marshall would treat it as an admission. If arrangements could be made for carrying on the public business at Monticello, why could they not be made for carrying it on at Richmond?

Perhaps temper had more to do with Jefferson's reasoning than he imagined. Nothing could be better calculated to nettle a philosophic President who believed the world, except within his own domain, to be too much governed, than the charge that he himself had played the despot and had trampled upon private rights; but that such charges should be pressed with the coarseness of Luther Martin, and should depend on the rulings of John Marshall, seemed an intolerable outrage on the purity of Jefferson's intentions. In such cases an explosion of anger was a common form of relief. Even President Washington was said to have sometimes dashed his hat upon the ground, and the second President was famous for gusts of temper.

" I have heard, indeed," wrote Jefferson,[1] " that my predecessor sometimes decided things against his Council by dashing and trampling his wig on the floor. This only proves, what you and I knew, that he had a better heart than head."

[1] Jefferson to William Short, June 12, 1807; Works, v. 93. Cf. Jefferson MSS.

Wigs were Federalist symbols of dignity and power. Republicans wore no wigs, and could use no such resource in moments of rage; but had President Jefferson worn the full paraphernalia of Federalism, — wig and powder, cocked hat and small sword, — he would never have shown his passion in acts of violence or in physical excitement. His sensitiveness relieved itself in irritability and complaints, in threats forgotten as soon as uttered, or in reflections tinged with a color of philosophic thought. His first impulse was to retaliate upon Martin and thrust him into the criminal dock. He wrote to Hay,[1] —

"Shall we move to commit Luther Martin as *particeps criminis* with Burr? Graybell will fix upon him misprision of treason at least. And at any rate his evidence will put down this unprincipled and impudent Federal bulldog, and add another proof that the most clamorous defenders of Burr are all his accomplices."

To the attorney-general he wrote in the same words:[2] "I think it material to break down this bulldog of Federalism." Jefferson's irritation rarely lasted long, and it evaporated with these words. Martin railed unmolested.

No one fretted by personal feeling could cope with the Rhadamanthine calm of John Marshall. The President could not successfully strike back; he was fortunate if he should succeed in warding off his enemies' blows. In the midst of these controversies and

[1] Jefferson to Hay, June 19, 1807; Works, v. 98.
[2] Jefferson to Rodney, June 19, 1807; Jefferson MSS.

irritations, June 15, General Wilkinson arrived. The audiences which in those days still crowded to the theatre and laughed at the extraordinary wit and morality of the " Beggar's Opera," found none of its possible allusions more amusing than the often-quoted line which seemed meant to point at James Wilkinson. " That Jemmy Twitcher should peach me, I own surprised me. 'Tis a plain proof that the world is all alike, and that even our gang can no more trust one another than other people." Wilkinson had not a friend ; even Daniel Clark turned against him. To break him down, to prove by his own confession that he was a pensioner of Spain and an accomplice with Burr, was the known object of the defence ; but the disgrace of Wilkinson would also discredit the President and shake the Administration which Wilkinson had saved. Whatever the consequences might be, Jefferson could not allow Wilkinson to suffer.

When Major Bruff, of the artillery, came from St. Louis to Washington early in March, 1807, three months before Burr's indictment, he made bitter complaints to the Secretary of War, accusing the general, under whose orders he served, of being a spy of Spain and a traitor with Burr.[1] General Dearborn listened without contradiction, and replied that there had been a time when General Wilkinson did not stand well with the Executive, but his energetic measures at

[1] Major Bruff's Testimony, Burr's Trial; Annals of Congress, 1807–1808, pp. 598–600.

New Orleans had regained him Executive confidence, and the President would sustain him; that after the actual bustle was over there might perhaps be an inquiry, but meanwhile Wilkinson must and would be supported. Attorney-General Rodney went even further.

"What would be the result," he asked Bruff, "if all your charges against General Wilkinson should be proven? Why, just what the Federalists and the enemies of the present Administration wish, — it would turn the indignation of the people from Burr on Wilkinson. Burr would escape, and Wilkinson take his place."

Rodney did not add, what was patent to all the world, that if Wilkinson were to be convicted, President Jefferson himself, whose negligence had left the Western country, in spite of a thousand warnings, at the General's mercy, could not be saved from the roughest handling. The President and his Cabinet shrank from Marshall's subpœnas because under the examination of Wickham, Botts, and Luther Martin they would be forced either to make common cause with the General, or to admit their own negligence. The whole case hung together. Disobedience of the subpœna was necessary for the support of Wilkinson; support of Wilkinson was more than ever necessary after refusing to obey the subpœna. The President accepted his full share in the labor. No sooner did he hear of Wilkinson's arrival, at the moment when his own subpœna was issued and defied, than he wrote a letter cal-

culated to give the General all the confidence he
needed : [1] —

" Your enemies have filled the public ear with slanders
and your mind with trouble on that account. The establishment of their guilt will let the world see what they
ought to think of their clamors ; it will dissipate the
doubts of those who doubted for want of knowledge, and
will place you on higher ground in the public estimate
and public confidence. No one is more sensible than
myself of the injustice which has been aimed at you.
Accept, I pray you, my salutations and assurances of
respect and esteem."

As an American citizen Jefferson had the right to
respect and esteem whom he pleased, and need not
even excuse his friendships. The world often loved
and cherished its worst rogues, — its Falstaffs, Mac-
heaths, and Burrs, — and Jefferson was not exempt
from such weakness ; but that his respect and esteem
for Wilkinson should require him to retain a pen-
sioned Spanish spy and a confederate with Burr and
Dayton at the head of the United States army during
several years of extreme public danger, was a costly
consequence to the people whose confidence Jefferson claimed and held. John Randolph saw this point
clearly, and his bloodhound instinct detected and followed, without hesitation, the trail that led to the
White House. Whether the chief-justice intended
it or not, he never struck Jefferson a blow so mischievous as when he directed the clerk to place

---

[1] Jefferson to Wilkinson, June 21, 1807; Works, v. 109.

John Randolph as foreman of the grand jury.[1] Randolph's nature revolted from Wilkinson; and if the President and the General could be gibbeted together, Randolph was the man to do it.

Such was the situation when the General was sworn and sent before the grand jury June 15, where his appearance, if his enemy could be believed, was abject.

"Under examination all was confusion of language and of looks," wrote Randolph to Nicholson.[2] "Such a countenance never did I behold; there was scarcely a variance of opinion among us as to his guilt. Yet this miscreant is hugged to the bosom of Government while Monroe is denounced."

Randolph ardently wished to indict the General at the same time with Burr; and while he strained every nerve to effect this purpose in the grand-jury room, Burr and his counsel in the court-room moved for an attachment against Wilkinson for attempting to obstruct the free course of justice by oppression of witnesses. The district-attorney resisted both attempts with all his authority; and June 24, to the disappointment of his enemies, Wilkinson escaped.

"Yesterday," wrote Randolph, June 25,[3] "the grand jury found bills for treason and misdemeanor against Burr and Blennerhassett *una voce*, and this day presented

[1] Wilkinson's Memoirs, ii. 6.

[2] Randolph to Nicholson, June 28, 1807; Nicholson MSS.

[3] Randolph to Nicholson, June 25, 1807; Nicholson MSS.

Jonathan Dayton, ex-senator, John Smith of Ohio, Comfort Tyler, Israel Smith of New York, and Davis Floyd of Indiana, for treason; but the mammoth of iniquity escaped, — not that any man pretended to think him innocent, but upon certain wire-drawn distinctions that I will not pester you with. Wilkinson is the only man that I ever saw who was from the bark to the very core a villain. The proof is unquestionable; but, my good friend, I cannot enter upon it here. Suffice it to say that I have seen it, and that it is not susceptible of misconstruction. Burr supported himself with great fortitude. He was last night lodged in the common town jail (we have no State prison except for convicts), where I daresay he slept sounder than I did. Perhaps you never saw human nature in so degraded a situation as in the person of Wilkinson before the grand jury; and yet this man stands on the very summit and pinnacle of Executive favor, while James Monroe is denounced."

In the debates of the next session, when Randolph followed up his attacks on Jefferson by trying to identify him with Wilkinson's misdeeds, a fuller account was given of the plea which saved Wilkinson from presentment.

"There was before the grand jury," said Randolph,[1] "a motion to present General Wilkinson for misprision of treason. This motion was overruled upon this ground, — that the treasonable (overt) act having been alleged to be committed in the State of Ohio, and General Wilkinson's letter to the President of the United States hav-

[1] Annals of Congress, Jan. 11, 1808; Session of 1807–1808, p. 1397.

ing been dated, though but a short time, prior to that
act, this person had the benefit of what lawyers would
call a legal exception, or a fraud; but I will inform the
gentleman that I did not hear a single member of the
grand jury express any other opinion than that which
I myself expressed, of the moral, not of the legal, guilt
of the party."

In the evidence taken by a Congressional committee in 1811 regarding Wilkinson,[1] several members of the grand jury were called to testify; and
their accounts showed that the motion to present
General Wilkinson for misprision of treason was
made by Littleton W. Tazewell, and supported by
Randolph and three or four other members of the
grand jury. One witness thought that the vote
stood 9 to 7.

Narrow though the loophole might be, Wilkinson
squeezed through it. The indictment of Burr was at
length obtained. The conspirators, who had at first
vehemently averred that Wilkinson would never dare
to appear, and who if he should appear intended to
break him down before the grand jury, were reduced
to hoping for revenge when he should come on the
witness-stand. Meanwhile, June 26, Burr pleaded
not guilty, and the court adjourned until August 3,
when the trial was to begin.

Thus far the President had carried everything be-

[1] Report of the Committee appointed to inquire into the
Conduct of General Wilkinson, Feb. 26, 1811, pp. 281, 298.
Cf. National Intelligencer, Aug. 3, 1807.

fore him. He had produced his witnesses, had sustained Wilkinson, indicted Burr, and defied Marshall's subpœnas. This success could not be won without rousing passion. Richmond was in the hands of the conspirators, and they denounced Jefferson publicly and without mercy, as they denounced Wilkinson and every other government officer.

" As I was crossing the court-house green," said an eye-witness,[1] " I heard a great noise of haranguing some distance off. Inquiring what it was, I was told it was a great blackguard from Tennessee, one Andrew Jackson, making a speech for Burr and damning Jefferson as a persecutor."

Hay wrote to the President, June 14 : [2] —

" General Jackson, of Tennessee, has been here ever since the 22d, denouncing Wilkinson in the coarsest terms in every company. The latter showed me a paper which at once explained the motive of this incessant hostility. His own character depends on the prostration of Wilkinson's."

This paper was no doubt Jackson's secret denunciation to Claiborne. Young Samuel Swartwout, who had some reason to complain of the ridiculous figure he had been made to cut, jostled Wilkinson in the street, and ended by posting him for a coward. John Randolph echoed Luther Martin's tirades against the President. Randolph was in despair at Jefferson's success.

[1] Parton's Life of Burr, ii. 107.
[2] Hay to Jefferson, June 14, 1807 ; Jefferson MSS.

" My friend," he wrote to Nicholson,[1] " I am standing on the soil of my native country divested of every right for which our fathers bled. Politics have usurped the place of law, and the scenes of 1798 are again revived. Men now see and hear, and feel and think, *politically*. Maxims are now advanced and advocated which would almost have staggered the effrontery of Bayard or the cooler impudence of Chauncey Goodrich when we were first acquainted."

All this work was but skirmishing. The true struggle had still to come. So long as the President dealt only with grand jurors and indictments, he could hardly fail to succeed ; but the case was different when he dealt directly with Chief-Justice Marshall and with the stubborn words of the Constitution, that " no person shall be convicted of treason unless on the testimony of two witnesses to the same overt act, or on confession in open court." The district-attorney was ready with a mass of evidence, but the chief-justice alone could say whether a syllable of this evidence should be admitted ; and hitherto the chief-justice had by no means shown a bias toward the government. Hay was convinced that Marshall meant to protect Burr, and he wrote to the President on the subject : [2] —

" The bias of Judge Marshall is as obvious as if it was stamped upon his forehead. I may do him injustice, but

[1] Randolph to Nicholson, June 25, 1807; Adams's Randolph, p. 221.

[2] Hay to Jefferson, Aug. 11, 1807; Jefferson MSS.

I do not believe that I am, when I say that he is endeavoring to work himself up to a state of f[irmness?] which
will enable [him] to aid Burr throughout the trial without
appearing to be conscious of doing wrong. He seems to
think that his reputation is irretrievably gone, and that
he has now nothing to lose by doing as he pleases. His
concern for Mr. Burr is wonderful. He told me many
years ago, when Burr was rising in the estimation of the
Republican party, that he was as profligate in principle
as he was desperate in fortune. I remember his words ;
they astonished me. Yet when the grand jury brought
in their bill, the chief-justice gazed at him for a long
time, without appearing conscious that he was doing so,
with an expression of sympathy and sorrow as strong
as the human countenance can exhibit without palpable
emotion."

August 3 the court opened its session and the
trial began. Not until August 17 was the jury im-
panelled ; and meanwhile a new figure appeared at
Burr's side. Blennerhassett arrived in Richmond
August 4, and was brought before the court August
10. He began at once a private journal of the trial,
which remained the only record of what passed
among the conspirators. As each witness appeared,
Blennerhassett told the gossip regarding him.

" The once redoubted Eaton," [1] who was put first upon
the stand, " has dwindled down in the eyes of this sarcastic town into a ridiculous mountebank, strutting about
the streets under a tremendous hat, with a Turkish sash
over colored clothes, when he is not tippling in the

[1] Blennerhassett Papers, p. 315.

taverns, where he offers up with his libations the bitter effusions of his sorrows."

" Old sly-boots " Dayton,[1] he said, was lurking about corners.

Wilkinson [2] " exhibited the manner of a sergeant under a court-martial rather than the demeanor of an accusing officer confronted with his culprit. His perplexity and derangement, even upon his direct examination, has placed beyond all doubt ' his honor as a soldier and his fidelity as a citizen.' "

These comments were sharp, yet the pages of Blennerhassett's diary were not so severe upon any of the witnesses for the government as they were upon Burr himself. Blennerhassett had wakened to the discovery that Burr was, after all, but a vulgar swindler. The collapse of Burr's courage when confronted by Cowles Meade and the Mississippi militia at Cole's Creek January 17 ; his desertion of Blennerhassett and his flight toward Spanish territory ; the protest of the bills which he had drawn on pretended funds in New York, and which Blennerhassett had indorsed under Allston's guaranty ; the evident wish of Allston to repudiate this guaranty as he had repudiated Burr ; and the ruin which had fallen on Blennerhassett's property at the island, — taught the Irishman how thoroughly he had been duped : [3] —

[1] Blennerhassett Papers, p. 397.
[2] Blennerhassett Papers, p. 422.
[3] Blennerhassett Papers, p. 373.

" The present trial cannot fail to furnish ample testimony, if not to the guilt, at least to the defect of every talent under the assumption of which this giddy adventurer has seduced so many followers of riper experience and better judgment than myself."

Yet Burr's mastership in deportment, his superficial dignity, his cheerfulness and sanguine temperament, and the skill with which he managed legal tactics, made an impression on Blennerhassett's mind : —

"As a jockey might restore his fame in the course after he had injured it on the tight-rope, so, perhaps, the little ' Emperor' at Cole's Creek may be forgotten in the attorney at Richmond." [1]

For a few days the trial went on undisturbed, while the government put Eaton, Truxton, Peter Taylor, the Morgans, and a number of other witnesses on the stand to prove an overt act of treason at Blennerhassett's island ; but nothing short of Blennerhassett's own confession could place the matter in a clear light, and Burr's chief fear was evidently that Blennerhassett should turn State's evidence. To prevent this, Allston was persuaded to pay the more pressing demands against Blennerhassett, and Burr exerted himself to conciliate him. On the other hand, Jefferson seemed to hope that he could be won over.[2] Duane, of the " Aurora," visited him in prison August 23, and offered to serve as an intermediary

[1] Blennerhassett Papers, p. 343.
[2] Jefferson to Hay, Aug. 20, 1807 ; Works, v. 174.

with the government.[1]   Had matters gone as the
President hoped, something might have come of this
manœuvre; but before further pressure could be
employed, the chief-justice struck the prosecution
dead.

August 19 Burr's counsel suddenly moved to arrest
the evidence. The government, they said, had gone
through all its testimony relating to the overt act
charged in the indictment; it admitted that Burr
was hundreds of miles distant from the scene; and
as the district-attorney was about to introduce col-
lateral testimony of acts done beyond the jurisdiction of the court, it became the duty of the defence
to object.

For ten days this vital point was argued. All the
counsel on either side exerted themselves to the utmost. Wickham's opening speech on the nature of
treason was declared by as good a judge as Lyttleton
Tazewell to be "the greatest forensic effort of the
American bar."[2] Luther Martin spoke fourteen hours,
beginning with an almost passionate allusion to his
idol Theodosia. William Wirt exhausted his powers
of argument and oratory, and in the course of his
address made the rhetorical display which became
familiar to every American, and which introduced
a sort of appeal to Blennerhassett to turn against
the more guilty crew who were trying to sacrifice
him to save themselves: —

[1] Blennerhassett Papers, p. 356.
[2] Grigsby's Tazewell, p. 73.

" Who is Blennerhassett?   A native of Ireland, a man
of letters, who fled from the storms of his own country
to find quiet in ours."

George Hay was neither so efficient nor so dex-
terous as Wirt, and either intentionally or by awkwardness succeeded in giving the impression of
threatening the court : [1] —

" Mr. Bott says that we are now advocating opinions
which on Fries' trial we condemned. . . . I beg leave to
assure the gentleman that the censure which the judge
drew on himself was not on account of his opinions, however incorrect they might be, but for his arbitrary and
irregular conduct at the trial, which was one of the
principal causes for which he was afterward impeached.
He attempted to wrest the decision from the jury, and
prejudge the case before hearing all the evidence in it,
— the identical thing which this court is now called on
by these gentlemen to do."

That Hay, knowing well Jefferson's thoughts and
the magic that hung about the word " impeachment," should have used these words inadvertently
seemed hardly credible. If he did so, his clumsi-
ness was as offensive as the threat could have been,
for the idea of impeachment was in the air of
the court-house. Burr's counsel at once retaliated.[2]
" It was very kind of the gentleman to remind the
court of the danger of a decision of the motion
in favor of the prisoner." Hay protested that he
had spoken innocently, and the chief-justice said

1 Burr's Trial, ii. 193.   2 Burr's Trial, ii. 238.

that the allusion had not been taken as personal ;
but the unpleasant impression remained. " The gentleman plainly insinuated the possibility of danger
to the court," persisted the defence ; and Luther
Martin added,[1] —

" I do not know whether it were intended by this observation that your honors should be apprehensive of an
impeachment in case you should decide against the
wishes of the government. I will not presume that it
was used with that view, but it is susceptible of being
so misunderstood, however innocently or inadvertently it
may have been made."

August 31 the chief-justice read his decision. Much
the longest of Marshall's judicial opinions ; elaborately
argued, with many citations, and with less simple
adherence to one leading thought than was usual
in his logic, — this paper seemed, in the imagination
of Marshall's enemies, to betray a painful effort
to reconcile his dictum in Bollman's case with the
exclusion of further evidence in the case of Burr.
To laymen, who knew only the uncertainties of law ;
who thought that the assemblage on Blennerhassett's
island was such an overt act as might, without violent
impropriety, be held by a jury to be an act of levying
war ; and who conceived that Burr, although absent
from the spot, was as principal present in a legal
sense such as would excuse a jury in finding him
guilty, — an uneasy doubt could not fail to suggest
itself that the chief-justice, with an equal effort of

[1] Burr's Trial, ii. 369.

ingenuity, might have produced equal conviction in a directly opposite result. On the other hand, the intent of the Constitution was clear. The men who framed that instrument remembered the crimes that had been perpetrated under the pretence of justice ; for the most part they had been traitors themselves, and having risked their necks under the law they feared despotism and arbitrary power more than they feared treason. No one could doubt that their sympathies, at least in 1788, when the Constitution was framed, would have been on the side of Marshall's decision. If Jefferson, since 1788, had changed his point of view, the chief-justice was not under obligations to imitate him.

" If it be said that the advising or procurement of treason is a secret transaction which can scarcely ever be proved in the manner required by this opinion, the answer which will readily suggest itself is that the difficulty of proving a fact will not justify conviction without proof."

At the close of his decision the chief-justice, with simple dignity which still compels respectful admiration, took up the gauntlet which the district-attorney had flung at his feet. As though turning from the crowd in the court-room to look for a moment directly into the eyes of the President, the threatened chief-justice uttered a few words that were at once answer and defiance : —

" Much has been said in the course of the argument on points on which the Court feels no inclination to comment particularly, but which may perhaps not improperly receive some notice.

" That this Court dares not usurp power is most true ; that this Court dares not shrink from its duty is not less true. No man is desirous of placing himself in a disagreeable situation ; no man is desirous of becoming the peculiar subject of calumny ; no man, might he let the bitter cup pass from him without self-reproach, would drain it to the bottom ; but if he has no choice in the case, — if there is no alternative presented to him but a dereliction of duty or the opprobrium of those who are denominated the world, — he merits the contempt as well as the indignation of his country who can hesitate which to embrace. . . .

" No testimony relative to the conduct or declarations of the prisoner elsewhere and subsequent to the transactions on Blennerhassett's island can be admitted ; because such testimony, being in its nature merely corroborative, and incompetent to prove the overt act in itself, is irrelevant until there be proof of the overt act by two witnesses."

On the following day, September 1, District-Attorney Hay abandoned the case, and the jury entered a verdict of " Not guilty." Hay instantly reported to Monticello the result of his efforts, and added criticisms upon Marshall : [1] —

" Wirt, who has hitherto advocated the *integrity* of the chief-justice, now abandons him. This last opinion has opened his eyes, and he speaks in the strongest terms of reprobation."

[1] Hay to Jefferson, Sept. 1, 1807 ; Jefferson MSS.

September 4 Jefferson replied in the tone which always accompanied his vexation : [1] —

" Yours of the 1st came to hand yesterday. The event has been what was evidently intended from the beginning of the trial ; that is to say, not only to clear Burr, but to prevent the evidence from ever going before the world. But this latter case must not take place. It is now, therefore, more than ever indispensable that not a single witness be paid or permitted to depart until his testimony has been committed to writing. . . . These whole proceedings will be laid before Congress, that they may decide whether the defect has been in the evidence of guilt, or in the law, or in the application of the law, and that they may provide the proper remedy for the past and the future."

Accordingly, although the trial for treason was at an end, the district-attorney pressed the indictment for misdemeanor ; and until October 19 the chief-justice was occupied in hearing testimony intended for use not against Burr, but against himself. Then at last the conspirators were suffered to go their way, subject to legal proceedings in Ohio which the government had no idea of prosecuting ; while the President, mortified and angry, prepared to pursue Marshall instead of Burr. The Federalists, who always overrated the strength of party passions, trembled again for the Judiciary ; but in truth nothing was to be feared. The days of Jefferson's power and glory had passed forever, while those of Marshall had barely

[1] Jefferson to Hay, Sept. 4, 1807 ; Works, v. 187. Cf. Jefferson MSS.

begun. Even on the testimony, the President's case was far from being so clear as he had hoped and expected. His chief witness, Wilkinson, could only with difficulty be sustained ; and the district-attorney, who began by pledging himself before the court to show the falsity of the charges which had been brought against the, General, ended by admitting their truth.

" The declaration which I made in court in his favor some time ago," wrote Hay to the President at the close,[1] " was precipitate ; and though I have not retracted it, everybody sees that I have not attempted the task which I in fact promised to perform. My confidence in him is shaken, if not destroyed. I am sorry for it, on his own account, on the public account, and because you have expressed opinions in his favor ; but you did not know then what you will soon know, and what I did not learn until after — long after — my declaration above mentioned."

The hint was strong. If Wilkinson were discredited, Jefferson himself was in danger. To attack the Supreme Court on such evidence was to invite a worse defeat than in the impeachment of Chase. Meanwhile the country had graver dangers to think about, and enemies at its doors who were not to be curbed by proclamations or impeachments.

[1] Hay to Jefferson, Oct. 15, 1807 ; Jefferson MSS.

END OF VOL. I.